MICHELIN

MOTORING ATLAS

Great Britain & Ireland

Tourism Department

MICHELIN

MICHELIN the world's leading manufacturer of tyres, is also a well known name in the field of tourist publications ; its annual sales of maps and guides exceed 16 million in over 70 countries.

Acting on the belief that motoring would have a great future, the Michelin brothers decided to offer the motorist a touring service, an innovative step at the turn of the century : free or inexpensive publications designed to provide information, assistance and encouragement.

At the wheel, touring, on holiday – these three aspects of travel were met by a simple response – a trio of complementary publications to be used together.

The first of these, the Red Guides, which are published annually, present a selection of hotels and restaurants, with a wide range of prices and facilities. It is, however, probably their award of the stars for good cooking that has established their international reputation ; as well as the wealth of essential touring information included in them. There are several guides covering Europe, including the Red Guide to France which alone has sold over 20 million copies to date. Readers have such faith in their reliability that the Red Guides are foremost among reference books in this field.

The role of the Michelin Green Guides is to provide tourists with information to help them explore and enjoy the countries, regions and cities of Western Europe and North America. The guides describe the sights, the countryside and picturesque routes ; they also contain maps, plans and practical information as well as illustrations and photographs which whet one's appetite for travel. There are over 70 titles covering Europe and North America, which are published in French and other European languages and are revised regularly.

"The principal mapping in this Atlas of Great Britain and Ireland is an enlargement of the 1:400 000 sheet map series covering these countries. In addition we have 14 pages of comprehensive Route Planning mapping to help you prepare your journey. There are 103 pages of mapping, 49 town plans and an index of approximately 10 000 place names. The same grid system as on the sheet maps is used in this Atlas in order that it can be used in conjunction with our Hotel and Restaurant Guides "Great Britain and Ireland" and "Ireland" and also with our Green Guides "Great Britain", "Ireland", "Scotland", "London" and "The West Country"."

It is our intention to continue our service to our readers by annually updating the information contained within the Atlas. We should welcome your comments and suggestions in order that we may take your wishes into account when preparing the next edition.

Thank you in advance. May we wish you a safe journey.

MICHELIN maps and guides
complement one another :
use them together !

Contents

Plans of cities and principal towns

Distances in Great Britain and Ireland

All distances are quoted in miles and kilometres.

    miles in red

    kilometres in blue

The distances quoted are not necessarily the shortest but have been based on the roads which afford the best driving conditions and are therefore the most practical.

Example:

Oxford – Killarney:

	Oxford – Fishguard	214 m.	or	344 km.
+	*Rosslare – Killarney*	157 m.	or	252 km.
		371 m.	or	596 km.

Ireland

Kilometres

Upper triangle (kilometres):

Belfast	419	121	171	87	316	461	34	362	115	110	318	200	229	330
Cork		298	248	332	197	86	451	92	461	430	189	325	202	115
Drogheda			50	35	224	340	154	242	188	135	198	204	108	209
Dublin				85	223	291	203	192	231	179	148	216	107	159
Dundalk					250	375	119	276	165	112	232	171	135	243
Galway						215	342	106	279	251	264	143	133	219
Killarney							494	110	479	480	252	343	224	180
Larne								395	120	118	351	226	262	362
Limerick									369	342	198	233	116	126
Londonderry										53	379	136	254	394
Omagh											326	109	204	341
Rosslare												314	161	74
Sligo													154	286
Tullamore														132
Waterford														

Lower triangle (miles):

	Belfast	Cork	Drogheda	Dublin	Dundalk	Galway	Killarney	Larne	Limerick	Londonderry	Omagh	Rosslare	Sligo	Tullamore	Waterford
Cork	260
Drogheda	76	185
Dublin	107	154	31
Dundalk	54	207	22	53
Galway	197	123	139	139	156
Killarney	287	54	212	181	233	134
Larne	21	281	96	127	74	213	307
Limerick	225	57	150	119	172	66	68	246
Londonderry	72	287	117	144	102	173	298	75	230
Omagh	68	268	84	111	70	156	254	74	213	33
Rosslare	198	118	123	92	144	164	157	218	123	236	203
Sligo	125	202	127	135	107	89	213	141	145	85	68	195
Tullamore	143	126	68	67	84	83	139	163	72	158	127	100	96
Waterford	205	72	130	99	151	136	112	225	78	245	212	46	178	82

Miles

Great Britain

Kilometres

Upper triangle (kilometres), cities in order: Aberdeen, Birmingham, Brighton, Bristol, Cambridge, Cardiff, Carlisle, Dover, Dundee, Edinburgh, Exeter, Fishguard, Glasgow, Harwich, Holyhead, Hull, Inverness, Kyle of Lochalsh, Leeds, Liverpool, London, Manchester, Middlesbrough, Newcastle, Northampton, Norwich, Nottingham, Oban, Oxford, Penzance, Plymouth, Portsmouth, Southampton, Stranraer, Swansea, Thurso.

```
Aberdeen     700 968 828 754 866 370 941 112 201 951 859 241 872 747 585 168 296 529 581 878 567 445 374 775 802 639 290 812 1131 1019 943 914 377 922 354
Birmingham       264 138 157 176 333 320 589 483 262 330 486 276 268 231 739 768 194 166 186 145 289 340  83 263  85 630 108  442 329 239 210 503 232 925
Brighton             253 193 306 601 169 857 738 269 478 754 202 536 420 1007 1036 423 433  86 413 517 568 205 268 313 898 169 452 339  75  95 770 362 1193
Bristol                  272  70 460 316 716 610 123 242 613 330 395 372 866 895 336 293 196 272 430 481 185 372 226 757 120 303 191 152 121 630 126 1052
Cambridge                    325 425 194 642 550 373 497 577 107 417 234 806 859 243 314  92 266 329 380  86 107 143 722 133 582 469 221 217 594 381 992
Cardiff                          498 369 754 648 194 180 651 383 370 410 904 933 374 277 249 310 468 520 238 424 264 795 172 374 261 249 188 668  64 1090
Carlisle                             645 259 152 584 492 155 543 380 257 409 437 200 214 511 200 160  95 408 474 310 300 445 764 652 576 547 172 555 594
Dover                                    830 738 392 541 798 203 580 421 994 1080 431 478 120 457 516 568 235 269 343 942 233 575 462 225 227 815 425 1179
Dundee                                        89 840 747 124 761 636 474 204 278 417 470 767 456 334 263 664 691 527 199 701 1020 907 832 803 260 810 390
Edinburgh                                        733 641  75 669 529 382 253 327 325 363 635 349 242 171 532 599 435 199 594 913 801 725 696 203 704 439
Exeter                                               366 736 431 518 496 990 1018 459 416 297 395 554 605 314 472 350 881 249 179  73 208 173 753 250 1176
Fishguard                                                644 555 266 465 898 926 376 266 421 310 480 531 410 596 363 788 344 546 433 421 360 661 119 1084
Glasgow                                                      696 532 409 275 286 352 366 663 353 313 248 561 626 462 148 597 917 804 728 699 137 707 460
Harwich                                                          535 323 924 978 361 433 126 384 447 498 208 116 261 840 219 640 527 259 275 712 439 1110
Holyhead                                                             353 786 814 265 151 481 549 287 677 379 699 586 510 481 549 299 972
Hull                                                                     638 691  99 212 319 158 144 212 224 258 156 553 315 676 564 446 417 426 466 823
Inverness                                                                    131 581 620 917 606 498 427 814 855 691 189 851 1170 1058 982 953 411 960 187
Kyle of Lochalsh                                                                 634 648 945 635 572 501 843 908 744 200 880 1199 1086 1011 981 420 989 278
Leeds                                                                                124 319  70 104 155 216 292 119 497 279 640 527 410 381 369 430 766
Liverpool                                                                                343  57 227 278 240 379 166 511 277 596 484 408 379 383 300 806
London                                                                                       322 413 464 101 181 209 808  89 506 393 126 141 680 305 1103
Manchester                                                                                       173 224 220 314 117 497 257 576 463 388 358 369 366 792
Middlesbrough                                                                                         72 310 377 214 438 373 734 621 504 475 329 524 683
Newcastle                                                                                               362 429 265 366 425 785 673 556 526 265 576 612
Northampton                                                                                               192 106 705  72 494 382 203 174 577 294 1000
Norwich                                                                                                       204 170 239 681 568 325 316 643 480 1000 877
Nottingham                                                                                                       607 169 530 417 300 271 479 320 877
Oban                                                                                                                 742 1061 948 873 844 282 851 375
Oxford                                                                                                                    429 316 135 105 614 228 1037
Penzance                                                                                                                      125 390 356 933 430 1356
Plymouth                                                                                                                          278 243 821 317 1244
Portsmouth                                                                                                                            34 745 305 1168
Southampton                                                                                                                             716 244 1139
Stranraer                                                                                                                                  724 596
Swansea                                                                                                                                        1147
Thurso
```

Lower triangle (miles), same city order:

```
Birmingham       436
Brighton         602 165
Bristol          515  86 157
Cambridge        469  98 120 169
Cardiff          538 110 190  44 202
Carlisle         230 207 374 286 264 310
Dover            585 199 105 197 120 229 401
Dundee            70 366 533 445 399 469 161 516
Edinburgh        125 300 459 379 342 403  95 459  56
Exeter           591 163 167  77 232 121 363 244 522 456
Fishguard        534 205 297 151 309 112 306 465 399 227
Glasgow          150 302 469 381 359 405  97 496  77  47 458 400
Harwich          542 171 126 206  66 238 338 127 473 416 268 345 432
Holyhead         465 167 333 245 259 230 236 360 395 329 322 166 331 333
Hull             364 261 232 145 255 232 145 256 262 295 238 308 289 254 201 220
Inverness        105 460 626 539 501 562 254 618 127 158 615 558 171 575 489 397
Kyle of Lochalsh 184 477 644 556 534 580 272 671 173 204 633 576 178 608 506 430  81
Leeds            329 121 263 209 151 233 124 268 260 202 286 234 219 225 165  61 361 394
Liverpool        361 103 270 182 196 172 133 297 292 226 259 165 228 269  98 132 385 403  77
London           546 116  54 122  57 155 318  75 477 395 185 262 412  78 277 199 570 588 198 213
Manchester       353  90 257 169 165 193 125 284 284 217 246 193 219 239 123  99 377 395  44  36 201
Middlesbrough    277 180 322 268 205 291 100 321 208 151 344 298 194 278 229  90 310 356  65 141 257 108
Newcastle        233 212 353 299 236 323  60 353 164 106 376 330 154 310 261 132 265 311  97 173 289 140  45
Northampton      482  52 127 115  54 148 254 146 413 331 195 255 349 129 213 140 506 524 134 150  63 137 193 225
Norwich          499 164 167 231  67 264 295 168 430 372 294 371 389  72 316 160 531 565 182 236 112 195 235 267 119
Nottingham       397  53 195 141  89 164 193 214 328 271 217 226 288 162 179  97 430 463  74 103 130  73 133 165  66 127
Oban             180 392 558 471 449 494 186 586 118 124 548 490  92 522 421 344 117 124 309 317 502 309 272 228 438 479 377
Oxford           505  68 105  75  83 107 277 145 436 370 155 214 372 136 236 196 529 547 174 173  56 160 232 264  45 149 105 461
Penzance         703 275 281 189 362 233 475 357 634 568 112 339 570 398 434 420 727 745 398 371 314 358 456 488 307 423 330 660 267
Plymouth         633 205 211 119 292 163 405 287 564 498  46 269 500 328 364 350 657 675 328 301 244 288 386 418 237 353 260 590 197  78
Portsmouth       586 149  47  96 137 155 358 140 517 451 129 262 453 161 317 278 611 628 255 254  79 241 314 346 126 202 187 543  84 243 173
Southampton      568 131  56  77 135 117 340 141 499 433 108 224 435 172 299 260 592 610 237 236  88 223 296 327 108 197 169 525  66 221 151  21
Stranraer        235 313 479 391 370 415 107 506 162 127 468 411  85 443 342 265 256 261 230 238 423 230 205 165 359 400 298 176 382 580 510 463 445
Swansea          573 145 225  79 237  40 345 264 504 438 155  74 439 273 186 290 597 615 267 187 190 228 326 358 183 299 199 529 142 267 197 190 152 450
Thurso           220 575 742 654 616 678 369 733 242 273 731 674 286 690 604 512 116 173 477 501 686 493 425 381 622 647 545 233 645 843 773 726 708 371 713
```

Miles

Route planning

Key to 1:1 000 000 map pages
(1 in : 16 miles)

```
0        10       20       30       40 miles
├────────┼────────┼────────┼────────┤
0    10    20    30    40    50    60 km
```

1:1 000 000 map pages

The Primary Road network in England in currently under review. Certain roads may therefore change their status during the currency of this publication.

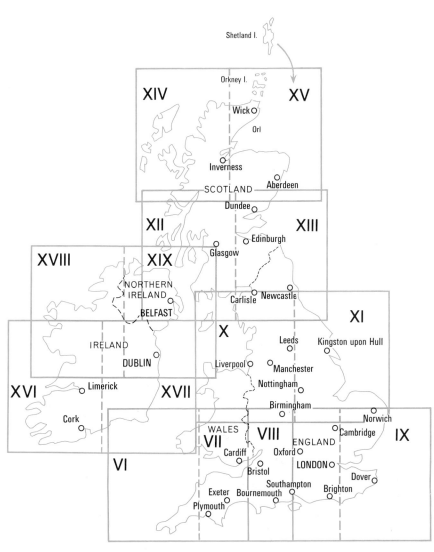

Route planning map legend

Road classification		Importance des routes	
Motorway	M 5	Autoroute (en Grande-Bretagne, la circulation sur autoroute est gratuite)	M 5
Dual carriageway with motorway characteristics		Double chaussée de type autoroutier	
Junctions : complete - limited	1 2 10	Échangeurs : complet - partiels	1 2 10
Primary route (GB) and national primary route (IRL) :		Primary route (GB) and National primary route (IRL) :	
Signposting for places on motorway and primary route networks	YORK Wells	Localités jalonnant un itinéraire autoroutier ou Primary et figurant sur la signalisation	YORK Wells
Official road classification : primary route (GB)	A 40 A 68	Numéros des routes : Primary route (GB)	A 40 A 68
National primary and secondary route (IRL)	N 2 N 59	National primary and secondary route (IRL)	N 2 N 59
National road network :		Route de liaison nationale :	
dual carriageway - 4 lanes		chaussées séparées - 4 voies	
2 wide lanes - 2 lanes		2 voies larges - 2 voies	
Regional road network :		Route de liaison interrégionale :	
dual carriageway		chaussées séparées	
2 or mote lanes - 2 narrow lanes		2 voies ou plus - 2 voies étroites	
Other roads :		Autres routes :	
Other selected regional road	A 258 T 53	Autre route de liaison interrégionale sélectionnée	A 258 T 53
Local road : surfaced - unsurfaced		Route locale revêtue - non revêtue	
In Scotland : narrow road with passing places		En Écosse : route très étroite avec emplacements pour croisement (passing places)	
Road under construction (when available : with scheduled opening date)	======	Route en construction (le cas échéant : date de mise en service prévue)	======
Distances (intermediate and total)		Distances (totalisées et partielles)	
on motorways - on others roads	14 10	sur autoroute - sur route	14 10
in miles	24	en miles	24
in kilometres	39	en kilomètres	39
Obstacles		Obstacles	
Road, bridge with toll		Route, pont à péage	
Steep hill (ascent in the direction of the arrow)		Forte déclivité (montée dans le sens de la flèche)	
Pass - altitude (in metres)	665	Col - altitude (en mètres)	665
Transportation		Transport	
Car ferry (seasonal services : in red)		Transport des autos (liaisons saisonnières : signe rouge)	
ferry	B - - - B	par bac	B - - - B
boat		par bateau	
Airport	✈	Aéroport	✈
Important isolated sights		Curiosités importantes isolées	
Ecclesiastical building - Historic house, castle - Ruins - Cave		Édifice religieux - Château - Ruines - Grotte	
Prehistoric monument - Other sights		Monument mégalithique - Autres curiosités	
Pleasant itinerary - National Forest Park, National park		Itinéraire agréable - Parc forestier national, parc national	

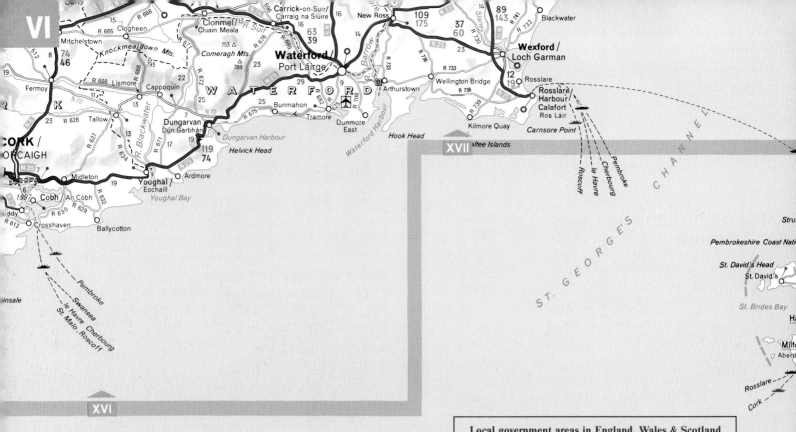

XVII

XVI

Local government areas in England, Wales & Scotland are subject to revision, with effect from april 1996

UNITARY AUTHORITIES

WALES

1 Aberconwy and Colwyn/Aberconwy a Cholwyn
2 Anglesey/Sir Fôn
3 Blaenau Gwent
4 Bridgend/Pen-y-bont ar Ogwr
5 Caerphilly/Caerffili
6 Cardiff/Caerdydd
7 Cardiganshire/Sir Aberteifi
8 Carmarthenshire/Sir Gaerfyrddin
9 Denbighshire/Sir Ddinbych
10 Flintshire/Sir y Fflint
11 Gwynedd
12 Merthyr Tydfil/Merthyr Tudful
13 Monmouthshire/Sir Fynwy
14 Neath Port Talbot/Castell-nedd Phort Talbot
15 Newport/Casnewydd
16 Pembrokeshire/Sir Benfro
17 Powys
18 Rhondda Cynon Taff/Rhondda Cynon Taf
19 Swansea/Abertawe
20 Torfaen/Tor-faen
21 Vale of Glamorgan/Bro Morgannwg
22 Wrexham/Wrecsam

CHANNEL ISLANDS

Alderney

Cap de la Hague

Cap Lévy

Weymouth

Guernsey

Cherbourg

Beaumont

St. Peter Port

les Pieux

Valognes

Sark

Bricquebec

Jersey

Carteret

Barneville

St Sauveur-le-V.

Portbail

la Haye-du-Puits

Gorey

Lessay

St Hélier

St Malo-de-la-Lande

Agon-Coutainville

Coutances

Montmartin

I. Chausey

St Malo

Bréhal

Granville

Portsmouth
Southampton
Poole
Rosslare
Cork

Newquay

St. Ives

Hayle

Truro

Redruth

Camborne

Penryn

St Just

Penzance

St. Michael's Mount

Sennen

Land's End

Helston

Falmouth

Mount's Bay

St. Kevern

Lizard

Lizard Point

Tresco

St. Martin's

Isles of Scilly

St. Mary's

Whitley Bay

Tynemouth
Jarrow **South Shields**
Hebburn

SUNDERLAND
Stanley
Washington
Chester-le-Street
Seaham
Houghton-le-Spring
Horden
Durham
Peterlee
Spennymoor
Sedgefield
Hartlepool
Newton Aycliffe
Billingham
Redcar
Stockton-on-Tees
Marske-by-the-Sea
Saltburn-by-the-Sea
Brotton
Darlington
Eaglescliffe
Middlesbrough
Guisborough
Loftus
Scotch Corner
Whitby

Cleveland Hills
454 △
North York Moors
National Park
Northallerton
Bedale
Helmsley
Scalby
Scarborough
Thirsk
Pickering
Ripon
Filey
Fountains Abbey
Easingwold
Malton
Norton
Boroughbridge
Wetwang
Gt. Driffield
Bridlington
Flamborough Head
Knaresborough
YORK
Beeford
Harrogate
Wetherby
H U M B E R S I D E
Harewood
Tadcaster
Leven
Hornsea
Market Weighton
LEEDS
Selby
Barlby
Beverley
Garforth
Castleford
Howden
KINGSTON-UPON-HULL
Snaith
Goole
Hedon
Withernsea
Dewsbury
Pontefract
Humber Bridge
Patrington
Wakefield
Barton-upon-Humber
Kilnsea
Thorne
Crowle
River Humber
Immingham Dock
Barnsley
Scunthorpe
Immingham
Bentley
Brigg
Great Grimsby
Spurn Head
Conisbrough
Doncaster
Humberside
Cleethorpes
Rotherham
Epworth
Caistor
Rotterdam / Zeebrugge
Maltby
Bawtry
SHEFFIELD
Gainsborough
Market Rasen
Louth
Mablethorpe
Dronfield
Worksop
Sutton-on-Sea
Staveley
East Retford
Wragby
Chesterfield
N O T T S
Tuxford
Lincoln
Sutton-on-Sea
Hardwick Hall
Ollerton
Horncastle
Alford
Clay Cross
Mansfield
L I N C O L N
Partney
Alfreton
Sutton-in-Ashfield
Woodhall Spa
Spilsby
Skegness
Ripley
Newark-on-Trent
Heanor
Southwell
Hucknall
NOTTINGHAM
Leadenham
Ilkeston
West Bridgford
Bingham
Sleaford
Boston
Long Eaton
Grantham
Hunstanton
Sheringham
Donington
Wells-next-the-Sea
Blakeney
Cromer
Burton-upon-Trent
Sutterton
Holt
Shepshed
Rempstone
The Wash
Sandringham House
Mundesley
Coalville
Loughborough
Melton Mowbray
Bourne
Spalding
Holbeach
Long Sutton
King's Lynn
Fakenham
North Walsham
N O R F O L K
Aylsham
LEICESTER
Stamford
Crowland
Wisbech
East Dereham
Low Street
Hinckley
Oakham
Eye
Guyhirn
Outwell
Swaffham
Acle
Oadby
Uppingham
Downham Market
Watton
NORWICH
Market Harborough
Corby
Whittlesey
March
Stradsett
Wymondham
E N G L A N D
Peterborough
Weldon
Oundle
Mundford
Attleborough
Bedworth
Rothwell
Desborough
C A M B R I D G E
Thrapston
Brandon
Bungay
Rugby
Kettering
Littleport
Thetford
Harleston

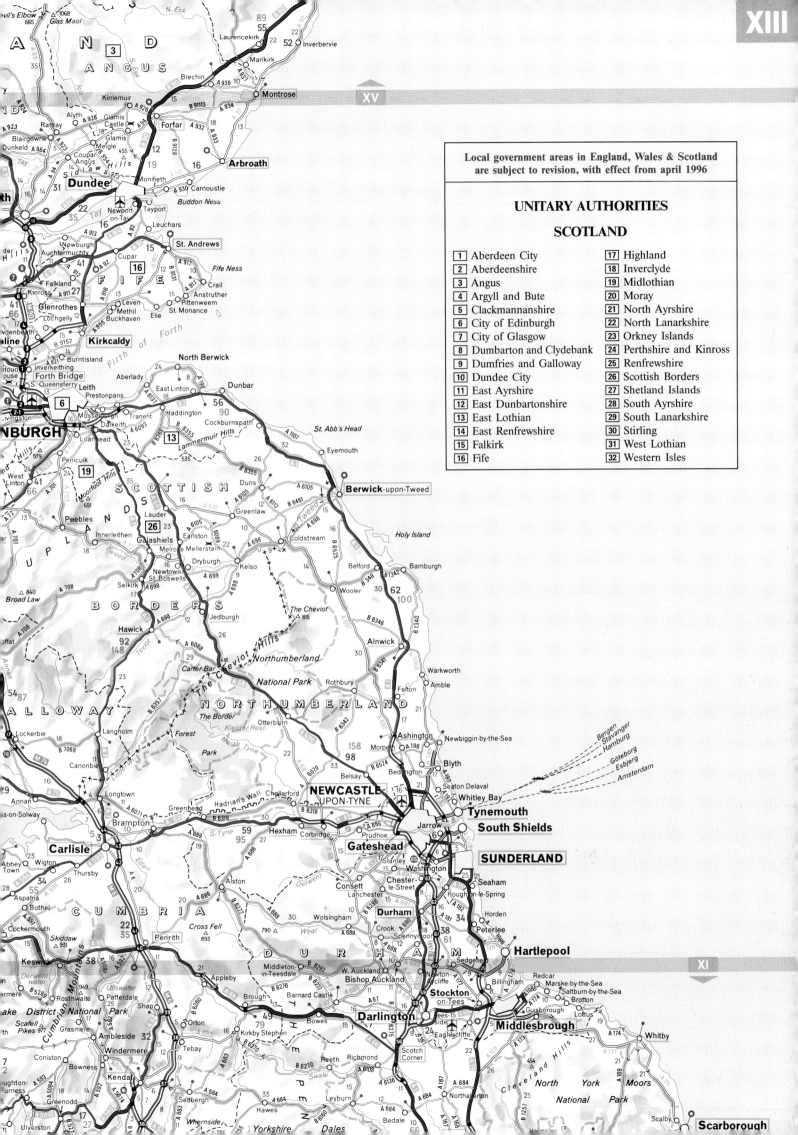

XV

Local government areas in England, Wales & Scotland are subject to revision, with effect from april 1996

UNITARY AUTHORITIES

SCOTLAND

1 Aberdeen City	17 Highland
2 Aberdeenshire	18 Inverclyde
3 Angus	19 Midlothian
4 Argyll and Bute	20 Moray
5 Clackmannanshire	21 North Ayrshire
6 City of Edinburgh	22 North Lanarkshire
7 City of Glasgow	23 Orkney Islands
8 Dumbarton and Clydebank	24 Perthshire and Kinross
9 Dumfries and Galloway	25 Renfrewshire
10 Dundee City	26 Scottish Borders
11 East Ayrshire	27 Shetland Islands
12 East Dunbartonshire	28 South Ayrshire
13 East Lothian	29 South Lanarkshire
14 East Renfrewshire	30 Stirling
15 Falkirk	31 West Lothian
16 Fife	32 Western Isles

XI

Cape Wrath
Butt of Lewis
Port of Ness
Whiten Head
Durness
Loch Eriboll
Kinlochbervie
A 838
20
Tongue
Col
LEWIS
Barvas
16 A 857
908 △ Foinaven
927 △ Ben Hope
Flannan I.
Carloway
A 858
12 A 857
292 △
Scourie
A 894
Laxford Bridge
A 838
B 838
Stornoway
Broad Bay
Portnaguran
Tiumpan Head
Kylestrome
Altnaharra
Ben Klibre
Garynahine
A 858
A 859
12 A 866
Eye Peninsula
THE MINCH
A 894
34
Inchnadamph
40
961 △
574 △
36
Eddrachillis Bay
A 837
19
Ben More Assynt
A 838
Loch Shin
Hushinish
B 887
Clisham
799 △
572 △
Kebock Head
Rubha Còigeach
Lochinver
998 △
Loch Broom
A 836
Tarbert
WESTERN
Coigach
743 △
18
A 835
Ledmore
Lairg
West Loch Tarbert
Toe Head
24
Harris
Leverburgh
A 859
Rubha Réidh
Ullapool
A 837
27 A 838
11
A 836
Rodel
Renish Point
ISLES
Laide
Gruinard Bay
12
A 835
Bonar Bridge
North Uist
Newtonferry
32
Gairloch
A 832
Dundonnell
1062 △
29
Beinn Dearg
1084 △
Easter
Tigharry
25
A 865
A 867
Lochmaddy
Sound of Harris
Waternish Point
A 855
Staffin
A 832
980 △
Sgurr Mór
1110 △
57
92
19
347 △
13
9
Uig
34
Wester
Ross
Ben Wyvis
A 835
1046 △
Balivanich
A 865
Benbecula
Dunvegan Head
Loch Snizort
The Storr
719 △
Rona
20
A 832
Loch Maree
Torridon
Liathach
1054 △
Kinlochewe
A 832
Achnasheen
A 890
15
Garve
Dingwall
A 862
Black
Creagorry
A 850
22
16
Dunvegan
A 863
Portree
Raasay
Sound of Raasay
896 △
A 886
24
Shieldaig
10 A 896
9
19
Glen Carron
A 832
Contin
Muir of Ord
A 831
A 862
Tore
South Uist
22
620 △
Bracadale
A 863
21
Idrigill Point
52
84
9
444 △
Lochcarron
15
1083 △
A 831
A 86
B 862
SEA OF
THE HEBRIDES
Loch Bracadale
Sligachan
Sconser
Scalpay
SKYE
17
Kyle of Lochalsh
Stromeferry
A 890
Cannich
A 831
Drumnadrochit
Ness
A 890
Daliburgh
Lochboisdale
Broadford
5
Dornie
Eilean Donan Castle
Carn Eige
1183 △
Loch Ness
17
The Cuillins
993 △
Kyleakin
10
Kylerhea
14
Glenelg
Shiel Bridge
A' Chràlaig
1120 △
HIGH
Invermoriston
A 887
Foyers
33
Whitebridge
Sound of Barra
Elgol
Isleornsay
17
50
80
Loch Quoich
A 87
69
43
7
Barra
A 888
383 △
Bayhirivagh
Canna
Ardvasar
Sound of Sleat
A 851
32
13
Invergarry
Fort Augustus
Monadhliath M
Carn Ban
942 △
King
Castlebay
Mallaig
Loch Nevis
Sgurr na Ciche
1040 △
Loch Arkaig
Loch Lochy
Glen Albyn
25
40
Newtonmore
Mingulay
Head
Rhum
812 △
Arisaig
19
Loch Morar
76
46
Glenfinnan
882 △
Caledonian Canal
15
Creag Meagaidh
1130 △
Laggan
A 86
Dalwhinnie
Sound of Arisaig
A 861
Spean Bridge
30
XII
Eigg
A 861
10
Loch Shiel
33
Fort William
Ben Nevis
1344 △
Ben Alder
1148 △
Loch Ericht
Pass of Drumoch
A 462
Coll
Kilchoan
528 △
Salen
B 8007
Strontian
888 △
Corran
Inchree
Onich
9
Ballachulish
Glen Coe
Kinloch Rannoch
Arinagour
Tobermory
B 8073
A 884
13
A 861
Kentallen
1141 △
Bidean nam Bian
33
Loch Rannoch
Schiehallion
Tiree
Dervaig
Sound of Mull
Lochaline
19
Portnacroish
Scarinish
L. Tua
Lochaline

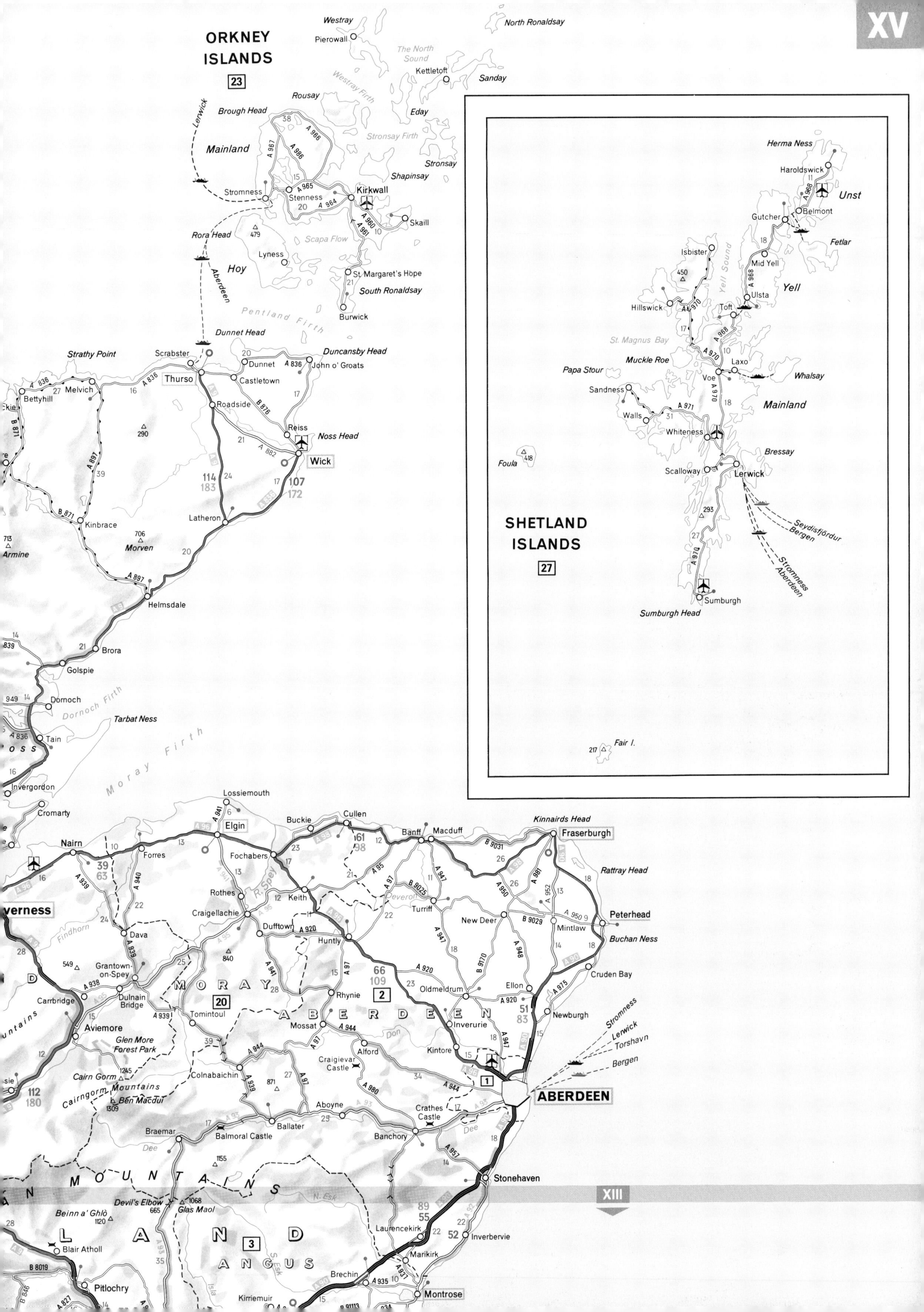

ORKNEY ISLANDS
23

Westray
Pierowall
North Ronaldsay
The North Sound
Kettletoft
Sanday
Rousay
Brough Head
Eday
Stronsay Firth
Westray Firth
Mainland
Lerwick
A 967
A 966
38
A 966
Shapinsay
Stronsay
15
Stenness
A 965
Kirkwall
A 964
20
Stromness
A 960
A 961
Skaill
10
Rora Head
479
Aberdeen
Lyness
Scapa Flow
St. Margaret's Hope
Hoy
21
South Ronaldsay
Pentland Firth
Burwick

Dunnet Head
Strathy Point
Scrabster
20
Duncansby Head
Dunnet
A 836
John o' Groats
Thurso
16
A 836
Castletown
27
Melvich
Roadside
B 876
17
Bettyhill
A 897
Reiss
290
A 882
Noss Head
A 836
39
21
Wick
B 871
114
24
183
B 871
17
107
Kinbrace
706
Latheron
172
713
Morven
20
Armine
A 897
Helmsdale

14
839
21
Brora
Golspie
949
14
Dornoch
Dornoch Firth
Tarbat Ness
16
Tain
OSS
A 836
Invergordon
Cromarty
Moray Firth

SHETLAND ISLANDS
27

Herma Ness
Haroldswick
11
Unst
A 968
Belmont
Gutcher
Fetlar
Isbister
Mid Yell
Yell Sound
450
A 968
18
A 970
Yell
Hillswick
Ulsta
17
Toft
St. Magnus Bay
A 968
Muckle Roe
Laxo
10
Papa Stour
Voe
A 970
Whalsay
Sandness
Walls
A 971
Mainland
31
A 971
18
Whiteness
Bressay
Foula
418
Scalloway
Lerwick
293
27
Seydisfjördur
Bergen
A 970
Stromness
Aberdeen
Sumburgh
Sumburgh Head
217
Fair I.

Lossiemouth
Kinnairds Head
A 941
6
Elgin
Buckie
Cullen
Banff
Macduff
Fraserburgh
Nairn
10
13
Fochabers
161
12
B 9031
Rattray Head
39
Forres
23
98
26
63
A 939
A 940
13
A 95
A 947
A 952
13
18
Rothes
12
Keith
B 9025
11
A 950
Peterhead
Findhorn
24
Craigellachie
Deveron
Turriff
A 950 9
Dava
Dufftown
A 920
22
New Deer
B 9029
Mintlaw
Buchan Ness
549
Huntly
A 97
18
A 948
14
18
Grantown-on-Spey
840
15
66
A 920
23
A 975
Cruden Bay
Carrbridge
A 938
Rhynie
109
Oldmeldrum
Ellon
A 920
51
Dulnain Bridge
A 939
20
Inverurie
Newburgh
83
15
Aviemore
Tomintoul
Mossat
A 944
Kintore
15
Stromness
12
39
A 97
A 944
Alford
18
A 947
Lerwick
1245
Colnabaichin
Craigievar Castle
34
A 944
Torshavn
Cairn Gorm
871
27
A 980
1
Bergen
112
Ben Macdui
A 93
Aboyne
Crathes Castle
17
ABERDEEN
180
1309
Ballater
25
Banchory
A 957
Braemar
Balmoral Castle
Dee
18
1155
N. Esk
Stonehaven
1068
89
XIII
Devil's Elbow
Glas Maol
55
Beinn a' Ghlò
665
22
52
Inverbervie
1120
3
Laurencekirk
22
Blair Atholl
ANGUS
Marykirk
A 935
10
B 8019
Brechin
Montrose
B 827
Pitlochry
Kirriemuir

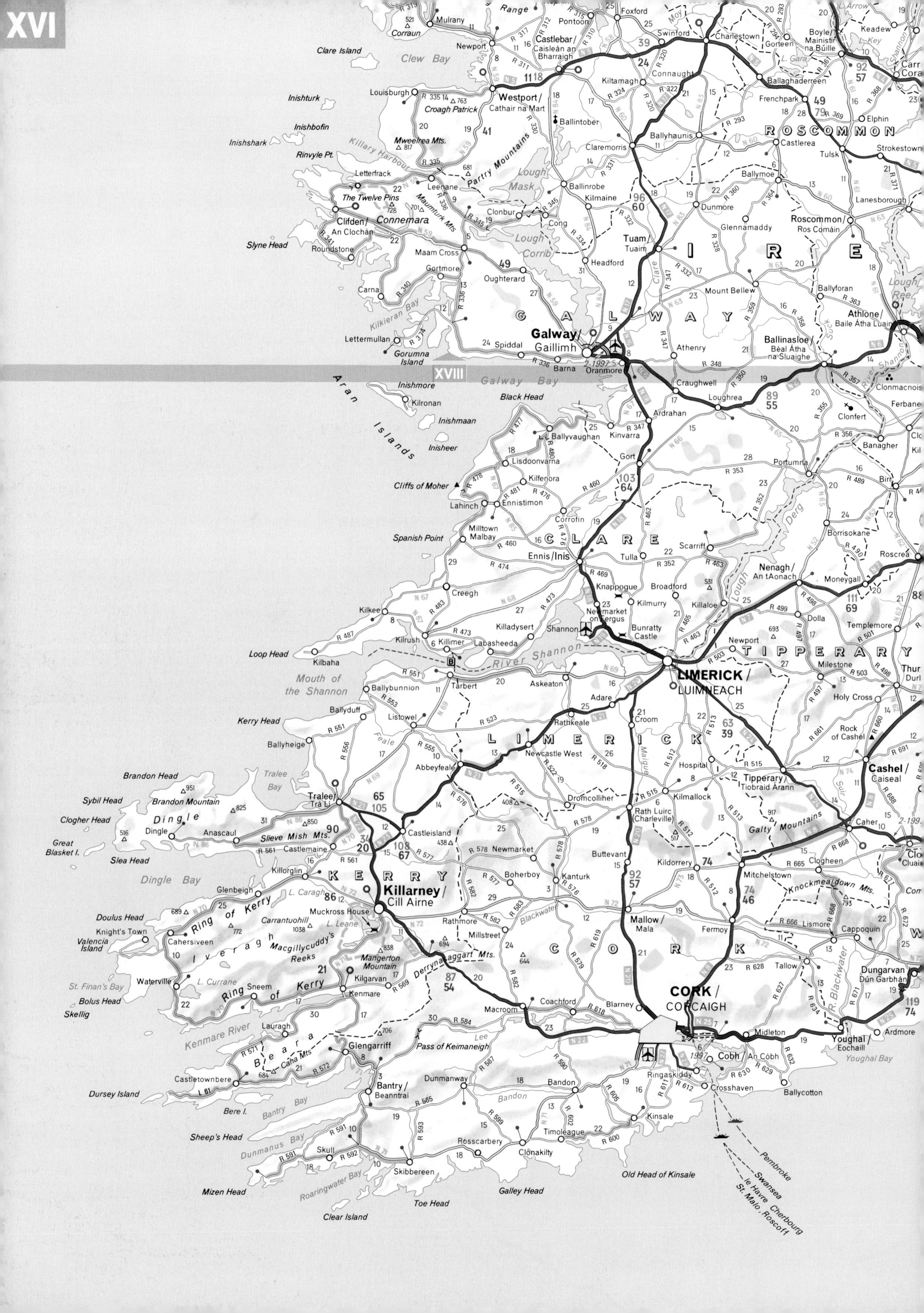

Range
Foxford
Mulrany
Corraun
Castlebar / Caisleán an Bharraigh
Newport
Swinford
Charlestown
Pontoon
Boyle / Mainistir na Búille
Keadew
Gorteen
Carr
Cora
L. Key
L. Arrow
Moy

Clare Island
Clew Bay
Westport / Cathair na Mart
Louisburgh
Croagh Patrick
Ballintober
Kiltamagh
Connaught
Charlestown
Ballaghaderreen
Frenchpark
Elphin
ROSCOMMON
Castlerea
Tulsk
Strokestown
Lanesborough

Inishturk
Inishbofin
Inishshark
Mweelrea Mts.
Rinvyle Pt.
Letterfrack
Leenane
Ballinrobe
Claremorris
Ballyhaunis
Dunmore
Roscommon / Ros Comáin
Glennamaddy
Ballyforan
Ballymoe

The Twelve Pins
Clifden / An Clochán
Connemara
Roundstone
Slyne Head
Maam Cross
Clonbur
Cong
Lough Mask
Kilmaine
Tuam / Tuaim
Mount Bellew
Ballinasloe / Béal Átha na Sluaighe
Athlone / Baile Átha Luain
Lough Ree

Carna
Gortmore
Oughterard
Headford
Lough Corrib
Athenry
CLARE
GALWAY

Lettermullan
Gorumna Island
Galway / Gaillimh
Spiddal
Barna
Oranmore
Craughwell
Clonmacnois
Ferbane

XVIII
Galway Bay

Aran Islands
Inishmore
Kilronan
Black Head
Loughrea
Ardrahan
Clonfert
Banagher

Inishmaan
Inisheer
Ballyvaughan
Kinvarra
Gort
Portumna
Birr

Cliffs of Moher
Lisdoonvarna
Kilfenora
Lahinch
Ennistimon
Corrofin
Borrisokane
Roscrea

Spanish Point
Milltown Malbay
CLARE
Ennis / Inis
Tulla
Scarriff
Nenagh / An tAonach
Moneygall
Templemore

Creegh
Kilkee
Killadysert
Knappogue
Kilmurry
Broadford
Killaloe
Newport
Dolla
Thurles / Durl

Kilrush
Killimer
Labasheeda
Shannon
Newmarket on Fergus
Bunratty Castle
TIPPERARY

Loop Head
Kilbaha
River Shannon
Tarbert
LIMERICK / LUIMNEACH
Milestone
Holy Cross

Mouth of the Shannon
Ballybunnion
Ballyduff
Listowel
Askeaton
Adare
Croom
Rock of Cashel

Kerry Head
Ballyheige
Feale
Rathkeale
Newcastle West
Hospital
Tipperary / Tiobraid Árann
Cashel / Caiseal

Brandon Head
Sybil Head
Brandon Mountain
Clogher Head
Dingle
Tralee Bay
Tralee / Trá Lí
Abbeyfeale
Dromcollogher
Kilmallock
Galty Mountains
Caher

Great Blasket I.
Slea Head
Slieve Mish Mts.
Anascaul
Castleisland
Newmarket
Rath Luirc (Charleville)
Cloheen
Clo
Cluai

Killorglin
Castlemaine
KERRY
Boherboy
Kanturk
Buttevant
Kildorrery
Mitchelstown
Knockmealdown Mts.

Glenbeigh
Ring of Kerry
Muckross House
Killarney / Cill Airne
Rathmore
Millstreet
Mallow / Mala
Fermoy
Lismore
Cappoquin

Doulus Head
Knight's Town
Cahersiveen
Valencia Island
Carrantuohill
L. Leane
Macgillycuddy's Reeks
Rathmore
Blackwater
CORK
Tallow

St. Finan's Bay
Waterville
L. Currane
Iveragh
Ring of Kerry
Kilgarvan
Mangerton Mountain
Derrynasaggart Mts.
Dungarvan / Dún Garbhán

Bolus Head
Skellig
Sneem
Kenmare
Macroom
Coachford
Blarney
Youghal / Eochaill
Ardmore

Kenmare River
Lauragh
Beara
Caha Mts.
Glengarriff
Pass of Keimaneigh
Lee
Cork / Corcaigh
Midleton

Dursey Island
Castletownbere
Bere I.
Bantry / Beanntraí
Dunmanway
Bandon
Ringaskiddy
Cobh / An Cóbh
Crosshaven
Ballycotton

Sheep's Head
Dunmanus Bay
Skull
Bantry Bay
Timoleague
Kinsale

Mizen Head
Roaringwater Bay
Skibbereen
Rosscarbery
Clonakilty
Old Head of Kinsale

Toe Head
Clear Island
Galley Head

Pembroke
Swansea
le Havre, Cherbourg
St. Malo, Roscoff

XVI

Key to map symbols   Légende

Roads — Routes

Motorway and service areas		Autoroute et aires de service
Dual carriageway with motorway characteristics		Double chaussée de type autoroutier
Junctions: complete - limited		Échangeurs : complet - partiels
Numbered junctions		Numéros d'échangeurs
Major road:		Route de liaison principale :
dual carriageway		à chaussées séparées
4 lanes - 2 wide lanes		à 4 voies - à 2 voies larges
2 lanes - 2 narrow lanes		à 2 voies - à 2 voies étroites
Regional road network		Routes de liaison régionale :
dual carriageway - 2 wide lanes		à chaussées séparées - à 2 voies larges
2 lanes - 2 narrow lanes		à 2 voies - à 2 voies étroites
Other roads: surfaced-unsurfaced		Autre route : revêtue - non revêtue
Road under construction		Route en construction
(when available: with scheduled opening date)		(le cas échéant : date de mise en service prévue)
Footpath - Long distance footpath or bridleway		Sentier - Sentier de grande randonnée ou piste cavalière
Roundabout - Pass, altitude (in metres)		Rond-point - Col, altitude (en mètres)
Distances on motorways or roads		Distances sur autoroute et route :
in miles - in kilometres	24 39	en miles - en kilomètres

Official road classification — Classement des itinéraires

United Kingdom:		Royaume-Uni :
Motorway	M 5	Autoroute
Primary route	A 38	Itinéraire principal
Other roads	A 190 B 629	Autres routes
Destination on primary route network	YORK	Localité jalonnant les itinéraires principaux
Republic of Ireland:		République d'Irlande :
Motorway	M 1	Autoroute
National primary and secondary route	N 5 N 59	Itinéraire principal
Other road	R 561	Autre route

Obstacles — Obstacles

In Scotland: narrow road with passing places		En Écosse : route très étroite avec emplacements pour croisement
Road: prohibited - subject to restrictions		Route : interdite - à circulation réglementée
Toll barrier - One-way road		Barrière de péage - Sens unique
On major and regional roads:		Sur liaisons principales et régionales :
Height limit (under 15'6" IRL, 16'6" GB)	11'9	Hauteur limitée (au-dessous de 15'6" IRL, 16'6" GB)
Weight limit (under 16t)		Charge limitée (au-dessous de 16 t)
(restrictions liable to alteration)		(Peuvent avoir été modifiées depuis la date d'édition)
Gradient:	1: 7-1: 5 +1: 5	Pentes :
(ascent in the direction of the arrow)	14-20% +20%	(les flèches dans le sens de la montée)

Railways — Voies ferrées

Standard gauge - Passenger station		Voie ferrée - Gare voyageurs
Steam railway - Industrial track		Voie touristique - industrielle
Level crossing, railway passing		Passage de la route :
under road, over road		à niveau - supérieur - inférieur
Industrial cable way - Chair lift		Transporteur industriel aérien - Télésiège

Car ferries — Transport des véhicules

Seasonal services: in red		Liaisons saisonnières : signe rouge
boat - hovercraft		par bateau - par aéroglisseur
ferry (maximum load in metric tons)	15	par bac (charge maximum en tonnes)
Pedestrians and cycles		Transport des piétons et cycles seulement

Towns - Administration — Localités - Administration

Town having a plan in the Michelin Red Guide		Localité dont le plan figure dans le Guide Rouge Michelin
Town included in the above Michelin Guide	Ambleside	Localité ayant des ressources sélectionnées dans ce même guide
Local government boundary (see list p. VI and XIII)		Division administrative locale (voir liste p. VI et XIII)
Scottish and Welsh borders	+-+-+-+-+	Limite de l'Écosse et du Pays de Galles
International border	++++++++	Frontière internationale

Other symbols — Signes divers

Telecommunications mast - Lighthouse		Émetteur de télécommunication - Phare
Power station - Quarry - Mine		Centrale électrique - Carrière - Mine
Factory - Refinery		Industrie - Raffinerie
Racecourse - Caravan and camping site		Hippodrome - Camping, caravaning
Racing circuit - Pleasure boat harbour		Circuit automobile - Port de plaisance
Golf course - National Forest Park, National Park		Golf - Parc forestier national, parc national
Ireland: Fishing - Youth hostel - Greyhound racetrack		Irlande : Pêche - Auberge de jeunesse - Cynodrome
Forest walk - Country park - Cliff		Sentier signalisé - Parc de loisirs - Falaise
Scenic route		Parcours pittoresque
Airport - Airfield		Aéroport - Aérodrome

Principal sights: see Michelin Guides — Principales curiosités : voir Guides Michelin

Ecclesiastical building - Ruins - Monument		Édifice religieux - Ruines - Monument
Historic house, castle		Château, manoir, palais
Prehistoric monument - Cave		Monument mégalithique - Grotte
Ireland: Celtic cross, cross slab - Round tower		Irlande : Croix celte - Tour ronde
Zoo - Nature reserve, bird sanctuary		Parc animalier, zoo - Réserve d'oiseaux
Gardens - Miscellaneous sights		Jardin, parc - Curiosités diverses
Panorama - Viewpoint		Panorama - Point de vue
Towns or places of interest, places to stay	Rye / Elgol	Localités ou sites intéressants, lieux de séjour

Bóithre

Mótarbhealach agus ionaid seirbhíse

Carrbhealach dúbailte le saintréithe mótarbhealaigh

Acomhail mótarbhealaigh : iomlán - teoranta
Vimhreacha ceangail
Mórbhóthar :
carrshlí dhéach
4 lána - 2 leathanlána
2 lána - 2 chunglána
Líonra réigiúnach bóithre :
carrshlí dhéach - 2 leathanlána
2 lána - 2 chunglána
Bóithre eile : réidh - gan réitiú
Bóthar á dhéanamh
(an dáta oscailte sceidealta, mas eol)
Cosán - Cosán fadsli
Timpeall - Bearnas is a airde (i méadair)

Faid ar mhótarshlíte, ar bóithre :
i mílte - i méadair

Ffyrdd

Traffordd a mannau gwasanaethu

Ffordd ddeuol â nodweddion traffordd

Cyfnewidfeyd : wedi'i chwblhau - cyfyngedig
Rhifau'r cyffyrdd
Prif ffordd gysylltu :
ffordd ddeuol
4 lôn - 2 lôn lydan
2 lôn - 2 lôn gul
Rhydwaith ffyrdd rhanbarthol :
ffordd ddeuol - 2 lôn lydan
2 lôn - 2 lôn gul
Ffyrdd eraill : â wyneb - heb wyneb
Ffordd yn cael ei hadeiladu
(Os cyfodi yr achos : dyddiad agor disgwyliedig)
Llwybr troed - Llwybr hir neu lwybr ceffyl
Cylchfan - Bwlch a'i uchder (mewn metrau)

Pellter ar ffyrdd a thraffyrdd :
mewn miltiroedd - mewn kilometrau

Aicmiú oifigiúil bóithre

An Ríocht Aontaithe :
Mótarshlí
Príomhbhealach
Bóithre eile
Ceann scríbe ar ghréasán bóithre príomha
i bPloblacht na hÉireann :
Mótarshlí
Príomhbhóithre agus fobhóithre náisiúnta
Bóthar

Dosbarthiad ffyrdd swyddogol

M 5	
A 38	
A 190	B 629
YORK	
M 1	
N 5	N 59
R 561	

Y Deyrnas Gyfunol :
Traffordd
Prif ffordd
Ffyrdd eraill
Cyrchfan ar rwydwaith y prif ffyrdd
Gweriniaeth Iwerddon :
Traffordd
Prif ffordd genedlaethol a ffordd eilradd
Ffyrdd eraill

Constaicí

Bóthar cúng le hionaid phasála (in Albain)
Bóthar : toirmeasctha - faoi theorannú
Bacainn dola - Bóthar aonslí
Ar phríomhbhóithre agus ar bhóithre réigiúnacha :
Teorainneacha airde (faoi 15'6'' IRL, faoi 16'6'' GB)
Teorann Mheáchain (faoi 16 t)
(teorannu - inathraithe)
Grádán :
(suas treo an gha)

1:7-1:5   +1:5
14-20%   +20%

Rhwystrau

Yn yr Alban : ffordd gul â mannau pasio
Ffordd : gwaharddedig - cyfyngiadau arni
Rhwystr Toll - Unffordd
Ar brif ffyrdd a ffyrdd rhanbarthol :
Terfyn uchder (llai na 15'6'' IRL, 16'6'' GB)
Terfyn pwysau (llai na 16 t)
(y cyfyngiadau'n agored i gael eu newid)
Graddiant
(esgyn gyda'r saeth)

Iarnróid

Leithead caighdeánach - Staisiún paisinéirí
Iarnród thraein ghaile - Ráille tionsclaíoch
Crosaire comhréidh, iarnród ag dul
faoi bhóthar, os cionn bóthair
Cáblashlí thionsclaíoch - Cathaoir cábla

Rheilffyrdd

Lled safonol - Gorsaf deithwyr
Rheilffordd ager - Trac diwydiannol
Croesfan rheilffordd :
rheilffordd yn croesi ffordd, o dan ffordd
Lein gêbl ddiwydiannol - Cadair esgyn

Longsheirbhísí

Seirbhísí séasúracha : dearg
Bád - Árthach foluaineach
Fartha (uas-ualach : tonnaí méadracha)
Coisithe agus lucht rothar

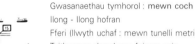

Llongau ceir

Gwasanaethau tymhorol : mewn coch
Ilong - Ilong hofran
Fferi (llwyth uchaf : mewn tunelli metrig)
Teithwyr ar droed neu feic yn unig

Bailte - Riarachán

Bailte a bhfuil a bplean in
Eolaí Dearg Michelin
Bailte a chuimsítear san
Eolaí Michelin sin
Teorainn Rialtais Áitiúil
Teorainn na hAlban agus teorainn na Breataine Bige

Teorainn idirnáisiúnta

Ambleside

- - - - - - - - -
+-+-+-+-+

++++++++++

Trefi - Gweinyddiaeth

Trefi â map ohonynt yn
Llyfr Coch Michelin
Trefi â gynhwysir yn
Llyfr Michelin uchod
Llywodraeth Leol
Ffin Cymru, ffin yr Alban

Ffin ryngwladol

Comharthaí Eile

Crann teileachumarsáide - Teach Solais
Stáisiún Giniúna - Cairéal - Mianach
Monarcha - Scaglann
Ráschúrsa - Láthair champa, láthair charbhán
Timpeall rásaíochta - Cuan bád aeraíochta
Machaire Gailf - Páirc Fhoraoise Náisiúnta, Páirc Náisiúnta
Éire : Iascaireacht - Brú chumann na hóige - Ráschúrsa con
Siúlóid fhoraoise - Páirc thuaithe - Aill
Bealach Aoibhinn

Aerfort - Aerpháirc

Symbolau eraill

Mast telathrebu - Goleudy
Gorsaf bŵer - Chwarel - Mwyngloddio
Ffatri - Purfa
Rasio Ceffylau - Leoedd i wersylla
Rasio Cerbydau - Harbwr cychod pleser
Cwrs golff - Parc Coedwig Cenedlaethol, Parc Cenedlaethol
Iwerdon : Pysgota - Hostel ieuenctid - Maes rasio milgwn
Llwybr coedwig - Parc gwledig - Clogwyn
Ffordd dygfeydd

Maes awyr - Maes glanio

Príomhionaid inspéise : féach Eolaithe Michelin

Foirgneamh Eaglasta - Fothrach - Séadchomhartha
Caisleán, teach stairiúil
Leacht meigiliteach - Pluais
Éire : Cros Cheilteach - Cloigtheach
Zú - Caomhnú nádúir, tearmannéan mara
Gáirdíní - Amhairc éagsúla

Lánléargas - Cothrom Radhairc

Bailte nó áiteanna inspéise baill lóistín

Rye
Elgol

Prif Olygfeydd : gweler Llyfr Michelin

Adeilag eglwysig - Adfeilion - Cofadail
Castell, tŷ hanesyddol
Heneb fegalithig - Ogof
Iwerdon : Croes Geltaidd - Tŵr crwn
Parc saffari, sŵ - Gwarchodfa natur
Gerddi, parc - Golygfeydd amrywiol

Panorama - Golygfan

Trefi new fannau o ddiddordeb, mannau i aros

C   D   E

Isles of Scilly (inset)

6°20

50°

A   B

34

32

Round Island
St. Martin's
Bryher
Tresco
Hugh Town
St. Mary's
Penzance
St. Agnes
Bishop Rocks
Isles of Scilly

6°20

Pentire Point
Padstow B.
Trevose Head
Trevone
Constantine Bay
St. Mer
Treyarnon
Little
Porthcothan
Petherick
Park Head
B 3276
Bedruthan Steps
Trenance
(△) Mawgan Porth
(△) Watergate Bay
Tregurrian (△)
B 3276
A 3059
(△) ▲ **Newquay**
A 3059
(△) Crantock
Trerice
A 392
8
(△) Holywell Bay
Holywell
A 3075
Fraddon
Penhale Point
Cubert
St. Newlyn
A 3076
East
9
Ligger or
Summerc
Perran Bay
Goonhavern
Mitchell
(△) Perranporth
B 3285
5½
A 3076
12
Perranzabuloe
Ladock
B 3284
A 30
St. Agnes Head
St. Agnes
5½
A 3075
Trispen
St. Agnes Head
192
Mithian
A 390
21
The Beacon
B 3277
14
22
13
Porthtowan
B 3284
6
Probus
(△) Portreath
Blackwater
15·3
A 39
Tin Streaming
Chacewater
Truro (△)
Hell's Mouth
Illogan
1½
A 390
Kea
St Michael
23   37
St. Day
Penkevil
St. Ives
Redruth
(△)
8
Come-to-Good
St. Ives Bay
Gwithian
Gwennap
B 3289
Ruan High
Camborne
7
Perranarworthal
Lanes
Zennor
Carbis Bay
Trelissick
Feock
Ve
247
Halsetown
A 3014
Praze-an-
Garden
10
Gurnard's Head
Hayle (△)
Beeble
252
Mylor
Penwith
B 3303
A 393
Bridge
B 3289
Portscatho
Pendeen Watch
B 3280
Stithians
13½
252
A 39
St-Just in Roseland
252
St. Erth
Leedstown (△)
10½
(△)
Madron
B 3302
2
Lamanva
Penryn
Cape Cornwall
Carleen (△)
205
B 3291
15·6
(△) St. Just
Ludgvan
8
St. Mawes
Trengwainton
Marazion
Wendron
5½
Zone Point
Sancreed
Relubbus
Mawnan
Falmouth (▲)
224
Rosudgeon
B 3302
Smith
Falmouth Bay
9   **Penzance**
194
14
Constantine
Glendurgan
Whitesand Bay
Newlyn
Breage
10
Mawnan
Cross-an-Wra
St Michael's
Praa
Sithney
Helford
Sennen
Mount
Sands
Mawnan
Land's End
Mousehole
Cudden Point
Helston
Gweek
Nare Point
B 3283
Culdrose
(△)
Gillan
St. Buryan
Lamorna
Porthleven
Helford
Manaccan
Longships
Gunwalloe
Mawgan
Porthallow
Gwennap Head
Mount's Bay
B 3293
Lizard
Porthgwarra
Poldhu Point
11
113
St. Keverne
Manacle Point
(△) Mullion
A 3083
B 3293
Isles of Scilly (St. Mary's)
B 3296
Peninsula
(△) Coverack
Mullion Cove
Kynance Cove
Black Head
Ruan Minor
Wolf Rock
Lizard
34
Lizard Pt.

C   D   E

Height limit (Feet/Metres)
Hauteur limitée (Pieds/Mètres)
Zulässige Gesamthöhe (Fuß/Meter)
Vrije hoogte (Voet/Meter)

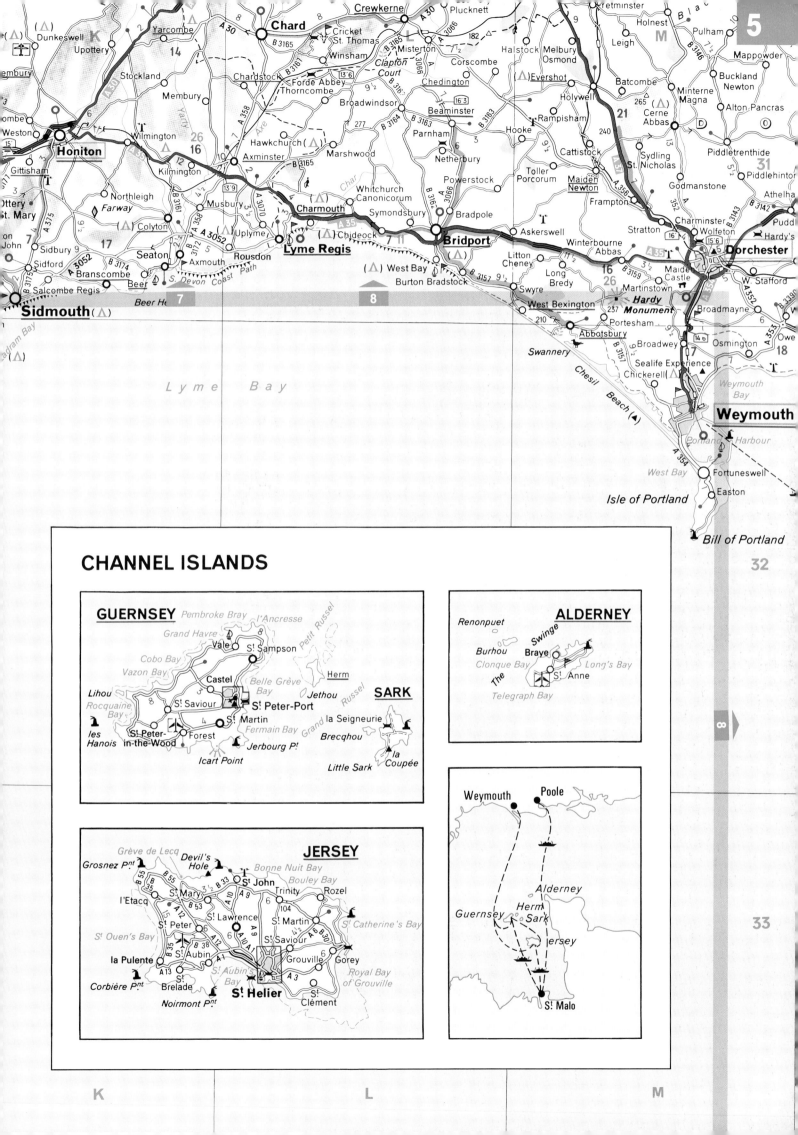

G

H

I

29

30

31

Lundy

(△▲) **Ilfracombe**
Berrynarbor *Heddon's Mouth* Woody Bay (△)
Lynton Lynmouth
Lee Chambercombe Combe Martin Hunter's Inn *Valley of the Rocks*
Morte Point Mortehoe A A 399 Parracombe A 39
Woolacombe (△) W. Down (△) 262 13 A 3123 Challacombe △ 487 B 3358 *Exmoo*
Morte Bay 210 480 △
Baggy Point **15** B 3230 **13** **12** A 39 Arlington Court 493 △
Putsborough Georgeham Muddiford Bratton A 39 Brayford
Croyde 4½ B 3231 Fleming 10
Saunton Braunton **Barnstaple** (△) E. Buckland
Braunton Wrafton Punchardon A 361 N. Molton
Burrows *Taw* 6 A 399
Fremington Goodleigh 9 A 361 9
Bishop's W. Buckland A 361 27
Barnstaple Appledore Instow Tawton Swimbridge 43 South Mo
or Westward Ho! Northam 69 A 39 Newton Chittlehampton B 3227
Bideford Bay Abbotsham **Bideford** Tracey 6½ 7 B 3226
Hartland Point Atherington Umberleigh (△) Alswear Bish
Hartland Quay Hartland Clovelly Fairy Cross Landcross A 3227 13½ Chittlehamholt Nym
Horn's Cross High Bickington *R. Taw* King's
Woolfardisworthy **40 25** Parkham Buckland St. Giles B 3217 12 Nympton
233 △ △ 216 Brewer B 3232 **40 64**
Welcome *Torridge* A 388 **Great** Burrington Chulmleigh
Cliffs W. Putford A 386 **Torrington** Beaford Eggesford Chawleigh
Morwenstow Stibb Cross Lit. Torrington **30 48** (△) Dolton Ashley B 3042
(△) Bradworthy Merton Ashreigney Wembworthy B 3220 4 Lapfo
Kilkhampton *Waldon* Milton Damerel B 3217 Winkleigh 21
Tamar 13 Iddesleigh Monkokehampton B 3220
Poughill *Lake* Shebbear Petrockstowe
Bude Stratton Chilsworthy Thornbury Sheepwash Hatherleigh Exbourne N. Tawton A 3072 Bow Colel
Bude Launcells (△) Bradford Black B 3216 Jacobstowe Sampford
Marhamchurch Holsworthy Torrington A 3072 Inwardleigh Courtenay Colebro
(△) Widemouth Bay Bridgerule (△) 13 3 A 3072 *Lew* Northlew Folly B 3219 Spreyton
Clawton 13½ Gate
beak Point (△) Poundstock Whitstone N. Tamerton Halwill (△) Okehampton
St. Gennys Week Junction Northlew Sticklepath S. Tawton
Crackington Haven (△) △ 166 St. Mary Ashwater Belstone S. Zeal Spinster's Roc
28 Jacobstow Boyton Bratton *Thrushel* Sourton Whiddon Down Castle Drew
259 △ Warbstow Clovelly Throwleigh Sandy Park
N. Petherwin St. Giles-on-the-Heath Bridestowe *High* Scorhill Castle
Ortery Werrington Broadwoodwidger **15** *Willhays* 621 △ Easton Drogo

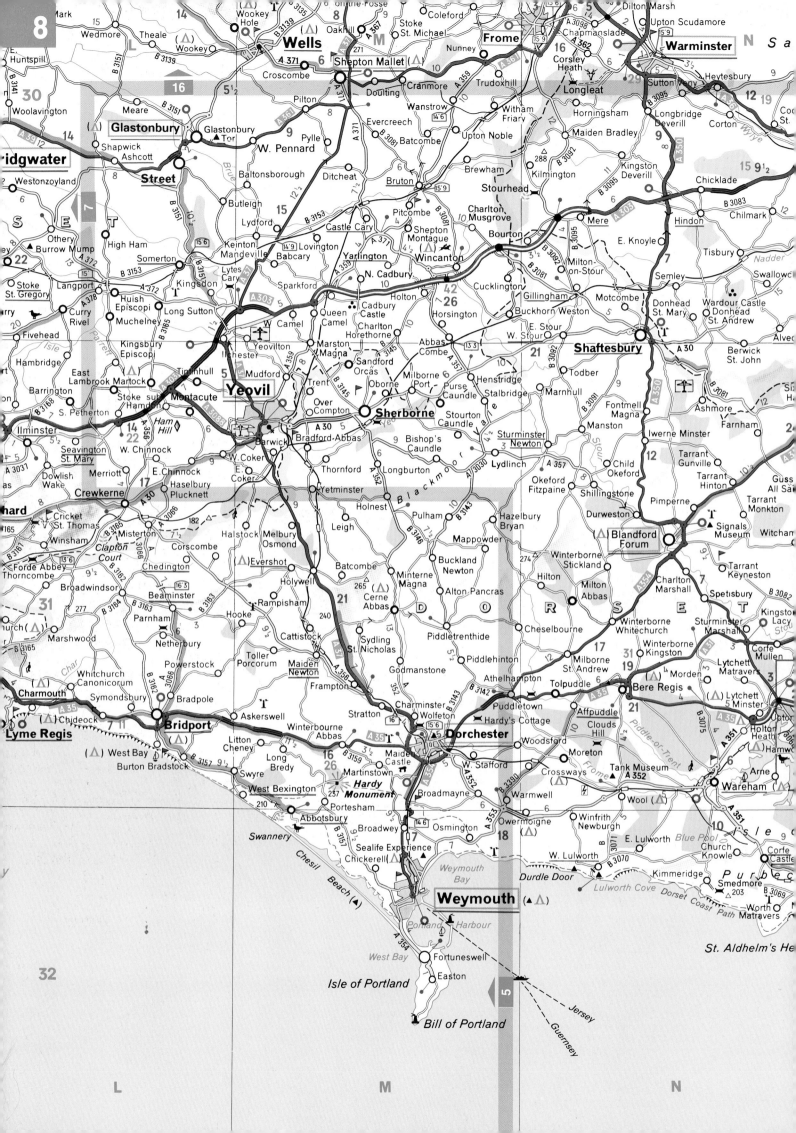

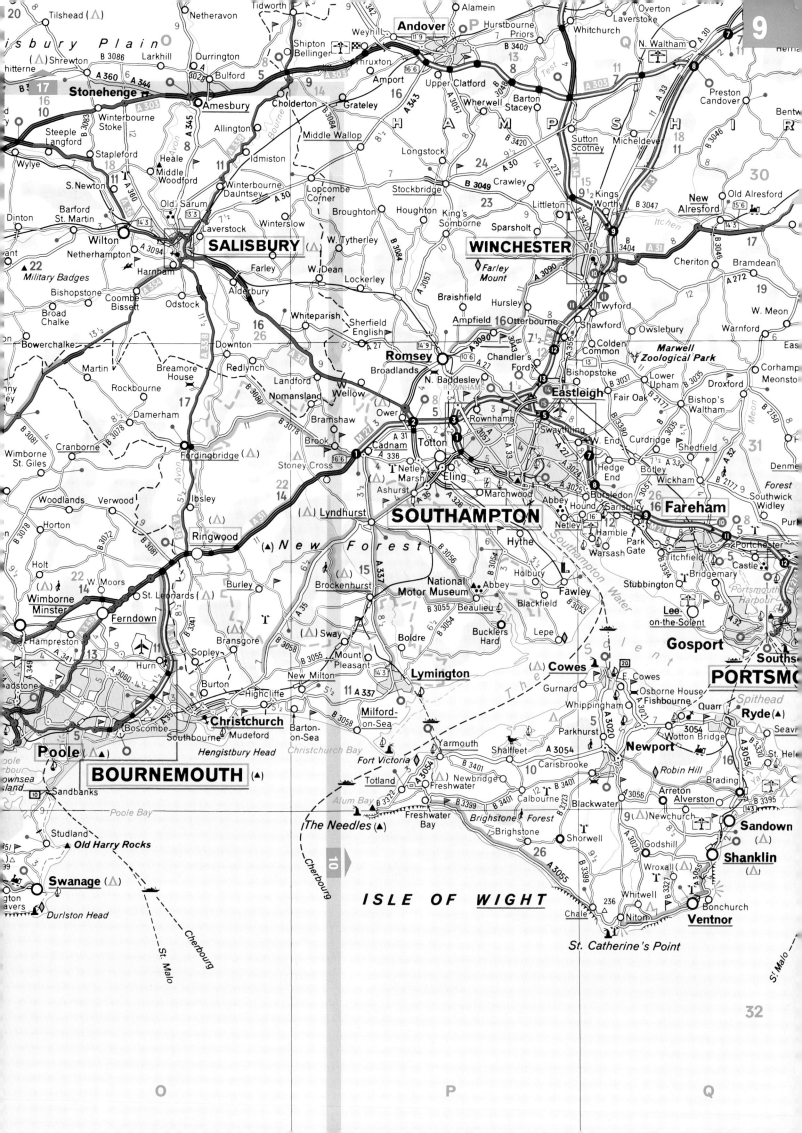

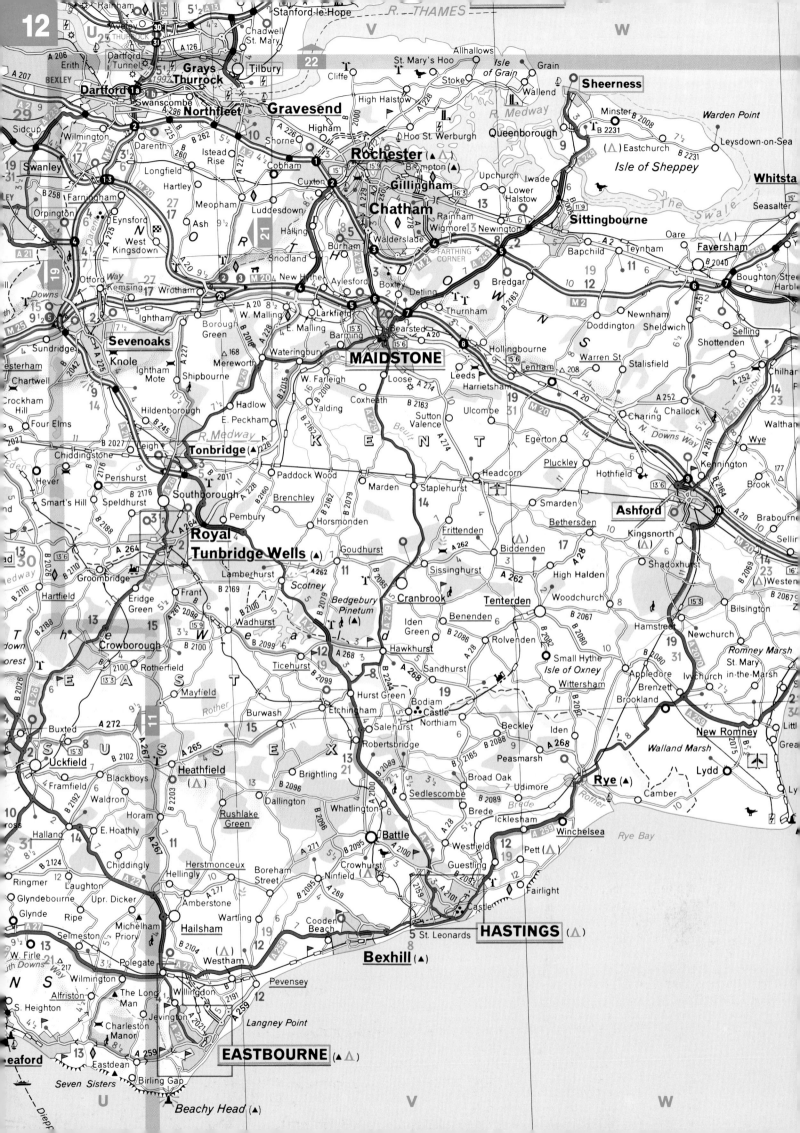

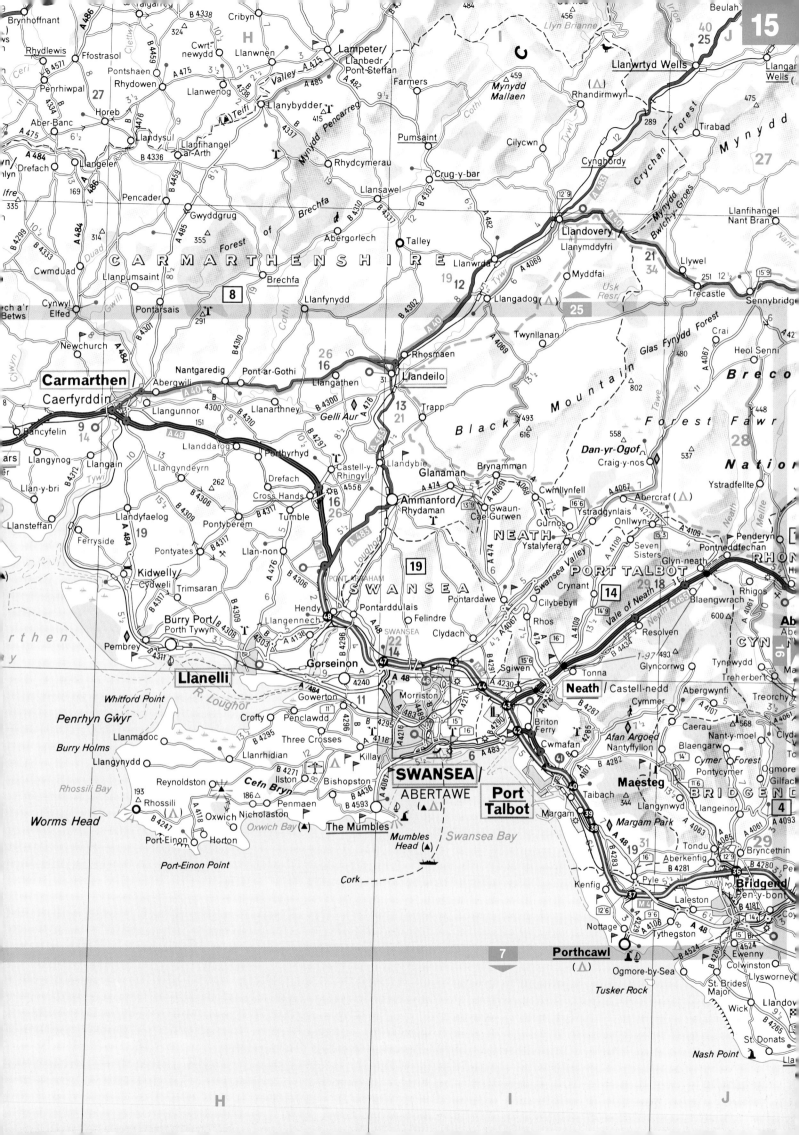

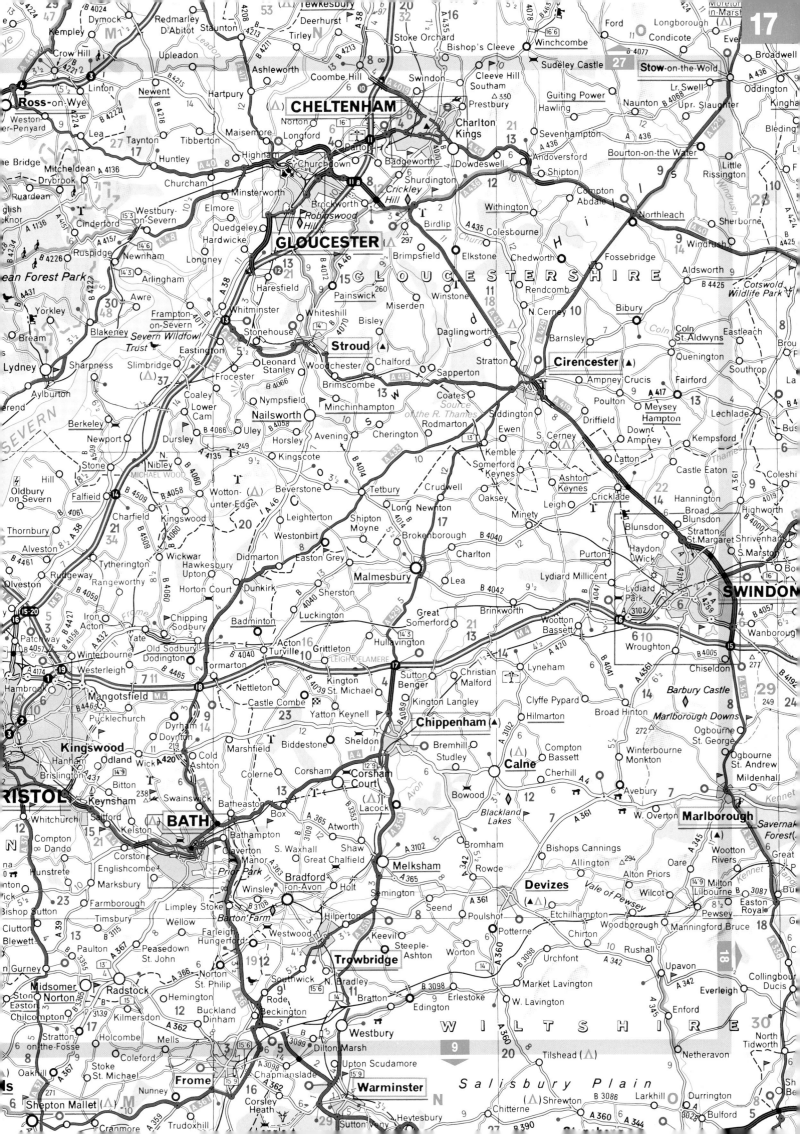

19

Chesham · Amersham · Beaconsfield · **Watford** · Bushey · **Potters Bar** · Borehamwood · Edgware · Mill Hill · Barnet · East Barnet · Cockfosters · Trent Park

Chorleywood · **Rickmansworth** · Northwood · Pinner · Wealdstone · **HARROW** · Harrow on the Hill · Wembley · Kingsbury · Hendon · Golders Green · Hampstead · Highgate

Gerrards Cross · Uxbridge · **HILLINGDON** · Ruislip · Eastcote · Northolt · Greenford · Perivale · **EALING** · Acton · Willesden · Harlesden · **KENSINGTON** · **CAMDEN** · Regent's Park

Slough · Langley · Iver · Yiewsley · West Drayton · Hayes · Southall · **HESTON** · Chiswick · **HAMMERSMITH** · **FULHAM** · Battersea · **CHELSEA** · **WESTMINSTER**

Eton · **Windsor** · Datchet · Colnbrook · **HEATHROW AIRPORT** · Cranford · **HOUNSLOW** · Isleworth · Brentford · Syon Park · **Richmond** · Barnes · Mortlake · Putney · **WANDSWORTH** · Clapham · **LAMBETH**

Old Windsor · Wraysbury · **Staines** · Stanwell · Bedfont · Feltham · Hanworth · Twickenham · **RICHMOND UPON THAMES** · Ham · Teddington · Wimbledon · Tooting · Streatham

Ascot · Sunningdale · Virginia Water · **Egham** · Ashford · **Sunbury** · Hampton · Bushy Park · **Hampton Court** · **KINGSTON UPON THAMES** · Surbiton · **MERTON** · Morden · Mitcham

Windlesham · Lyne · **Chertsey** · Addlestone · Shepperton · Walton-on-Thames · Molesey · Long Ditton · **Esher** · Malden · Worcester Park · Cheam · **SUTTON** · Carshalton · Wallington

Bisley · Chobham · Ottershaw · **Weybridge** · Hersham · Claygate · Chessington · Hook · **Ewell** · **Epsom** · Banstead · Purley

Woking · Pyrford · Byfleet · Wisley · Cobham · Stoke d'Abernon · Oxshott · Ashtead · Burgh Heath · Chipstead · Coulsdon

Guildford · Merrow · West Clandon · East Horsley · Great Bookham · Effingham · Fetcham · **Leatherhead** · Headley · Walton-on-the-Hill · Kingswood

Clandon Park · East Clandon · West Horsley · Mickleham · Box Hill · Buckland · Merstham · **Redhill**

Dorking · Brockham · Betchworth · **Reigate** · South Nutfield

Gatwick Airport, Crawley, Brighton · Worthing · Portsmouth · Farnham, Southampton · Basingstoke, Reading · Bristol · Oxford, High Wycombe, Aylesbury · Leeds, Birmingham · St Albans · Luton, Bedford · Grantham

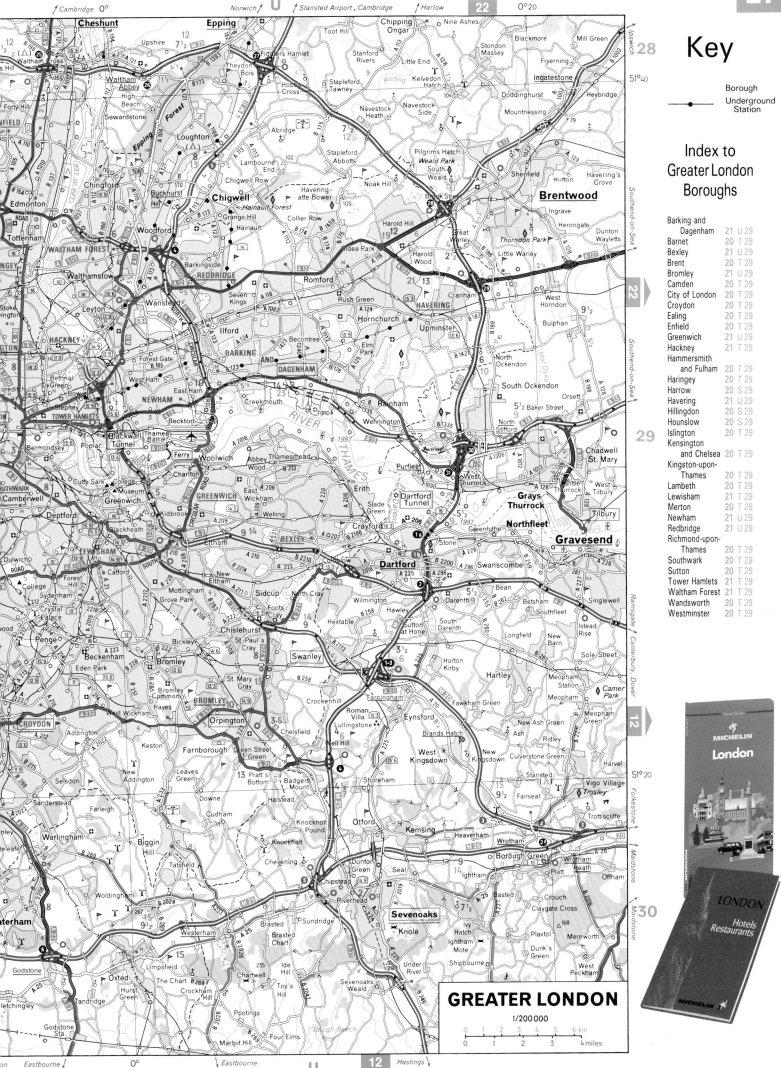

Key

	Borough
●—	Underground Station

Index to Greater London Boroughs

GREATER LONDON

1/200 000

0 1 2 3 4 5 6 km

0 1 2 3 4 miles

MICHELIN
London

LONDON
Hotels
Restaurants

MICHELIN

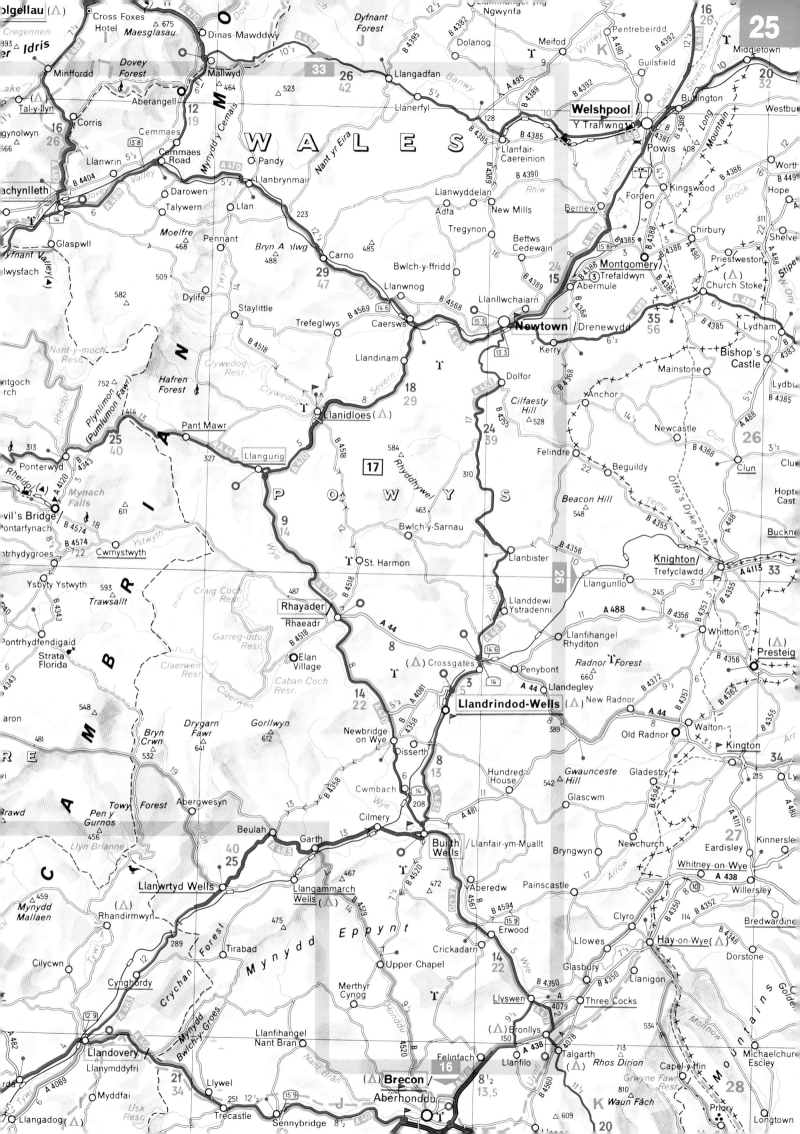

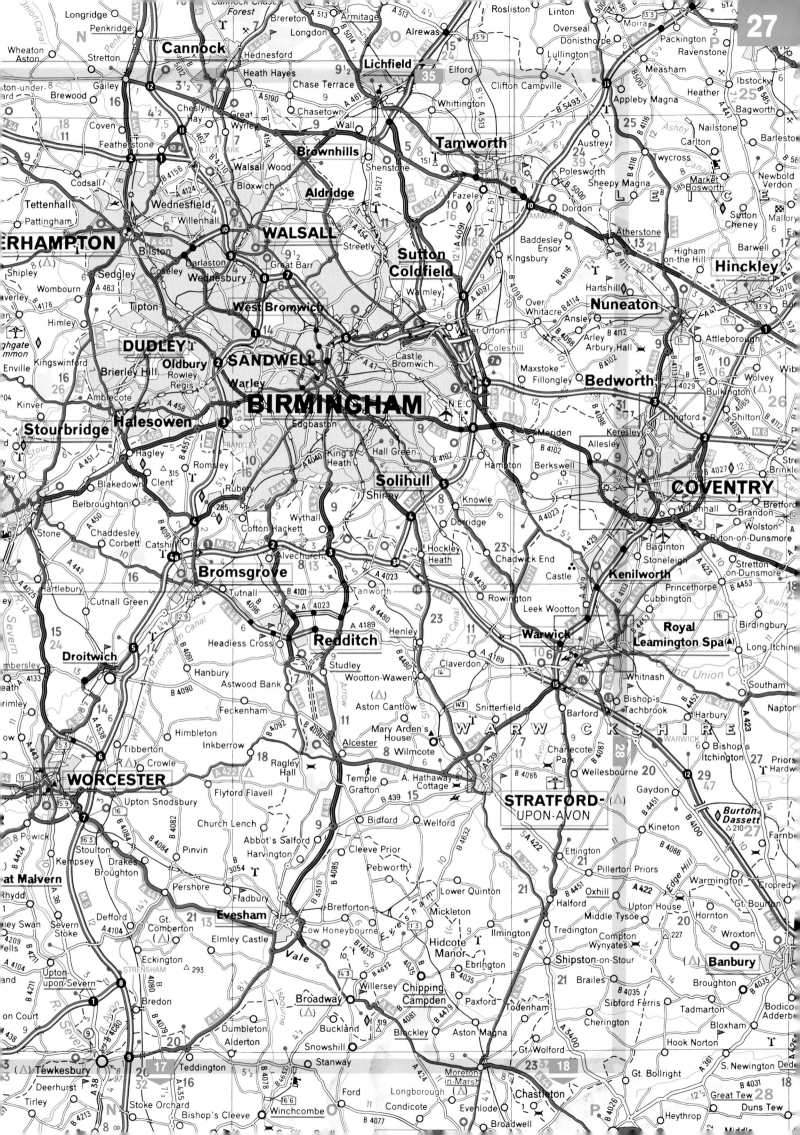

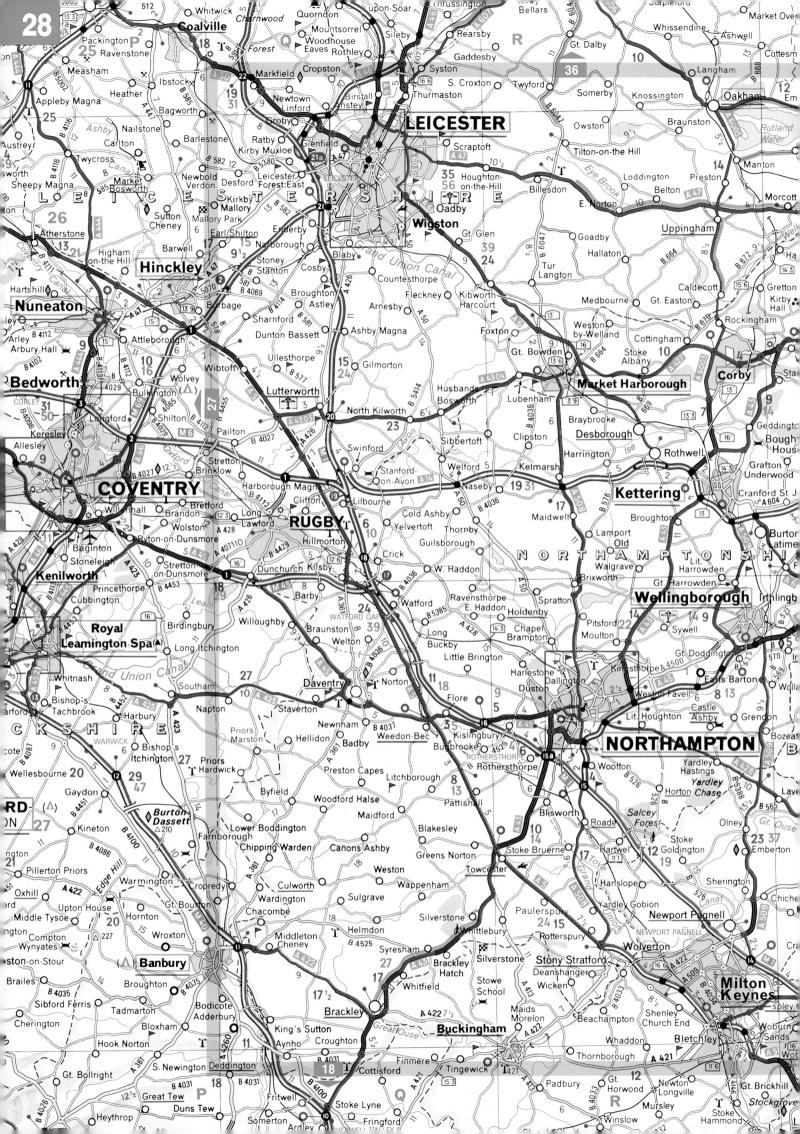

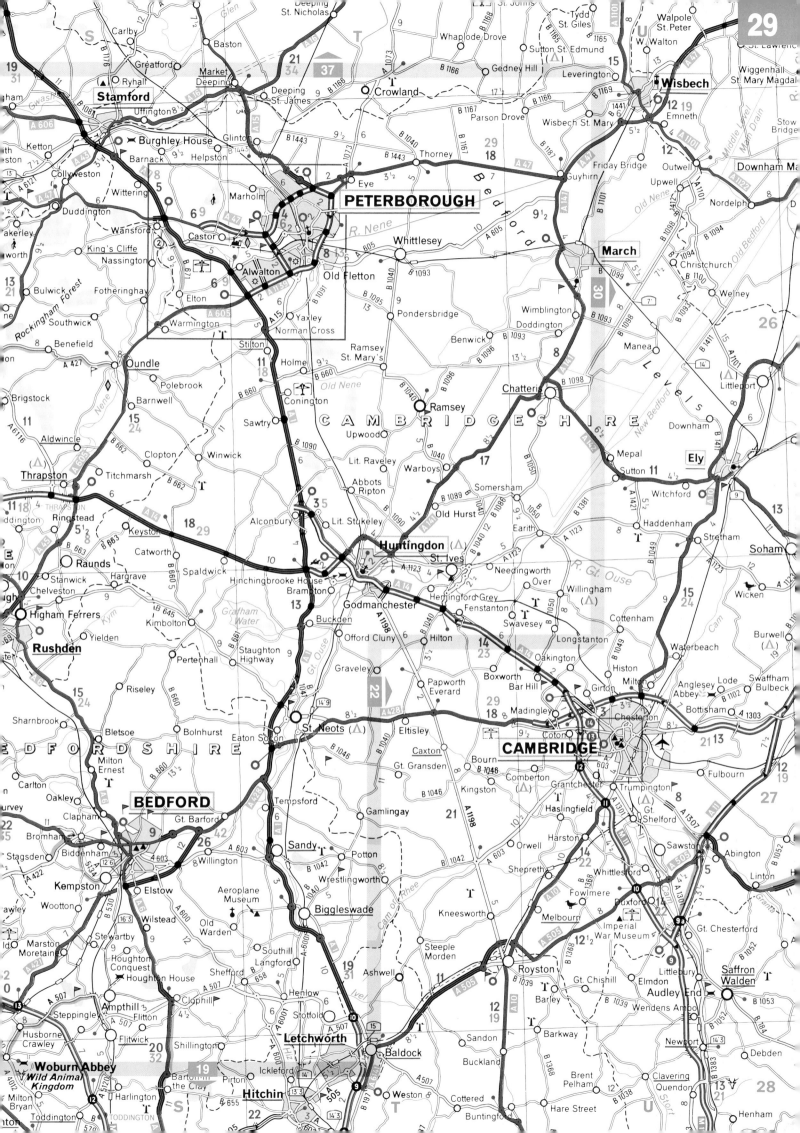

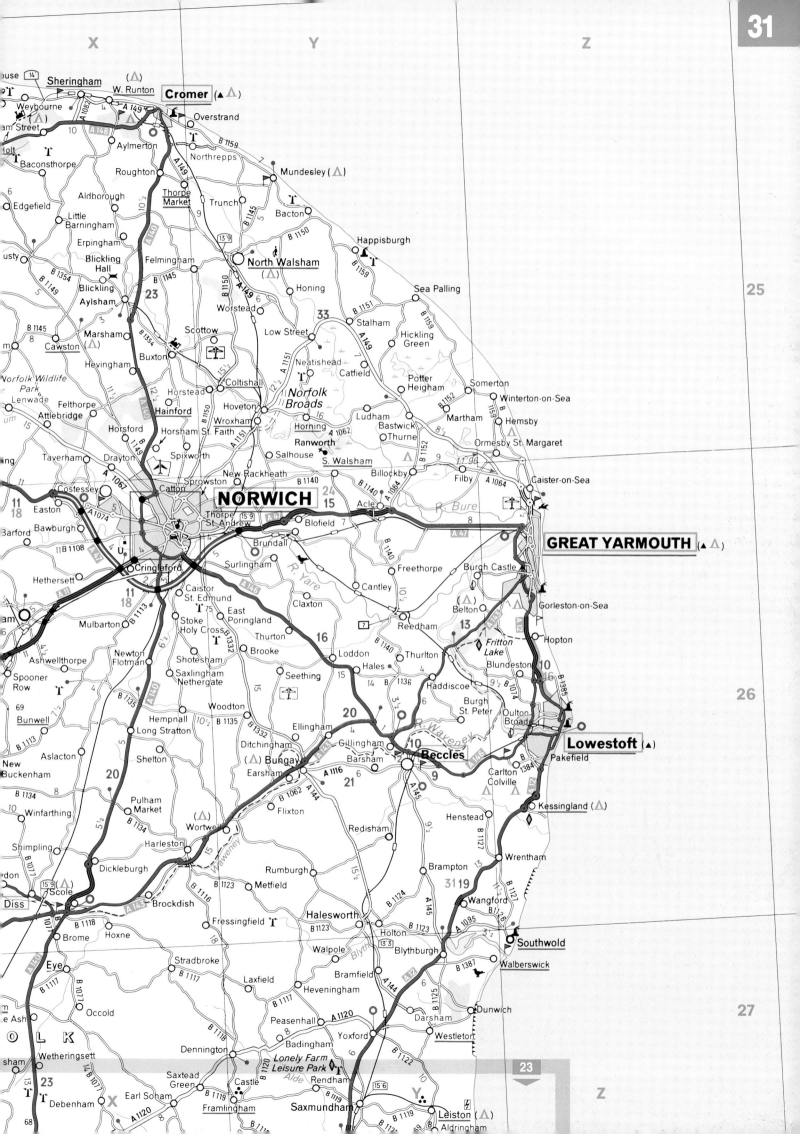

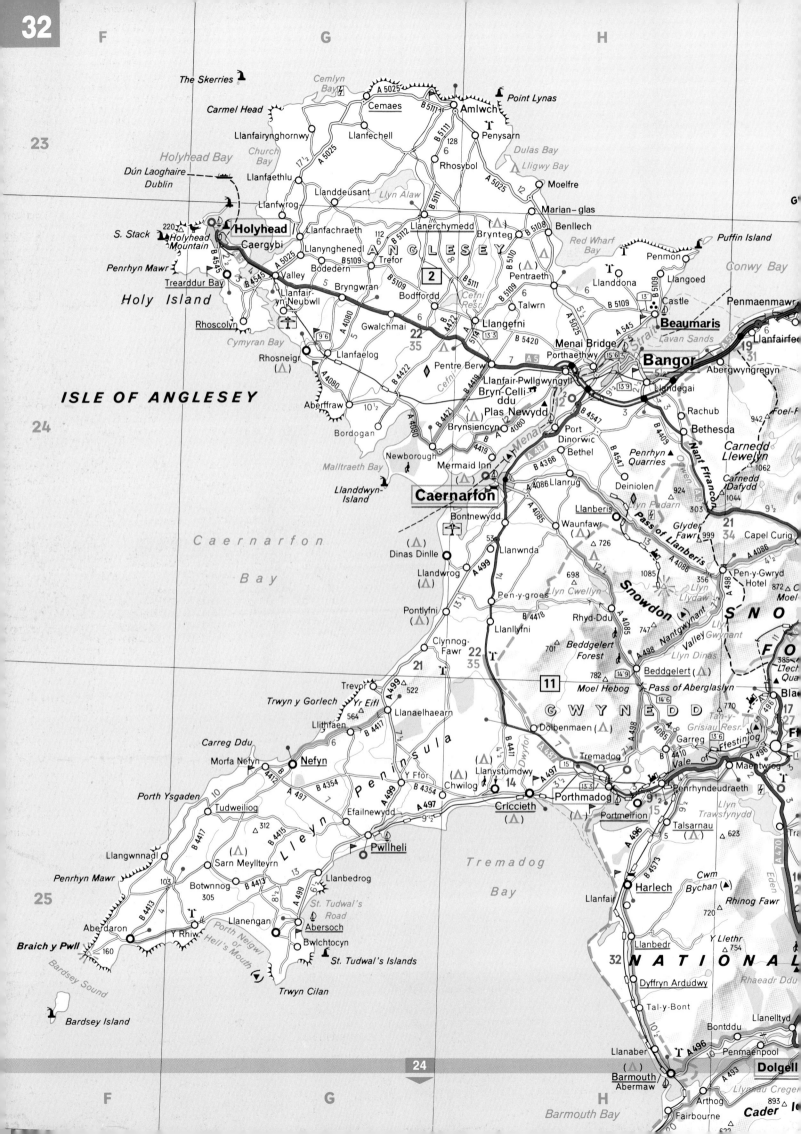

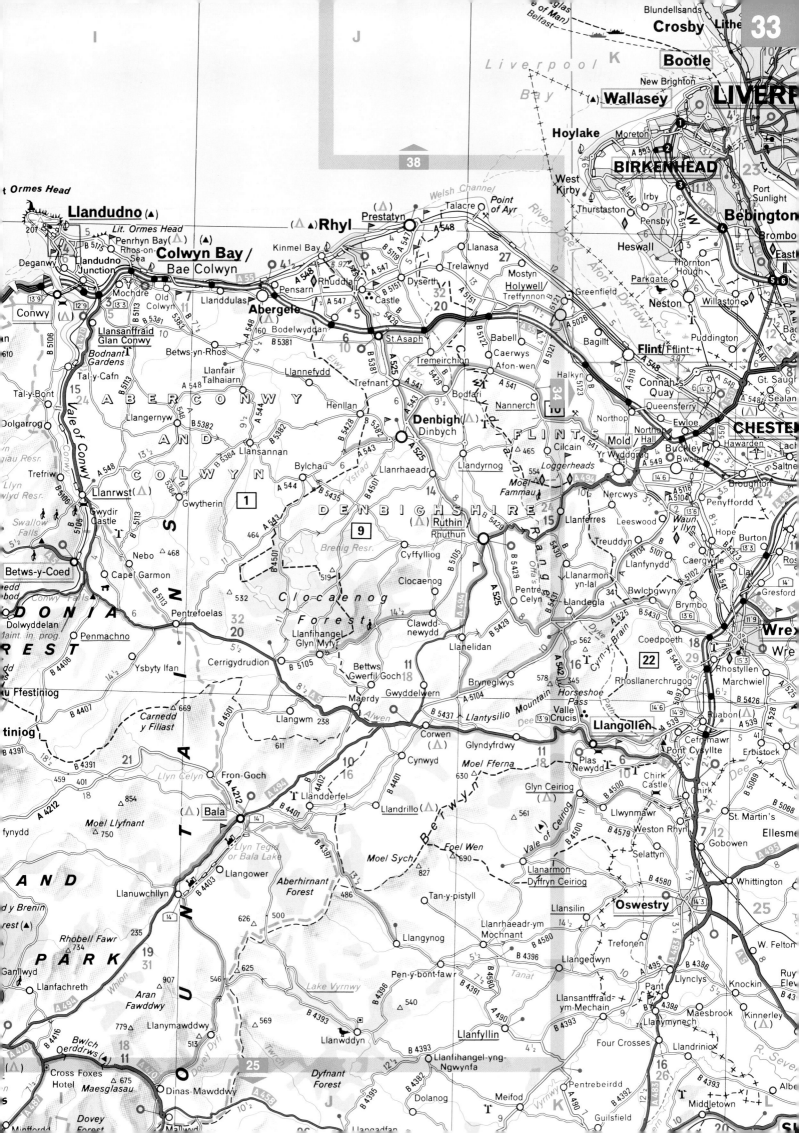

Blundellsands
Crosby Lithe
Bootle
LIVERP
New Brighton
Wallasey
Hoylake
Moreton
West Kirby
BIRKENHEAD
Port Sunlight
Bebington
Irby
Thurstaston
Pensby
Heswall
Parkgate
Neston
Willaston
Gt. Saugh
CHESTE

Liverpool Bay

Welsh Channel
Point of Ayr
Talacre
A 548
River Dee / Afon Dyfrdwy

t Ormes Head
Llandudno (▲)
Lit. Ormes Head
Penrhyn Bay (▲)
Rhos-on-Sea
Colwyn Bay /
Bae Colwyn
Deganwy
Llandudno Junction
Mochdre
Old Colwyn
Conwy
Pensarn
Abergele
Rhyl
Prestatyn
Kinmel Bay
Rhuddlan
Castle
Dyserth
Trelawnyd
Mostyn
Holywell / Treffynnon
Greenfield
Bagillt
Flint / Fflint
Connah's Quay
Queensferry
Northop Hall
Ewloe
Hawarden

Llanasa

Conwy
Llansanffraid Glan Conwy
Bodnant Gardens
Tal-y-Cafn
Betws-yn-Rhos
Bodelwyddan
St. Asaph
Tremeirchion
Afon-wen
Caerwys
Babell
Halkyn
Northop
Buckley
Bwlch
Mold / Yr Wyddgrug
Cilcain
Loggerheads
Moel Fammau
Llanarmon-yn-lal
Penyffordd
Hope
Burton

Trefriw
Dolgarrog
Llangernyw
Llanfair Talhaiarn
Llannefydd
Trefnant
Henllan
Denbigh (▲)
Dinbych
Bodfari
Nannerch
Nercwys
Treuddyn
Leeswood
Waun y llyn
Caergwrle

Tal-y-Bont
Vale of Conwy
Llanrwst (▲)
Llansannan
Bylchau
Llanrhaeadr
Llandyrnog
Ruthin
Rhuthun
Llanferres
Llanfynydd
Bwlchgwyn
Brymbo
Coedpoeth
Wrex
Wre

Betws-y-Coed
Gwydir Castle
Gwytherin
1
9
DENBIGHSHIRE
(▲) Ruthin
Rhuthun
Cyffylliog
Clocaenog
Clawdd-newydd
Llanelidan
Pentre Celyn
Llandegla
Rhostyllen
Marchwiel

Swallow Falls
Nebo
Capel Garmon
Clocaenog Forest
Llanfihangel Glyn Myfyr
Llangwm
Maerdy
Gwyddelwern
Bryneglwys
Valle Crucis
Llangollen
Ruabon (▲)
Cefnmawr
Pont Cysyllte

Dolwyddelan
Penmachno
Pentrefoelas
Cerrigydrudion
Bettws Gwerfil Goch
Corwen (▲)
Glyndyfrdwy
Horseshoe Pass
Llantysilio
Plas Newydd
Chirk Castle
Erbistock

tiniog
Ysbyty Ifan
Carnedd y Filiast
Fron-Goch
Cynwyd
Moel Fferna
Glyn Ceiriog
Chirk (▲)
Llwynmawr
St. Martin's

Llyn Celyn
Llanderfel
Llandrillo
Foel Wen
Llanarmon Dyffryn Ceiriog
Weston Rhyn
Selattyn
Gobowen

Moel Llyfnant
Bala
Llyn Tegid or Bala Lake
Moel Sych
Vale of Ceiriog
Whittington

fynydd
Llangower
Llanuwchllyn
Aberhirnant Forest
Tan-y-pistyll
Llansilin
Oswestry

y Brenin
rest (▲)
Rhobell Fawr
Llanfachreth
Aran Fawddwy
Llangynog
Llanrhaeadr-ym-Mochnant
Llanfyllin
Trefonen
Pant
Llynclys
Knockin

Dyfnant Forest
Pen-y-bont-fawr
Llansantffraid-ym-Mechain
Maesbrook
Kinnerley

Bwlch Oerddrws
Cross Foxes Hotel
Maesglasau
Dinas-Mawddwy
Llanymawddwy
Llanwddyn
Lake Vyrnwy
Llanfihangel-yng-Ngwynfa
Llangadfan
Meifod
Pentrebeirdd
Guilsfield
Llandrinio
Four Crosses
Llanymynech
Middletown

Dovey Forest
Dovey Dyfi
Dolanog
Aber

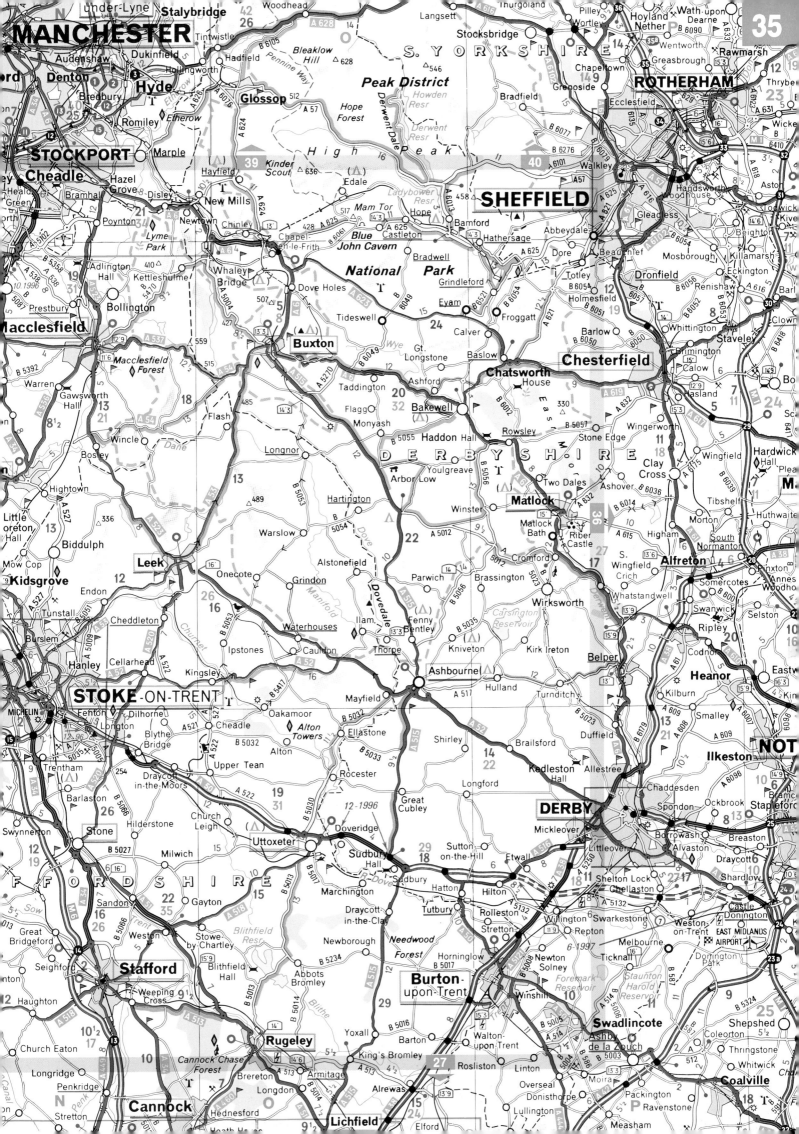

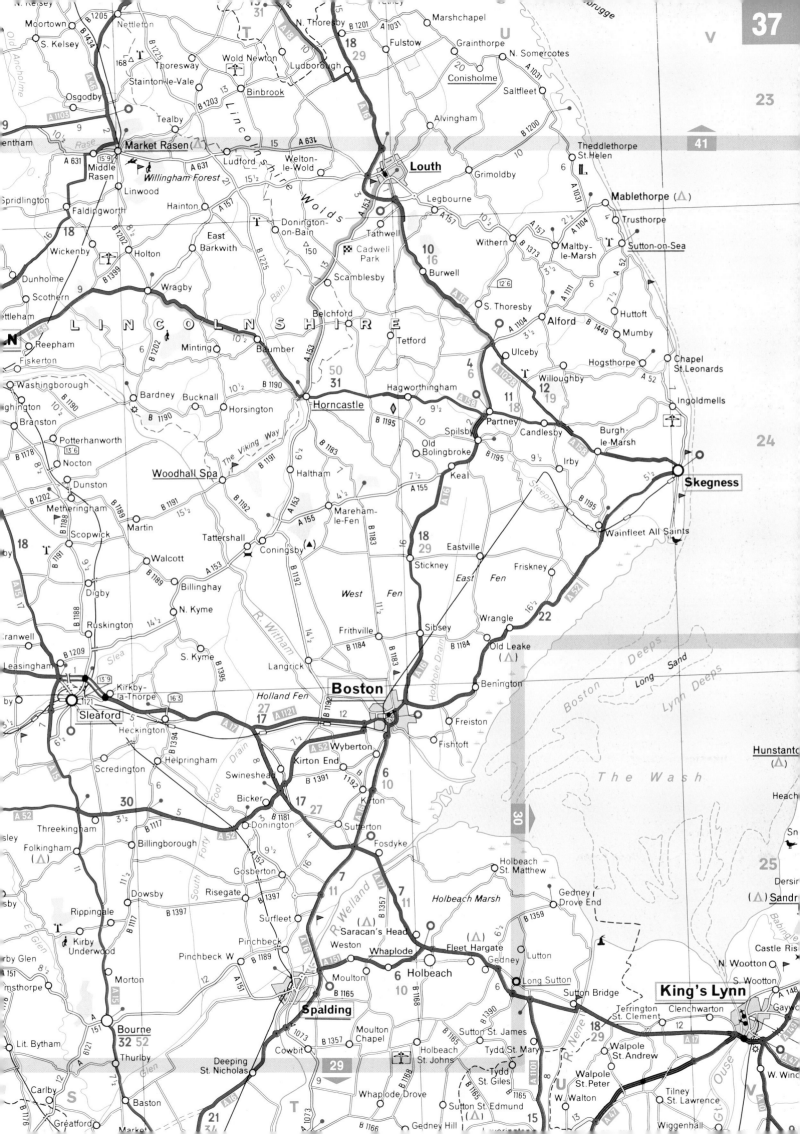

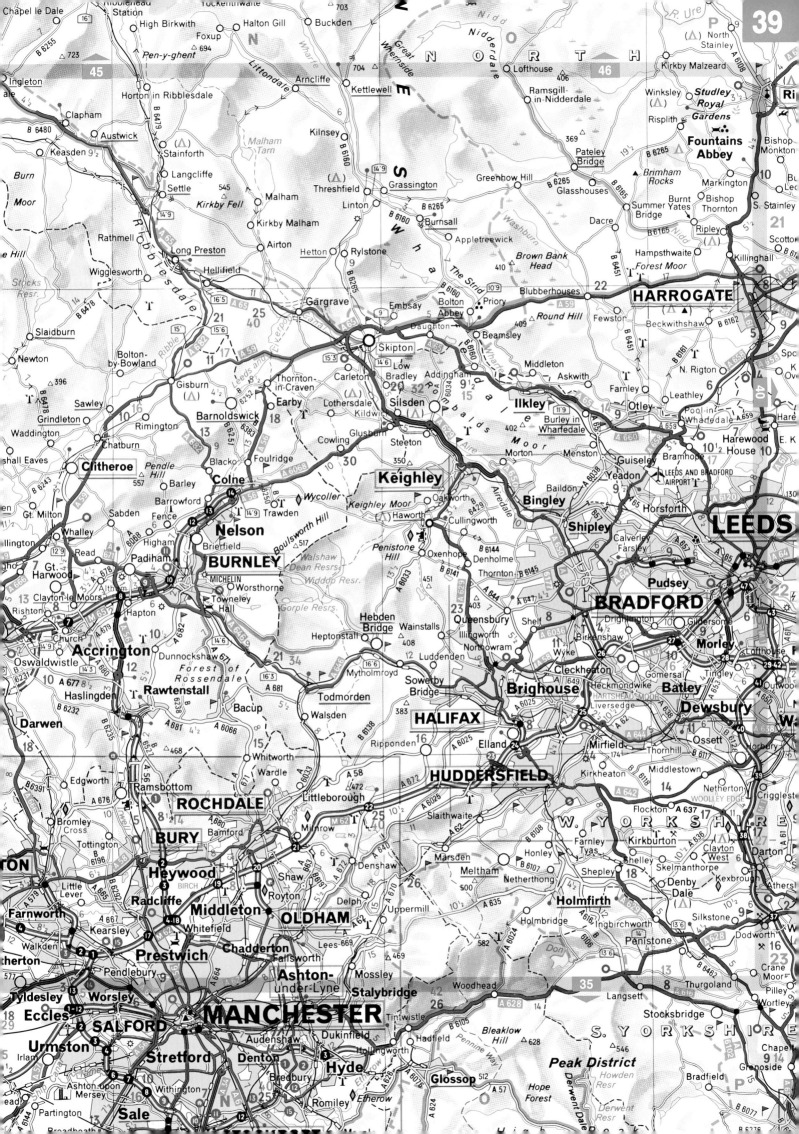

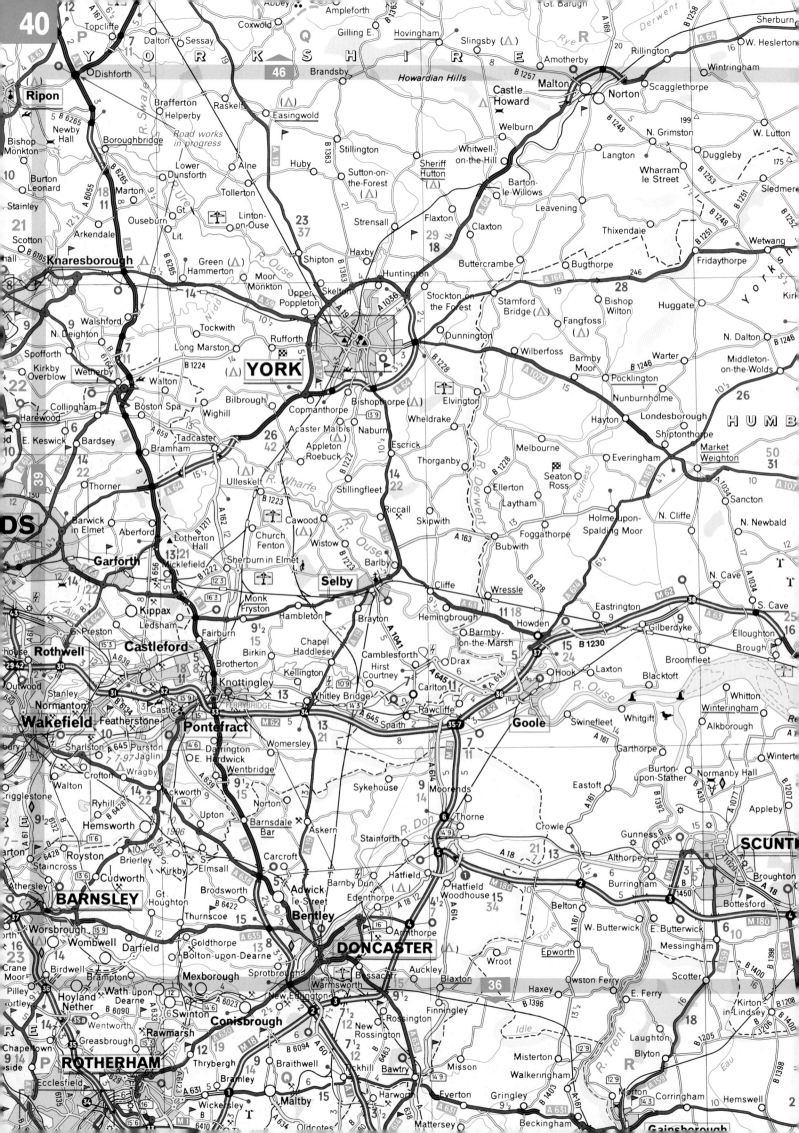

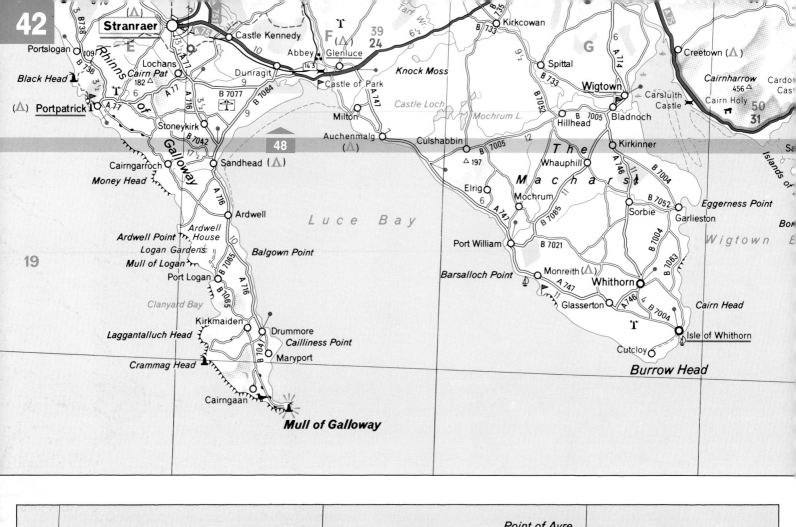

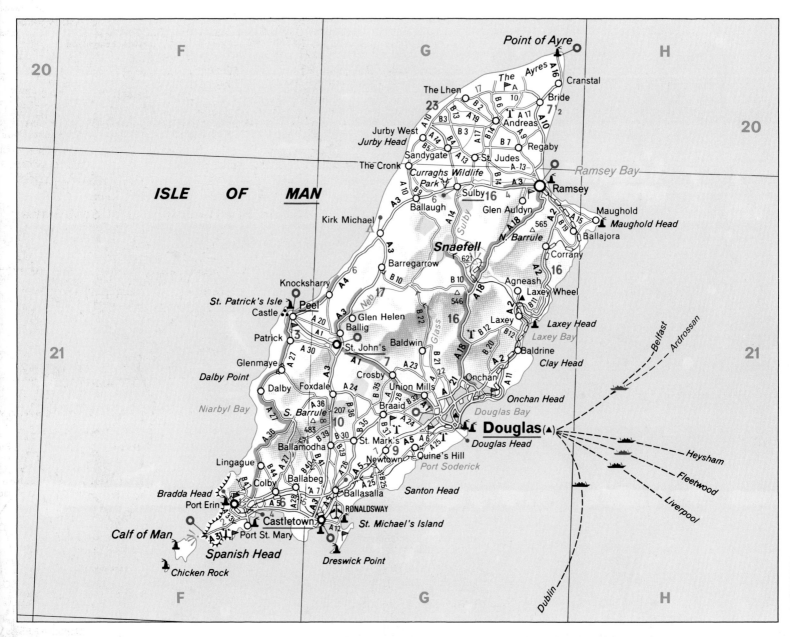

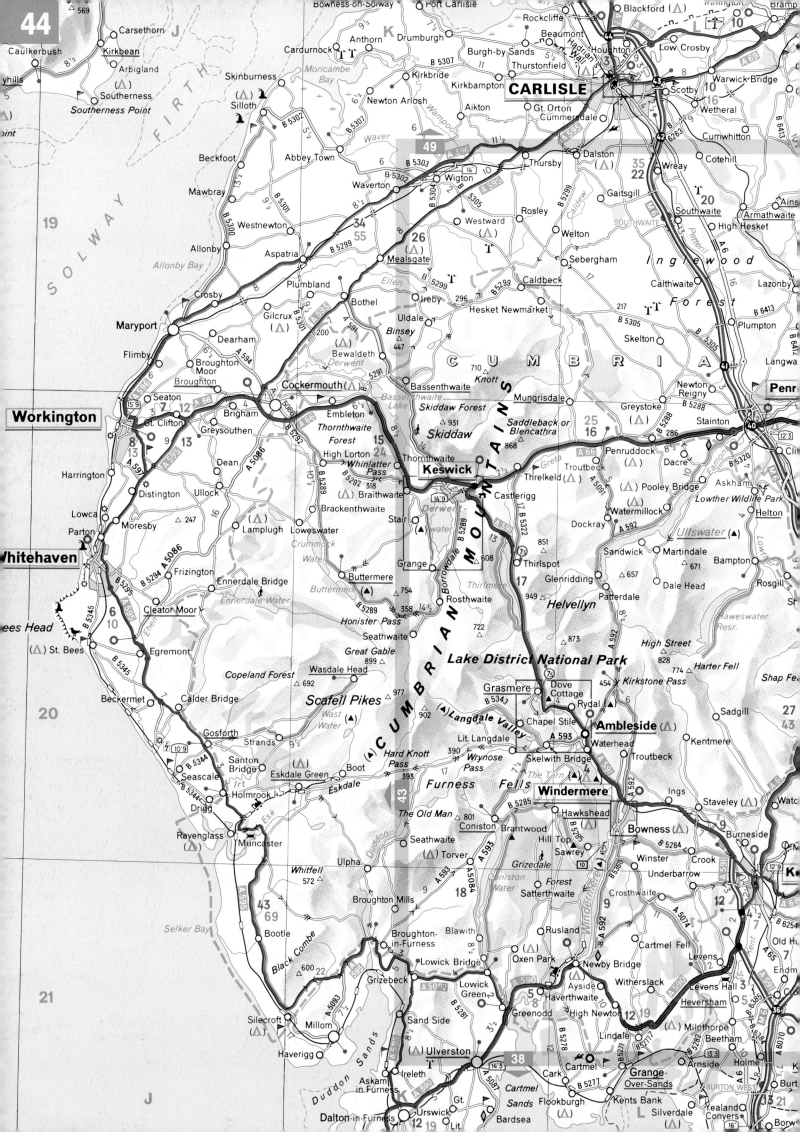

19

20

Staithes
Easington   Hinderwell
Kettleness
B 1266   A 174   Lythe
Scaling
Reservoir   22   Sandsend   **Whitby** (△)
Ugthorpe (△)   Abbey
A 171
299   Ruswarp
Lealholm   Sleights   ESK   B 1447
Egton   Hawsker
Glaisdale   Grosmont   (△)
B 1416   Robin Hood's Bay
Y o r k   M o o r s   206   Cleveland
Egton High Moor   288   21   Way
Goathland   Ravenscar
Wheeldale   A 169
Moor   Fylingdales Moor (△)   201   Staintondale
o n a l   P a r k   299   A 171
Derwent
sedale   Harwood Dale
bbey (△)   Langdale Forest   Cloughton
Cropton Forest   280
Hartoft End   Burniston
Langdale   A 165
Newton-on-   End   Scalby
Rawcliffe   Hackness
gham   Levisham
Cropton   **SCARBOROUGH** (▲ △)
(△)
ington   Wrelton   Dalby
A 170   Middleton   Forest   Wykeham Forest   Eastfield   7 1/2
(△) Pickering   Ayton   A 64
Normanby   Thornton   Ebberston   Wykeham   B 1261   Seamer   Cayton   B 1261
Flamingo   Dale   Allerston   (△)   Snainton   17   Lebberston   A 1039
Park   B 1415   B 1258   A 170   Brompton   6   Gristhorpe   Filey (△)
Yedingham   by Sawdon   Hertford   Filey Bay
Gt. Barugh   Kirby Misperton   The   Carrs   6 Muston
A 169   Derwent   Staxton   A 1039   Hunmanby
Sherburn   Ganton   (△)   41
Rye   B 1258   22   B 1249   Reighton
Amotherby   A 64   35   7   11
Rillington   W. Heslerton   Speeton
Wintringham   Foxholes   B 1229   15 9

21

R   S   T

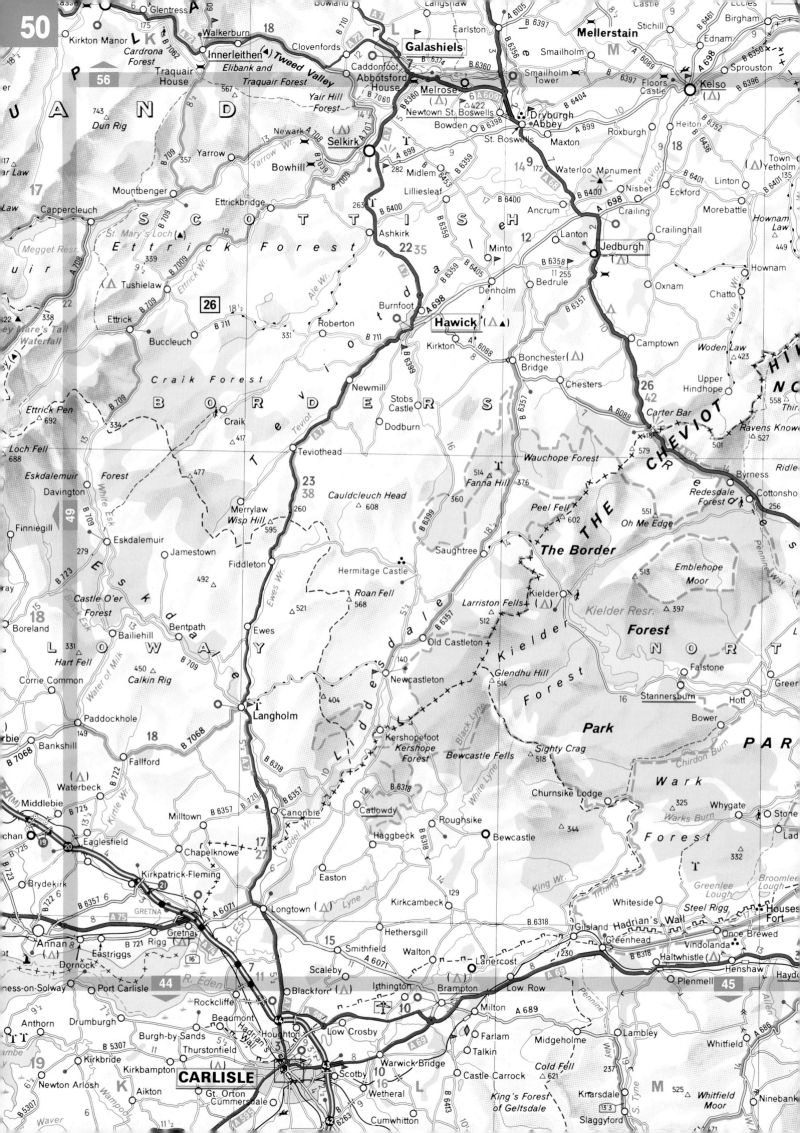

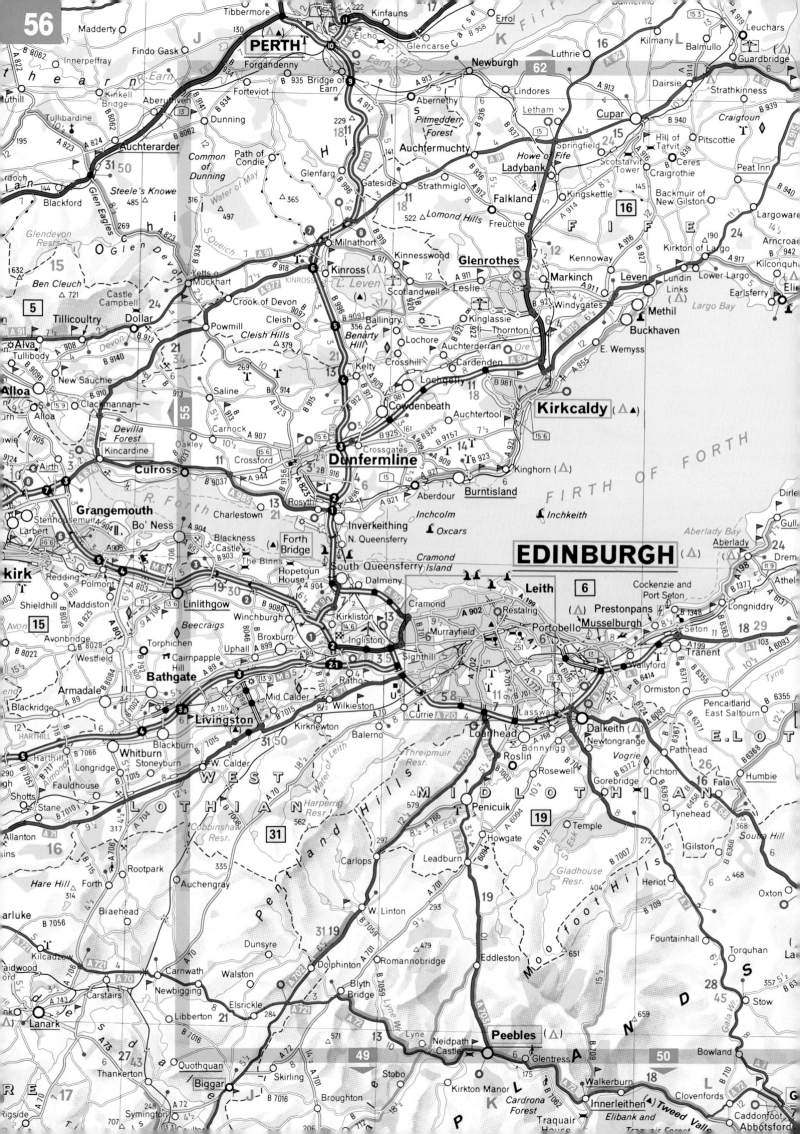

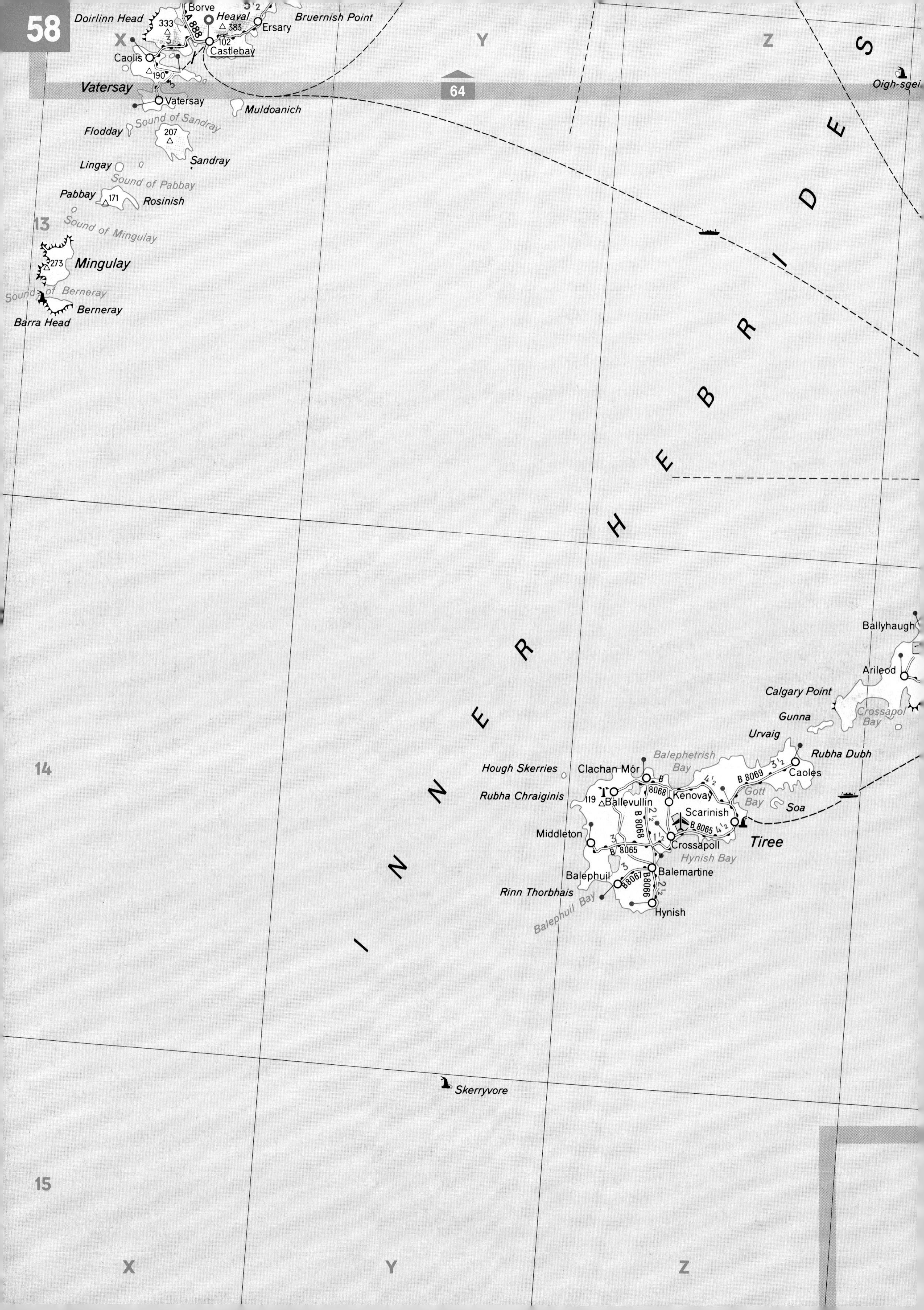

Doirlinn Head 333 Borve Heaval 2 Bruernish Point
△ 888 △ 383 Ersary
X 102
Caolis Castlebay

Y Z

▲ 64

Oigh-sgei

Vatersay

Vatersay
Muldoanich
Flodday 207
Lingay Sandray
Sound of Sandray

Pabbay △ 171 Rosinish
Sound of Pabbay

13 Sound of Mingulay

△ 273 Mingulay

Sound of Berneray

Berneray
Barra Head

H E B R I D E S

Ballyhaugh

Arileod

Calgary Point

Gunna Crossapol
Bay

Urvaig Rubha Dubh

14 Hough Skerries Clachan Mór Balephetrish B 8069 3½ Caoles
Bay
Rubha Chraiginis B 4½
119 8068 Kenovay Gott Soa
△ Ballevullin Bay
B 2½ Scarinish
Middleton 8068 1½ B 8065 4½
3 B 8065 Crossapoll Tiree
B 8065 Hynish Bay
Balephuil Balemartine
3 B8066
Rinn Thorbhais B8066 2½
Balephuil Bay Hynish

I N N E R

Skerryvore

15

X Y Z

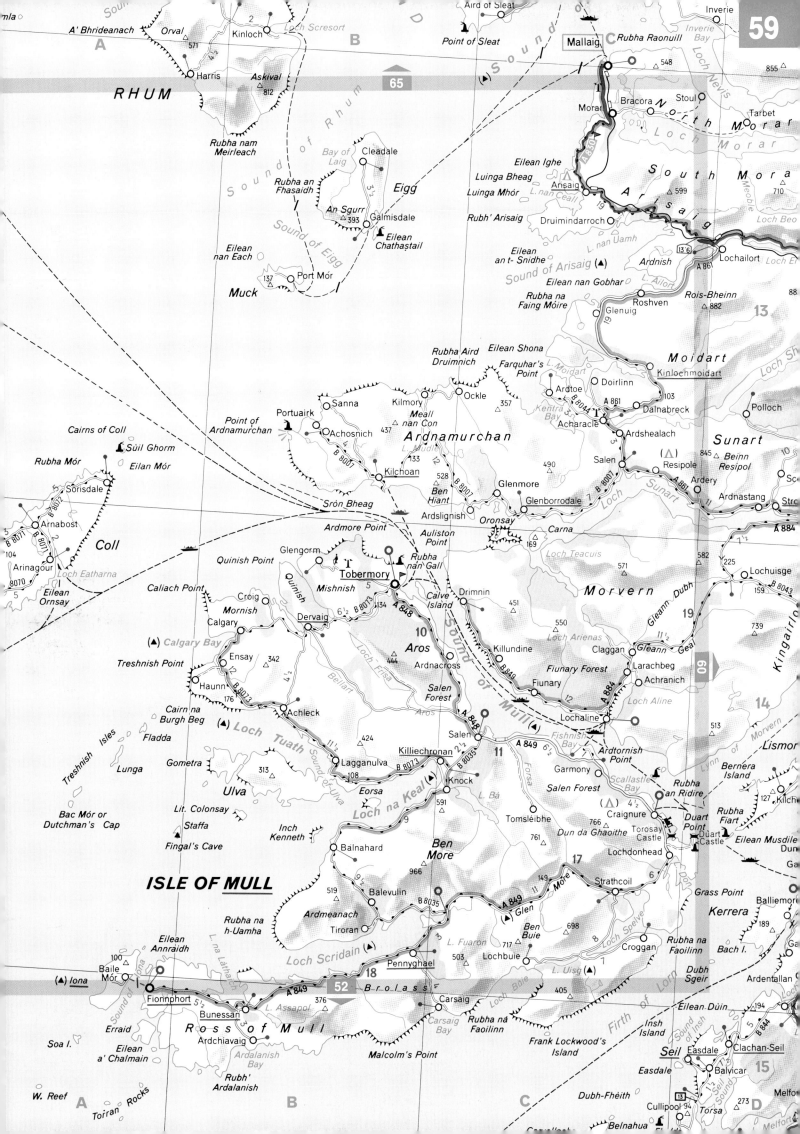

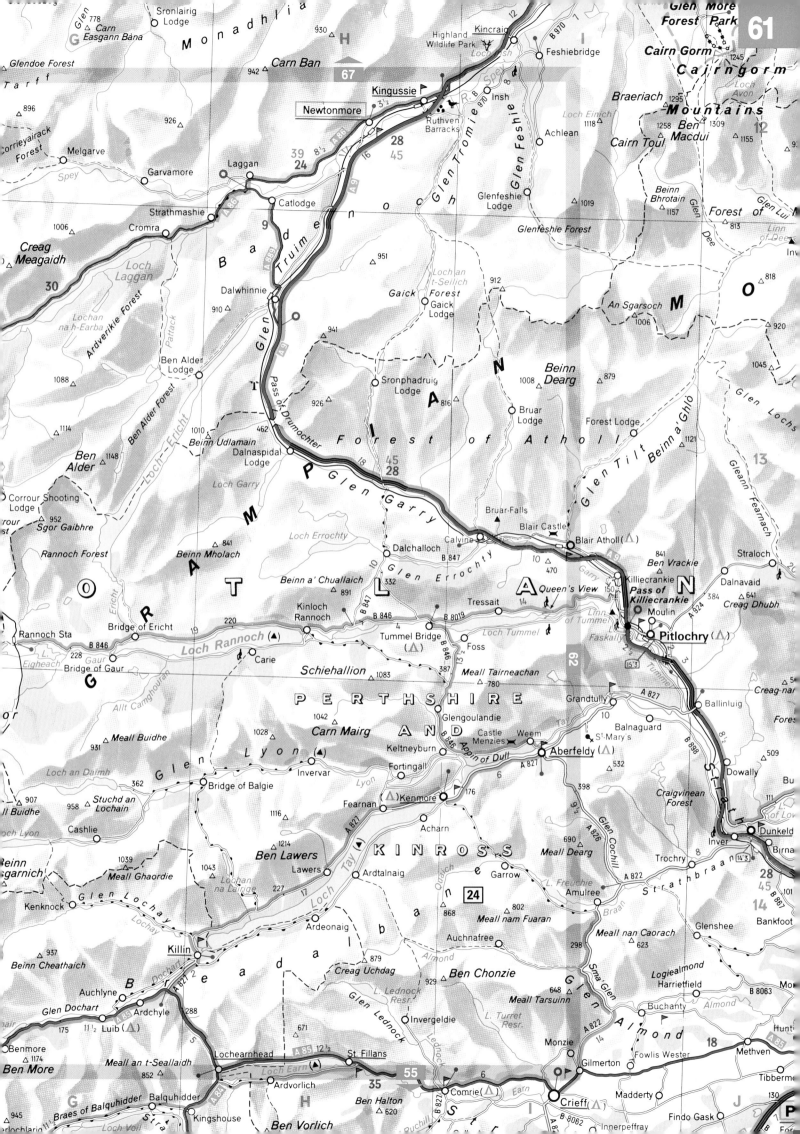

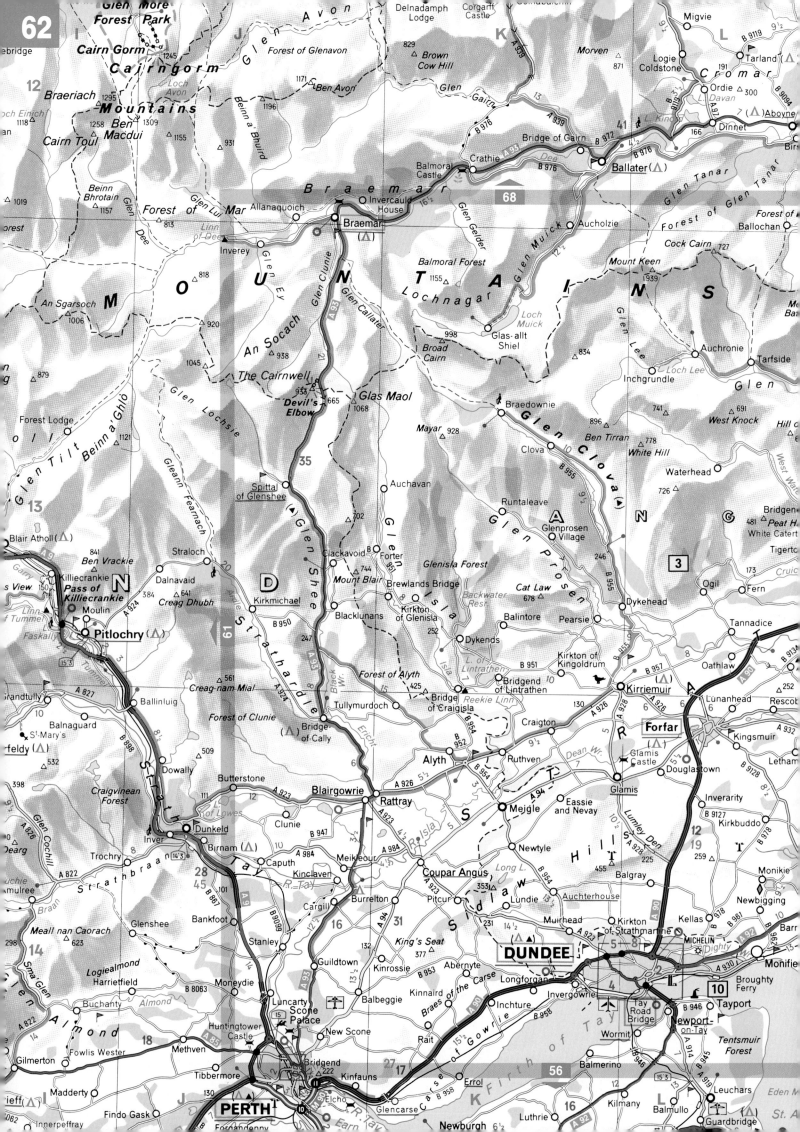

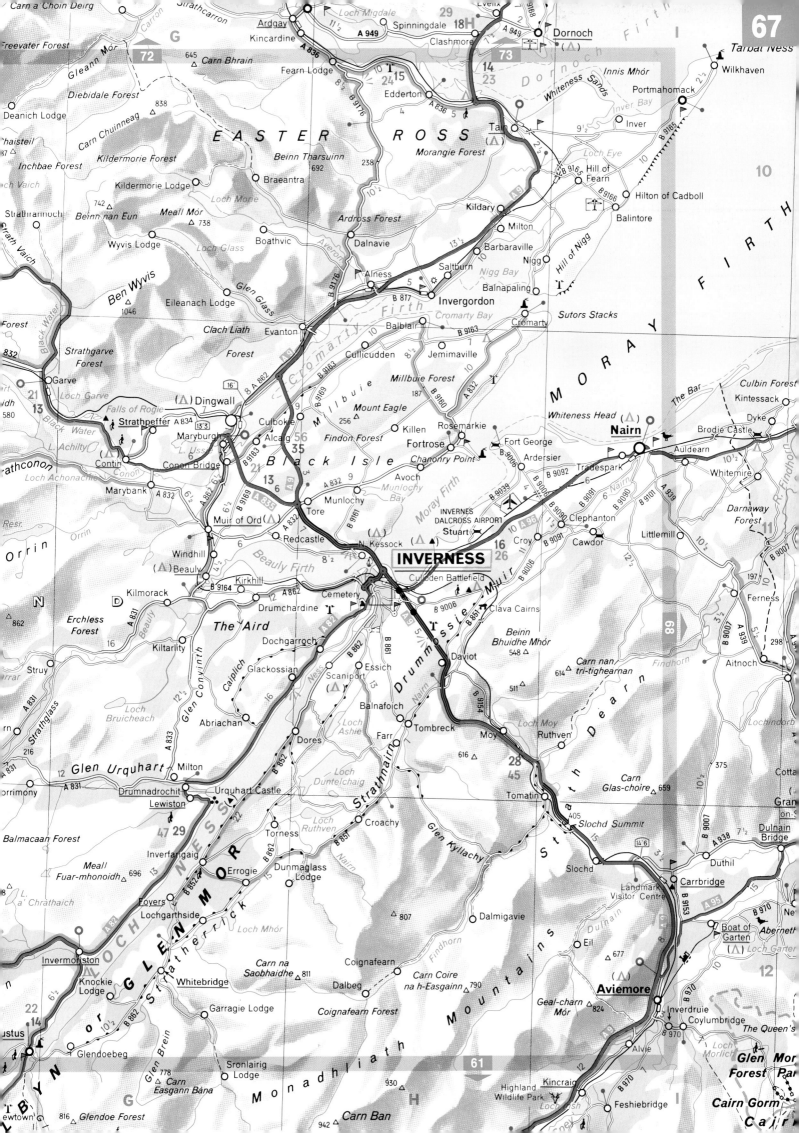

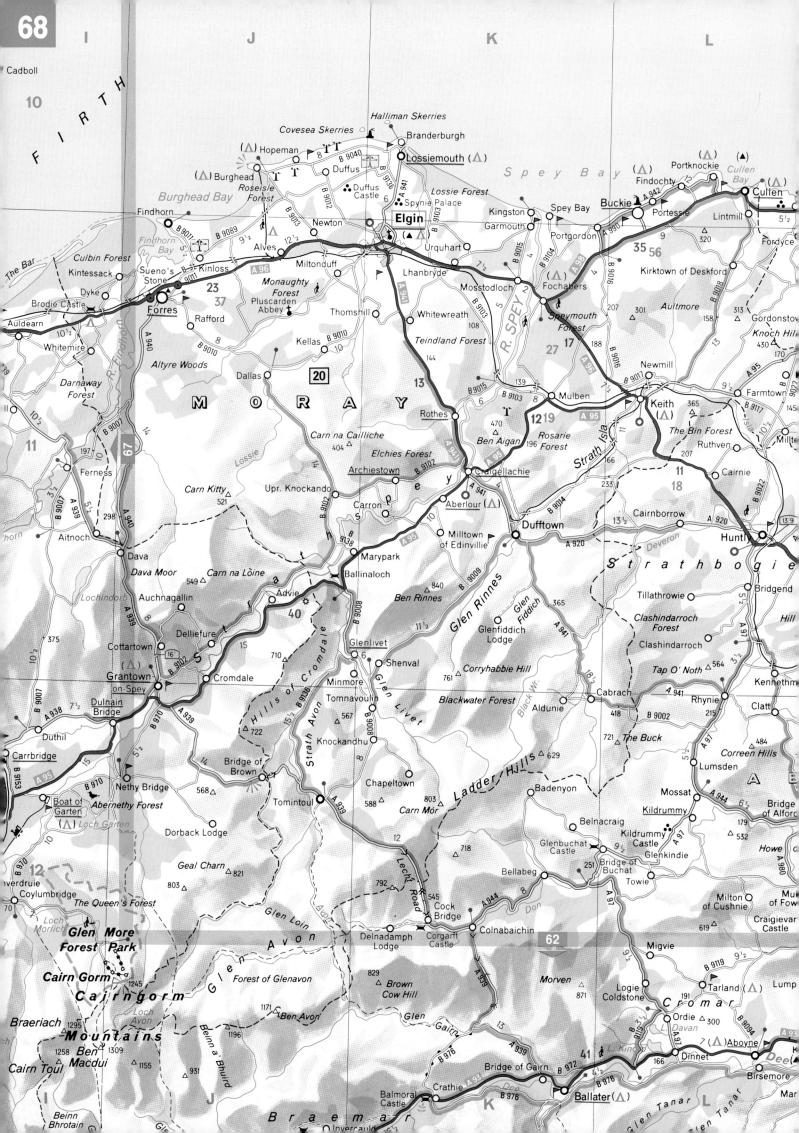

ISLE OF LEWIS
AND HARRIS

OUTER HEBRIDES

WESTERN ISLES

LEWIS

HARRIS

NORTH HARRIS

SOUTH HARRIS

Stornoway
Newmarket
Tong
Barvas
Arnol
Bragar
Shawbost
Galson
Borve
Shader
Col
Garenin
Carloway
Dun Carloway Broch
Tolsta Chaolais
Beinn Mholach 292
L. Urrahag
Loch Breivat
Little Bernera
Tobson
Breaclete
Pabay Mór
Gallan Head
West Loch Roag
East Loch Roag
Great Bernera
Breasclete
Callanish
Standing Stones
Eilean Kearstay
Crulivig
Garynahine
Aird Uig
Valtos
Miavaig
Timsgarry
Vuia Mór
Floday
Uig
Camas Uig
Mangersta
Islivig
Aird Brenish
Brenish
Enaclete
Suainaval 574
L. Grunavat
Loch Roag
Little Loch Roag
B 8011
B 8059
20
Achmore
L. nam Falcag
L. Octasay
Leurbost
Crossbost
Ranish
Barkin Isles
Laxay
Keose
Eilean Chaluim Chille
Cromore
Eilean Th
Marvig
Balallan
L. Erisort
Kershader
B 8060
Glenside
Gravir
L. Odhairn
Kebo
Arivruaich
L. Sgibacleit
Seaforth Head
Park or Pairc
Eishken
Lemreway
B 8060
Eilean Iubhard
Mealasta I.
L. Tamanavay
Caolas an Eilein
Kearstay
Bràigh Mór
Loch Resort
Morsgail Forest
Loch Langavat
Loch Airigh na h-Airde
L. Trealaval
281
492
401
Crionaig 467
Beinn Mhór 572
371
Scarp 308
303
Ulladale
Stùlaval 579
Tirga Mór 679
Hushinish
Hushinish Point
B 887
Forest of Harris
Amhuinnsuidhe
Meavaig
13
Clisham 799
Ardvourlie
Seaforth Island
Loch Seaforth
A 859
36
217
17½
Gasker
Taransay Glorigs
Soay Mór
Maaruig
Beinn Mhór
Crionaig
Eilean Mór a'Bhàigh
Sound of Shiant
Shiant Islands
Eilean
West Loch Tarbert
Taransay
Isay
Ardhasaig
Tarbert
Rhenigidale
Loch Trollamarig
Kyles Scalpay
334
Scotasay
Scalpay 104
Scalpay
Sound of Taransay
Luskentyre
South Harris Forest
Drinnishadder
Toe Head
Coppay
Scarista
Borve
24
16½
A 859
South Harris
365
398
Grosebay
Manish
Stockinish I.
Shillay
Sound of Shillay
Northton
L. Langavat
14
Pabbay 196
Brenish Point
Ensay
Spuir
Sound of Pabbay
Leverburgh
Finsbay
460
A 859
12½
Boreray
Berneray
Borve
Killegray
Langay
Gilsay
Groay
Renish Point
Rodel
Sgeir nam Maol
Fladda-chùain
Eilea

Butt of Lewis

B

C

D

8

Eilea

Eoropie
Port of Ness
Habost
Skigersta
B 8015
Cross
Dell
Ness

Loch Langavat

Cellar Head

Handa Isla

U

Eddrachillis
Bay

248
△
Muirneag
Tolsta
Tolsta Head

Point of Stoer
Culkein
Eilean
Chrona
Clashnessie
L 33
Lo

B 895
Gress

72

Stoer
Clachtoll
L. Crocach
B 869

Back
12½

9

Achmelvich
A 83

Tiumpan Head
Portnaguran
A 866

Baddidarach
In
L. Inver
Loc

Broad Bay
(▲)

THE MINCH

Soyea Island
A' Chleit
Kirkaig
Point
Inverkirkaig

Melbost
12
Garrabost
Eye Peninsula
Knock
Bayble
Chicken Head

Rubha Còigeach
Eilean Mór

Enard Bay
11½
Fio
Loch Sion

Rubha Mór
Reiff
Brae of Achnahaird
6
Badnagyle
Eilean
Mullagrach
Altandhu
Osgaig
Stac Polla
613 △

raidh

k Head

Isle Ristol
Polbain
L. Bad a' Ghaill

Glas-leac Mór
Tanera
Mór
Achiltibuie
Loch Lurgair
Badenscallie

Tanera Beg
Summer Is.
Horse I.
Culnacraig
△ 743
Ben
Coig

Eilean Dubh
Achduart
Stra

Priest Island
Bottle I.

Càrn nan Sgeir
I. Martin
Ine

Mhuire

Greenstone Point
Cailleach Head
Scoraig
Annat Bay
S
Eilea

Opinan
Rubha Beag
Mellon Udrigle
Stattic Point
Badluarach
Beinn
Stattic Point

Gob a' Gheodha
Gruinard
Island
Mungasdale
Little L
Caillea

Eilean Furadh Mór
Achgarve
Badcaul

Rubha Réidh
Mellon
Charles
Laide
Gruinard
Bay
ard Bay
Badl

Cove
66
Coast
A 832
Mungasda

296
An Cuaidh
Aultbea
Gruinard
Bay
A 832

B 8051
I. of Ewe
L. a' Bhaid-
Luachraich

Melvaig
Loch Ewe
L. Fada

B 8021
Midtown
9

65

Inverewe Gardens
Tournaig

B

C

N. Erradale
Poolewe
6

D

Trodday
Fisherfield

ORKNEY ISLANDS

Hoy

J · K · L · M

Flotta
Fara
Lyness
Flotta
Water Sound
Burray
Bow
St. Margaret's Hope
Causeway
Grim Ness
Langhorpe
Switha
Herston
Sound of Hoxa
Wateringhouse
Hurliness
South Walls
Cantick Head
Tor Ness
Swona
Burwick
South Ronaldsay
118
Cleat
Old Head
Brough Ness
B 9041

Pentland Firth

Langaton Point
Island of Stroma
Nethertown
Uppertown 51
Pentland Skerries

Dunnet Head

Stromness

Scarfskerry
St. John's Point
Brough
Gills
Mey
Duncansby Head
Canisbay
John o' Groats (△)
Holborn Head
St. John's Loch
20
A 836 11½
124
Dunnet Bay
Dunnet (△)
Barrock
Thurso Bay
82
A 836 5½
Castletown
Loch Heilen
Skirza
Freswick
Skirza Head
Thurso (△)
Slickly
Freswick Bay
6
141
B 876
13½
Auckengill
Bower
Lyth
Sortat
Keiss
Roadside
17
B 874
Myrelandhorn
8½
A 9
8
L. Scarmclate
Sinclair's Bay
Noss Head
grinmore
Banniskirk
Loch Watten
4½
B 870
Reiss
Girnigoe and Sinclair Castles
Spittal
A 9
5
Watten
B 876
Staxigoe
Mybster
B 870
A 882
B 874
A 9
North Head
hale
5½
Wick
8
Wick
21 Haster
South Head
Badlipster
Tannach
13
Loch Hempriggs
Grey Cairns of Camster
Thrumster
44
71
212
Sarcle
211
Ruard
13
A 9
37
Ulbster
60
Hill o' Many Stanes
287
Houstry
Lybster
W. Clyth
Latheron
Forse
Janetstown
73
Dunbeath
20
orgue
Berriedale
9

J · K

(Inset map)

4°20 · 3°

J · K · L

5
59° · Sule Skerry
Stack Skerry
Mull Head
Bow Head
Papa Westray
Noup Head
Pierowall
Westray
169
B 9066
The Nort
Midbea
Sound
Rapness
Westray Firth
Calfsound
Backa
3°20
101
Rousay
Wasbister
Egilsay
Eday
6
(▲) Brough of Birsay
250
Brinyan
Wyre
Stronsay
Brough Head
Birsay
B 9064
Gairsay
Firth
Kitchener Memorial
A 966
Georth
Gurness Broch
A 967
Twatt
B 9057
9½
Balfour
Sandgarth
Skara Brae
Dounby 221
L. of Harray
8½
Shapins
Yesnaby
A 966
Maes Howe
Finstown
Rennibister
59°
Ring of Brodgar
A 965
268½
Kirkwall
Mainland
Stenness
Wideford Hill Cairn
Stromness
A 964
Orphir
Moness
Graemsay
Cava
St. Mary's
Lamb Holm
479
Rackwick
St. Mary's
Rose Ness
Old Man of Hoy
Fara
Scapa Flow
Causeway
Burray
Rora Head
Lyness
Flotta
Causeway
7
Hoy
Tor Ness
South Walls
St. Margaret's Hope
Lerwick Aberdeen
118
Burwick
South Ronald.
Old Head
Pentland Firth
Stroma
Pentland Skerries
Dunnet Head
58°40'
Scarfskerry
Gills
Duncansby Head
Scrabster
Dunnet (△)
A 836
John o' Groats (△)
Thurso
Castletown
5½
J · K · L

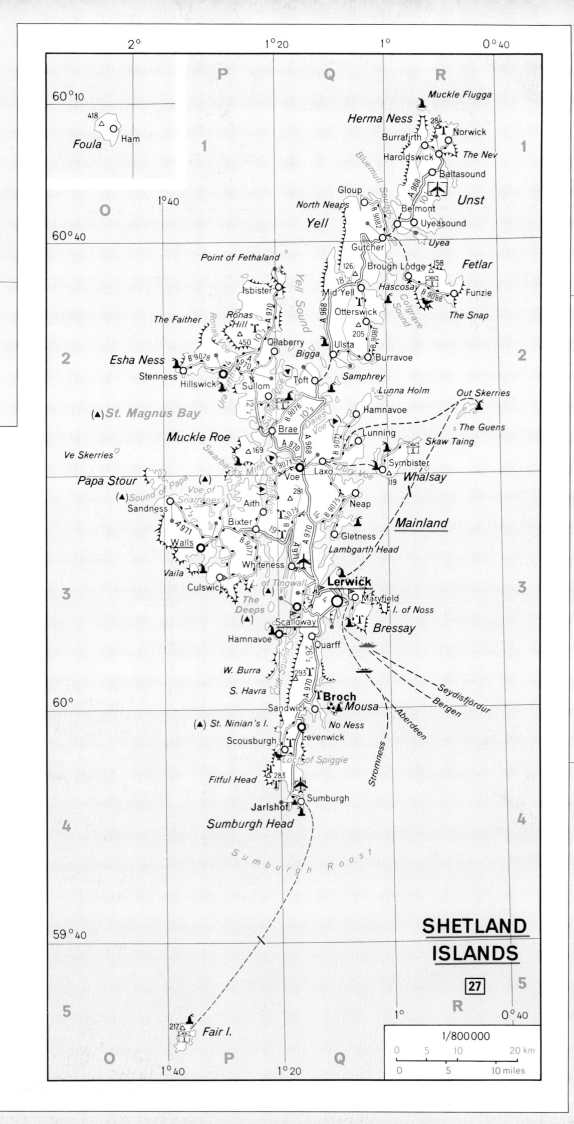

SHETLAND
ISLANDS

27

1/800 000

| 0 | 5 | 10 | 20 km |
| 0 | 5 | 10 miles |

Shetland Islands labels:

Muckle Flugga
Herma Ness
Burrafirth
Haroldswick
Norwick
284
The Nev
Baltasound
Unst
Gloup
North Neaps
Belmont
Uyeasound
Yell
Gutcher
Uyea
Point of Fethaland
Brough Lodge
158
Fetlar
Isbister
126
Hascosay
Funzie
The Faither
Mid Yell
The Snap
Ronas Hill
Otterswick
205
450
Ollaberry
Ulsta
Esha Ness
Bigga
Burravoe
Stenness
Toft
Samphrey
Hillswick
Sullom
Lunna Holm
Hamnavoe
Out Skerries
(▲) St. Magnus Bay
Brae
Lunning
The Guens
Muckle Roe
169
Skaw Taing
Ve Skerries
Voe
Symbister
Papa Stour
Laxo
119
Whalsay
(▲) Sound of Snarraness
281
Neap
Mainland
Sandness
Aith
Gletness
Bixter
Lambgarth Head
Walls
Whiteness
Vaila
L. of Tingwall
Culswick
Lerwick
Maryfield
The Deeps
I. of Noss
Scalloway
Bressay
Hamnavoe
Quarff
W. Burra
293
S. Havra
Broch
Mousa
Sandwick
No Ness
(▲) St. Ninian's I.
Levenwick
Scousburgh
Fitful Head
283
Loch of Spiggie
Sumburgh
Jarlshof
Sumburgh Head
Sumburgh Roost
Seydisfjördur
Bergen
Aberdeen
Stromness
Fair I.
217

Foula inset:
418
Foula
Ham

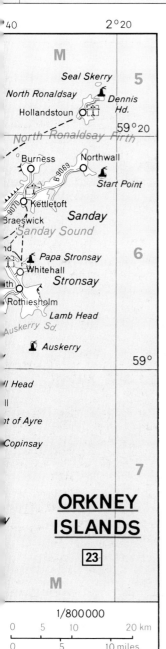

ORKNEY
ISLANDS

23

1/800 000

| 0 | 5 | 10 | 20 km |
| 0 | 5 | 10 miles |

Orkney Islands labels:

Seal Skerry
North Ronaldsay
Dennis Hd.
Hollandstoun
North Ronaldsay Firth
Burness
Northwall
Start Point
Kettletoft
Sanday
Braeswick
Sanday Sound
Papa Stronsay
Whitehall
Stronsay
Rothiesholm
Lamb Head
Auskerry Sd.
Auskerry
Head
nt of Ayre
Copinsay

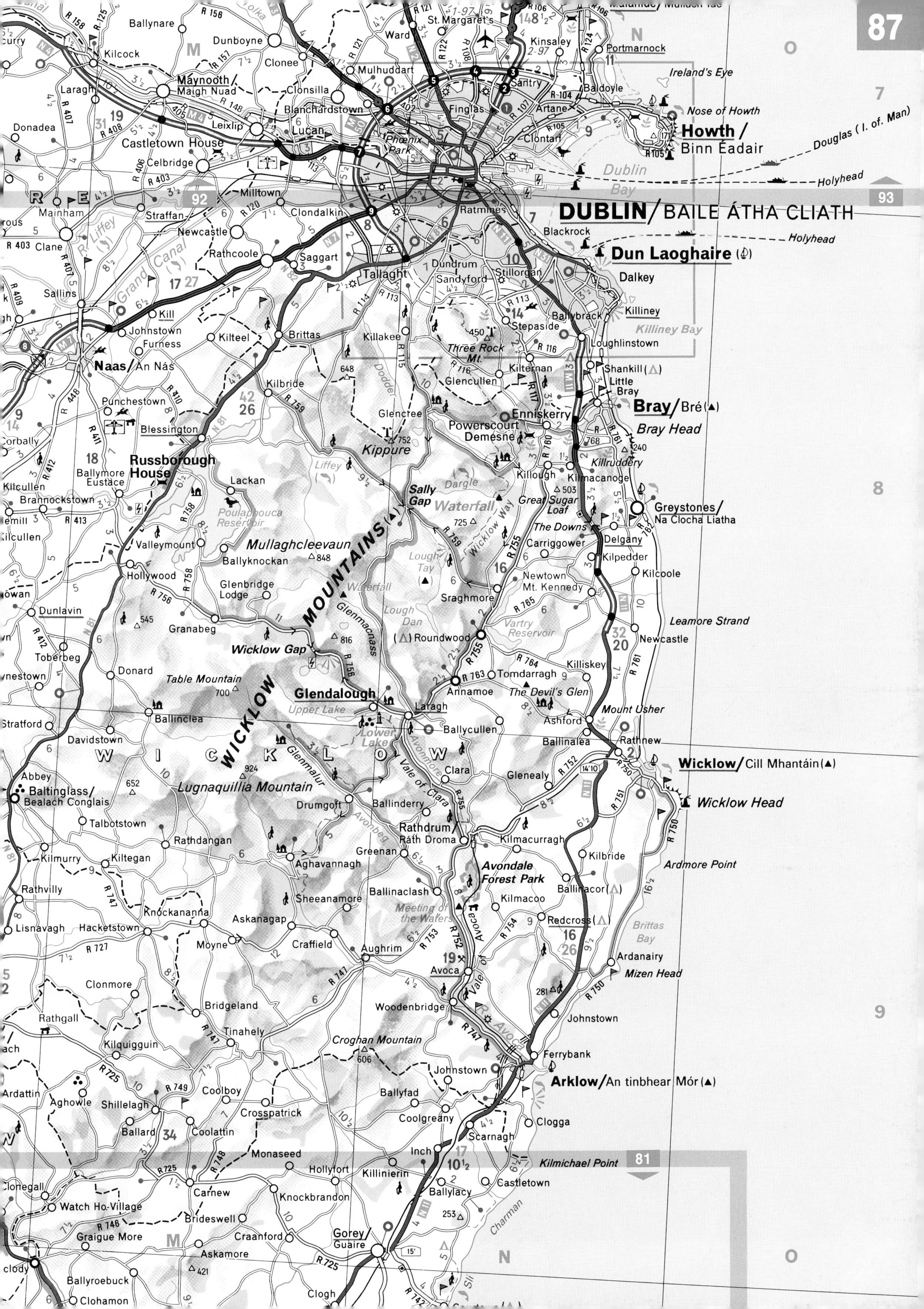

DUBLIN / BAILE ÁTHA CLIATH

Howth / Binn Éadair
Ireland's Eye
Nose of Howth
Portmarnock
Baldoyle
Kinsaley
Santry
Artane
Clontarf
St. Margaret's
Ward
Finglas
Mulhuddart
Dunboyne
Clonee
Blanchardstown
Clonsilla
Maynooth / Maigh Nuad
Leixlip
Lucan
Kilcock
Laragh
Donadea
Castletown House
Celbridge
Milltown
Clondalkin
Straffan
Newcastle
Rathcoole
Saggart
Tallaght
Mainham
Clane
Sallins
Kill
Johnstown
Furness
Naas / An Nás
Brittas
Kilteel
Kilbride
Punchestown
Blessington
Russborough House
Ballymore Eustace
Lackan
Ballyknockan
Valleymount
Hollywood
Glenbridge Lodge
Granabeg
Dunlavin
Toberbeg
Donard
Table Mountain
Ballinclea
Stratford
Davidstown
Baltinglass / Bealach Conglais
Talbotstown
Rathdangan
Kiltegan
Kilmurry
Rathvilly
Lisnavagh
Hacketstown
Knockananna
Moyne
Craffield
Askanagap
Aghowle
Shillelagh
Coolboy
Crosspatrick
Coolattin
Ballard
Monaseed
Hollyfort
Killinierin
Carnew
Knockbrandon
Brideswell
Craanford
Askamore
Gorey / Guaire
Watch Ho-Village
Graigue More
Clonegall
Ballyroebuck
Clohamon
Clonmore
Bridgeland
Tinahely
Kilquigguin
Rathgall
Ardattin
Ballyfad
Coolgreany
Clogga
Scarnagh
Castletown
Inch
Ballylacy
Clogh
Mullaghcleevaun
Kippure
Sally Gap
Waterfall
Wicklow Gap
Glendalough
Laragh
Annamoe
Roundwood
Sraghmore
Lough Dan
Lough Tay
Powerscourt Demesne
Enniskerry
Killough
Killruddery
Great Sugar Loaf
Kilmacanoge
Greystones / Na Clocha Liatha
The Downs
Delgany
Carriggower
Kilpedder
Kilcoole
Newtown Mt. Kennedy
Leamore Strand
Newcastle
Killiskey
Tomdarragh
The Devil's Glen
Mount Usher
Ashford
Ballinalea
Rathnew
Wicklow / Cill Mhantáin
Wicklow Head
Glenealy
Clara
Ballycullen
Vale of Clara
Rathdrum / Ráth Droma
Greenan
Ballinderry
Avondale Forest Park
Kilmacurragh
Kilbride
Ardmore Point
Ballinaclash
Kilmacoo
Ballinacor
Redcross
Drumgoft
Aghavannagh
Sheeanamore
Meeting of the Waters
Avoca
Ardanairy
Mizen Head
Brittas Bay
Woodenbridge
Croghan Mountain
Johnstown
Ferrybank
Arklow / An tinbhear Mór
Lugnaquillia Mountain
Glenmalur
WICKLOW MOUNTAINS
WICKLOW
Poulaphouca Reservoir
Liffey
Dargle
Vartry Reservoir
Kilmichael Point
Dun Laoghaire
Dalkey
Killiney
Killiney Bay
Blackrock
Loughlinstown
Shankill
Little Bray
Bray / Bré
Bray Head
Ratmines
Dundrum
Sandyford
Stillorgan
Stepaside
Ballybrack
Kilternan
Glencullen
Three Rock Mt.
Killakee
Kilternan
Glencree
Dublin Bay
Douglas (I. of Man)
Holyhead

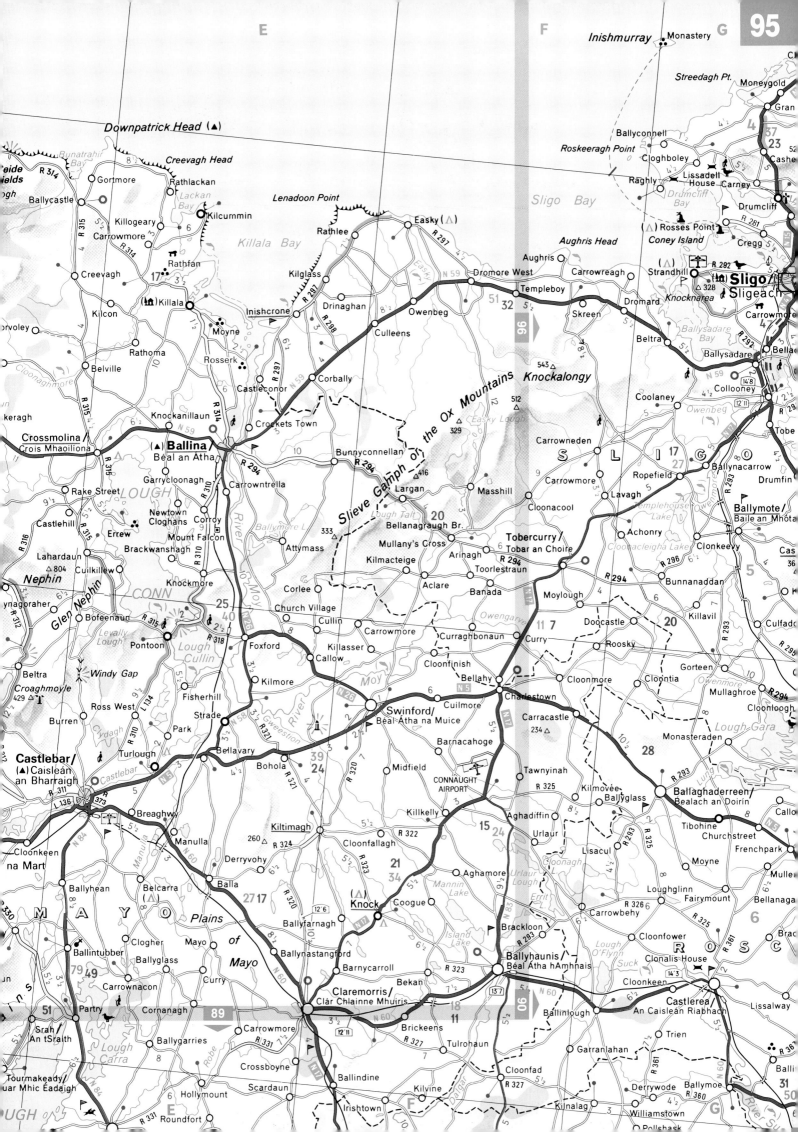

F G H

2

Tory Island / Toraigh
West Town
East Town

Tory Sound

Horn Head

Inishbofin /
Inis Bó Finne

Dunfanaghy
Portnabla
Ballym

Bloody Foreland Head

Meenlaragh
R 257
Brinlack
Bun na Leaca
Meenaclady
316
R 256
Ray
Gortahork
Gort an Choirce
Falcarragh /
An Fál Carrach
Cashelm
Crees

Gola Island /
Gabhla
Gweedore
Derrybeg
Tievealehid
431
Muckish Moun
582
Altan
Lough
Cloghaneely
670

Owey Island /
Llaighe
Bunbeg /
An Bun Beag
Middletown
R 258
Gweedore /
Gaoth Dobhair
Dore
R 251
Errigal Mountain
752
Glenveagh
National

58
36

Cruit
Island
Inishfree
Bay
R 257
Clady
Nacung
St. Colmcille Ora
Park

Torneady Point
Rosses
Bay
Kincasslagh
R 259
Annagary
Crolly /
Croithlí
Dunlewy
Derryveagh Mts.
445

Aran or
Aranmore Island /
Árainn Mhór
Leabgarrow
228
The
Rosses
Loughanure
Meencorwick
683
Slieve
Snaght
538
Glendowan
Mts
R 254
Glendowa
Gleann Dom

Ballintra
Burtonport /
Ailt an Chorráin
519
Anure
Owenator
396
Commeen
Barra
Ulster Way

Rutland
Island
Meela
Dunglow /
An Clochan Liath
Lough
Croangar
Owenwee
Breenagh

Inishfree Upper
R 259
Meenatotan
R 252
Doocharry /
An Dúchoraidh
R 254
Owenwee
Gweebarra
28
Kingarrow

Crohy Head
Maghery
Derrydruel
384
R 252
Fintown /
Baile na Finne
R 250
Bellanamore
Cark

Meenacross
Trawenagh
Bay
17
27
Ballynacarrick
Lettermacaward /
Leitir Mhic an Bhaird
Aghla Mountain
596
Meenanarwa
Clogh
An C

Roaninish
Gweebarra
Bay
Dooey Point
Derrylough
Finn
N Commeen / E
An Coimín

Dunmore Head
(Λ) Portnoo
Clooney
Gweebarra
Bridge
335
D
O
Graffy
R 253
Altnapaste

Dawros Head
Naran
Maas
5
Stracashel
568

Rossbeg
Loughros More
Bay
Kilclooney
R 261
N 56
R 250
Glenties
Tangaveane
602

Loughros Point
Glendorragha
443
Crannogeboy
Owenea
N 56
Kilrean
R 253
Lavagh More
672
Carnaween
521
Croaghnageer
547

Port
Slievetooey
Maghera
Laconnell
Ardara
Owentocker
Meenybraddan
672
Blue Stack Mountains
29
18

Glen Head
St.
Columbkille
374
Stravally
Lough
Nalughraman
48
30
Neck of the Ballagh
502
Barnesmore Gap
M

Glen Bay
Rossan Point
Malin More
Glencolumbkille /
Gleann Cholm Cille
Crove
Glengesh
Pass
Meentullynagarn
Tullynaha
Lough
Eske
13

Malin Beg /
Málainn Bhig
Meenaneary /
Mín na Aoire
473
Croagh
Eanyl
Letterbarra
Barnesmore
438

O'Birne
Island
Meenavean
Carrick /
An Charraig
493
Frosses
N 15
Copany

Trabane
Strand
Slieve League
Cliff
601
R 263
Crownarad
Inver
N 56
2
Donegal /
Dún na nGall
330

Carrigan Head
Teelin
Kilcar
Shalwy
R 263
Largy
Killybegs /
Na Cealla Beaga
Dunkineely
Mountcharles
Laghy
R 232

Muckros Head
Fintragh
Bay
Mac
Swyne's
Bay
Inver
Bay
Tullyvoos
Mullinasole
Lou
De

Drumanoo Head
Doorin
Point
Bridgetown
26

F G H

3

4

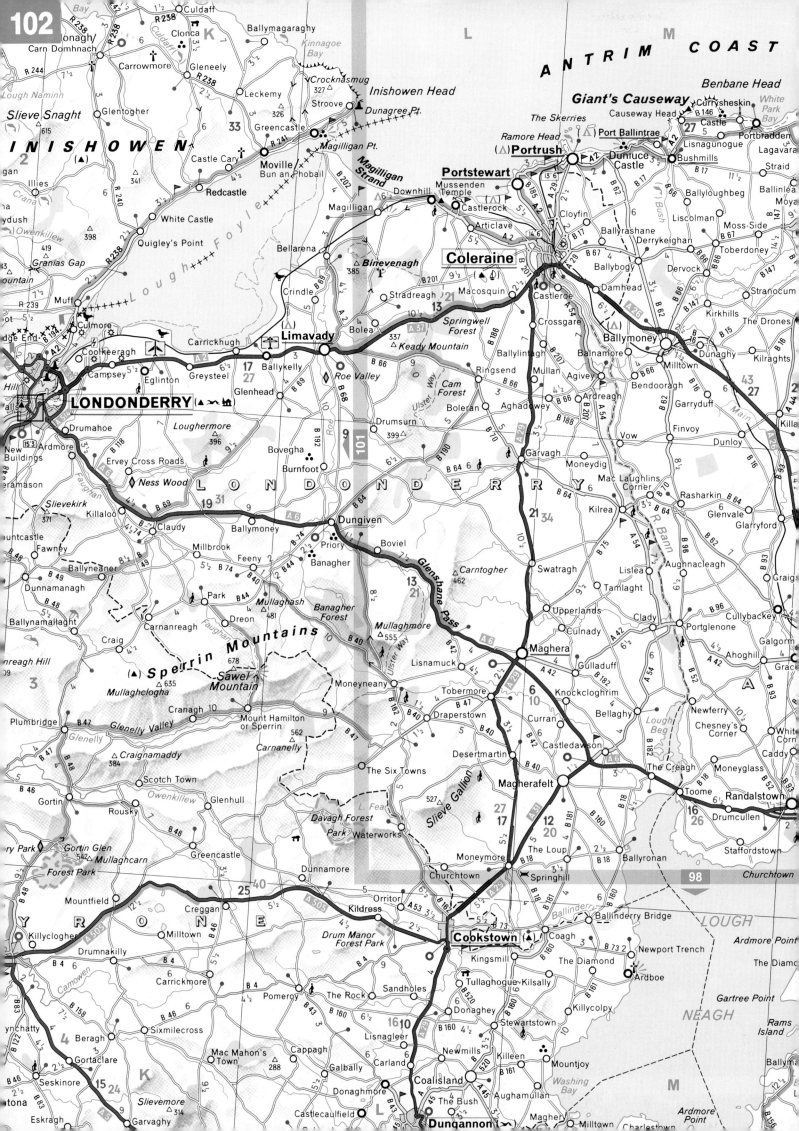

How to use this index

Page number
Map co-ordinate common
to all Michelin publications

County abbreviations

ENGLAND

Symbols on townplans

Roads

Motorway, dual carriageway
Major thoroughfare
Street: Unsuitable for traffic, subject to restrictions - Pedestrian
Shopping street - Car park
Car ferry - Lever bridge

Sights - Hotels - Restaurants
(See Michelin Red Guide)

Place of interest and its main entrance
Cathedral - Church or chapel
Reference letter locating a sight
Reference letter locating a hotel or a restaurant

Various signs

Tourist information centre - Hospital
Cathedral - Church - Cemetery
Garden, park, wood - Stadium
Golf course: visitors unrestricted - restricted
Public building located by letter:
Local government Offices - Town Hall
Police (Headquarters) - Museum
Theatre - University, polytechnics
Main post office with poste restante, telephone
Underground station

London

Borough - Area   **BRENT** SOHO
Borough boundary - Area boundary
Underground station

Légende des plans de ville

Voirie

Autoroute, route à chaussées séparées
Grandes voies de circulation - Sens unique
Rue impraticable, réglementée - Rue piétonne
Rue commerçante - Parc de stationnement
Bac pour autos - Pont mobile

Curiosités - Hôtels - Restaurants
(Voir le Guide Rouge Michelin)

Bâtiment intéressant et entrée principale
Cathédrale - Église ou chapelle
Lettre identifiant une curiosité
Lettre identifiant un hôtel ou un restaurant

Signes divers

Information touristique - Hôpital
Cathédrale - Église - Cimetière
Jardin, parc, bois - Stade
Golf : Ouvert à tous - Réservé
Bâtiment public repéré par une lettre :
Administration du comté - Hôtel de Ville
Police (commissariat central) - Musée
Théâtre - Université, grande école
Bureau principal de poste restante, téléphone
Station de métro

Londres

Nom d'arrondissement - de quartier
Limite d'arrondissement - de quartier
Station de métro

Comnarthaí ar phleanna bailte

Bóithre

Mótarbhealach, carrbhealach dúbailte
Príomh-thrébhealach - Bóthar aonslí
Sráid : neamhoiriúnach do thrácht, ach í stáit speisialta - coisithe
Sráid siopadóireacha - Carrchlós
Bád fartha feithiclí - Droichead starrmhaidí

Ionaid inspéise - Óstáin - Bialanna
(Féach Eolaí Dearg Michelin)

Ionad inspéise agus an priomhbhealach isteach
Ardeaglais - Eaglais nó séipéal
Ionad inspéise curtha in iúl le litir thagartha
Óstán nó bialann curtha in iúl le litir thagartha

Comharthaí Éagsúla

Ionad eolais turasóireachta - Ospidéal
Ardeaglais - Eaglais - Reilig
Gairdín, páirc, coill - Staidiam
Galfchúrsa : gan bac ar chuairteoirí - cuairteoirí faoi theorannú
Foirgneamh poiblí curtha in iúl le litir thagartha :
Oifigí rialtais áitiúil - Halla baile
Póitíní (ceanncheathrú) - Músaem
Amharclann - Ollscoil, polaiteicnicí
Príomhoifig phoist le poste restante, teileafón
Stáisiún traenach faoi thalamh

Londain

Buirg - Limistéar   **BRENT** SOHO
Teorainn bhuirge - Teorainn limistéir
Stáisiún traenach faoi thalamh

Symbolau ar gynlluniau'r trefi

Ffyrdd

Traffordd, ffordd ddeuol
Prif ffordd drwodd - Unffordd
Stryd : Anaddas i draffig, cyfyngedig - Cerddwr
Stryd siopa - Parc ceir
Fferi geir - Pont liferi

Golygfeydd - Gwestai - Tai bwyta
(Gweler Llyfr Coch Michelin)

Man diddorol a'i brif fynedfa
Eglwys Gadeiriol - Eglwys neu gapel
Llythyren gyfeirio sy'n dynodi golygfa
Llythyren gyfeirio sy'n dynodi gwesty neu dŷ bwyta

Arwyddion amrywiol

Canolfan croeso - Ysbyty
Eglwys Gadeiriol - Eglwys - Mynwent
Gardd, parc, coedwig - Stadiwm
Cwrs golff : dim cyfyngiad ar ymwelwyr - cyfyngiad ar ymwelwyr
Adeilad cyhoeddus a ddynodir gan lythyren :
Swyddfeydd llywodraeth leol - Neuadd y Dref
Yr Heddlu (pencadlys) - Amgueddfa
Theatr - Prifysgol, Colegau Politechnig
Prif swyddfa bost gyda poste restante, ffôn
Gorsaf danddaearol

Llundain

Bwrdeistref - Ardal
Ffin Bwrdeistref - Ffin yr Ardal
Gorsaf danddaearol

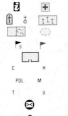

Great Britain

A

Abbas Combe	8	M 30
Abberley	26	M 27
Abbey	13	X 30
Abbey Dore	26	L 28
Abbey Town	44	K 19
Abbeydale	35	P 23
Abbeystead	38	L 22
Abbots Bromley	35	O 25
Abbots Langley	20	S 28
Abbotsbury	8	M 32
Abbotsford House	50	L 17
Abbotskerswell	4	J 32
Aberaeron	24	H 27
Aberaman	16	J 28
Aberangell	25	I 25
Abercarn	16	K 29
Aberchirder	69	M 11
Abercynon	16	J 28
Aberdare/Aberdâr	16	J 28
Aberdaron	32	F 25
Aberdaugleddau/ Milford Haven	14	E 28
Aberdeen	69	N 12
Aberdour	56	K 15
Aberdour Bay	69	N 10
Aberdovey/ Aberdyfi	24	H 26
Abereiddy	14	E 28
Aberfeldy	61	I 14
Aberffraw	32	G 24
Aberford	40	P 22
Aberfoyle	55	G 15
Abergavenny/ Y-Fenni	16	K 28
Abergele	33	J 24
Abergwaun/ Fishguard	14	F 28
Abergwesyn	25	I 27
Abergwyngregyn	32	H 24
Abergynolwyn	24	I 26
Aberhonddu/ Brecon	25	J 28
Aberlady	56	L 15
Aberlemno	62	L 13
Aberlour	68	K 11
Abermaw/ Barmouth	32	H 25
Abernethy	56	K 15
Aberpennar/ Mountain Ash	16	J 28
Aberporth	24	G 27
Abersoch	32	G 25
Abersychan	16	K 28
Abertawe/Swansea	15	I 29
Aberteifi/Cardigan	24	G 27
Abertillery	16	K 28
Aberuthven	55	J 15
Aberystwyth	24	H 26
Abingdon	18	Q 28
Abinger Common	19	S 30
Abington (South Lanarkshire)	49	I 17
Abington (Cambs.)	29	U 27
Aboyne	62	L 12
Abridge	21	U 29
Accrington	39	M 22
Achallader	60	F 14
Achanalt	66	F 11
Achaphubuil	60	E 13
Acharn	61	H 14
Achavanich	73	J 8
Achiltibuie	72	D 9
Achmelvich	72	E 9
Achmore	66	D 11
Achnasheen	66	E 11
Achnashellach Forest	66	E 11
Achray (Loch)	55	G 15
Achriesgill	72	F 8

Acklington	51	P 18
Ackworth	40	P 23
Acle	31	Y 26
Acomb	51	N 19
Acrise Place	13	X 30
Acton Turville	17	N 29
Adderbury	28	Q 27
Addingham	39	O 22
Addlestone	20	S 29
Adlington	38	M 23
Adlington Hall	35	N 24
Advie	68	J 11
Adwick-le-Street	40	Q 23
Ae (Forest of)	49	J 18
Affric (Glen)	66	F 12
Afon Dyfrdwy/ Dee (River)	33	K 24
Ailort (Loch)	59	C 13
Ailsa Craig	48	E 18
Ainort (Loch)	65	B 12
Ainsdale	38	K 23
Ainwick	51	O 17
Aird (The)	67	G 11
Airdrie	55	I 16
Airigh na h-Airde (Loch)	70	Z 9
Airth	55	I 15
A La Ronde	4	J 32
Albourne	11	T 31
Albrighton	27	N 26
Albyn or Mor (Glen)	60	F 12
Alcester	27	O 27
Alconbury	29	T 26
Aldbourne	18	P 29
Aldbrough	41	T 22
Aldbury	19	S 28
Alde (River)	23	Y 27
Aldeburgh	23	Y 27
Aldenham	20	S 28
Alderley Edge	35	N 24

Alderney (Channel I.)	5	
Aldershot	19	R 30
Aldridge	27	O 26
Aldringham	23	Y 27
Aldwick	10	R 31
Alexandria	55	G 16
Alfold Crossways	11	S 30
Alford (Aberdeenshire)	69	L 12
Alford (Lincs.)	37	U 24
Alfreton	35	P 24
Alfrick	26	M 27
Alfriston	12	U 31
Aline (Loch)	59	C 14
Alkborough	40	S 22
Alkham	13	X 30
Allendale Town	45	N 19
Allerston	47	S 21
Alligin Shuas	66	D 11
Alloa	55	I 15
Alloway	48	G 17
All Stretton	26	L 26
Alltan Fhèarna (Loch an)	73	H 9
Almond (Glen)	61	I 14
Almondbank	62	J 14
Almondsbury	17	M 29
Alness	67	H 10
Alnmouth	51	P 17
Alnwick	51	O 17
Alpheton	22	W 27
Alphington	4	J 31
Alpraham	34	M 24
Alrewas	35	O 25
Alsager	34	N 24
Alsh (Loch)	66	D 12
Alston	45	M 19
Alswear	6	I 31
Altarnun	3	G 32
Altnacealgach	72	F 9

Altnaharra	72	G 9
Alton (Hants.)	10	R 30
Alton (Staffs.)	35	O 25
Alton Towers	35	O 25
Altrincham	34	M 23
Alum Bay	9	P 31
Alva	55	I 15
Alvechurch	27	O 26
Alvediston	8	N 30
Alves	68	J 11
Alvie	67	I 12
Alyth	62	K 14
Amberley	11	S 31
Amble	51	P 18
Amblecote	27	N 26
Ambleside	44	L 20
Amersham	19	S 28
Amesbury	9	O 30
Amlwch	32	G 23
Ammanford/ Rhydaman	15	I 28
Ampleforth	46	Q 21
Ampthill	29	S 27
Amroth	14	G 28
An Riabhachan	66	E 11
An Socach	62	J 13
An Teallach	66	E 10
Ancroft	57	O 16
Andover	18	P 30
Andoversford	17	O 28
Andreas	42	G 20
Angle	14	E 28
Anglesey (Isle of)	32	F 24
Anglesey Abbey	29	U 27
Angmering	11	S 31
Annan	50	K 19
Annan (River)	49	J 17
Annat (Northum.)	66	D 11
Annat Bay	72	E 10
Anne Hathaway's Cottage	27	O 27
Annfield Plain	46	O 19
Anstey	28	Q 25
Anston	36	Q 23
Anstruther	57	L 15
Antony House	3	H 32
Appin	60	E 14
Appleby	45	M 20
Appleby Magna	27	P 25
Appledore (Devon)	6	H 30
Appledore (Kent)	12	W 30
Appleford	18	Q 29
Aran Fawddwy	33	I 25
Arber Low	35	O 24
Arberth/Narberth	14	F 28
Arbirlot	63	M 14
Arbroath	63	M 14
Arbury Hall	27	P 26
Archiestown	68	K 11
Ard (Loch)	55	G 15
Ardarroch	66	D 11
Ardcharnich	66	E 10
Ardechive	60	E 13
Ardeonaig	61	H 14
Ardersier	67	H 11
Ardfern	54	D 15
Ardgay	67	G 10
Ardgour	60	D 13
Ardingly	11	T 30
Ardivachar	64	X 11
Ardleigh	23	W 28
Ardlui	54	F 15
Ardlussa	52	C 15
Ardmore Point	65	A 11
Ardnamurchan	58	B 13
Ardnave Point	52	B 16
Ardrishaig	54	D 15
Ardrossan	54	F 17
Ardvasar	65	C 12
Ardverikie Forest	61	G 13
Argyll	54	D 15
Argyll Forest Park	54	F 15
Arienas (Loch)	59	C 14
Arinagour	59	A 14
Arisaig	59	C 13
Arivruaich	70	Z 9
Arkaig (Loch)	60	E 13
Arkengarthdale	45	O 20
Arklet (Loch)	55	G 15
Arlingham	17	M 28
Arlington Court	6	I 30

Armadale (West Lothian)	55	I 16
Armadale Bay	65	C 12
Armadale (Highland)	73	H 8
Armitage	35	O 25
Armthorpe	40	Q 23
Arncliffe	39	N 21
Arncott	18	Q 28
Arnesby	28	Q 26
Arnisdale	66	D 12
Arnol	70	A 8
Arnold	36	Q 25
Arnside	44	L 21
Aros	59	B 14
Arran (Isle of)	53	E 17
Arreton	10	Q 31
Arrochar	54	F 15
Arun	11	S 31
Arundel	11	S 31
Ascot	20	R 29
Ascott House	19	R 28
Ascrib Islands	65	A 11
Asfordby	36	R 25
Ash (Kent)	13	X 30
Ash (Surrey)	19	R 30
Ash Mill	7	I 31
Ashbourne	35	O 24
Ashburton	4	I 32
Ashbury	17	P 29
Ashby de la Zouch	35	P 25
Ashcott	8	L 30
Ashford (Derbs.)	35	O 24
Ashford (Kent)	12	W 30
Ashford (Surrey)	20	S 29
Ashie (Loch)	67	H 11
Ashingdon	22	W 29
Ashington (Northum.)	51	P 18
Ashington (West Sussex)	11	S 31
Ashover	35	P 24
Ashperton	26	M 27
Ashtead	21	T 30
Ashton-in-Makerfield	38	M 23
Ashton Keynes	17	O 29
Ashton-under-Lyne	39	N 23
Ashton-upon-Mersey	39	M 23
Ashwell	29	T 27
Askam in Furness	44	K 21
Askern	40	Q 23
Askernish	64	X 12
Askerswell	8	L 31
Askham	44	L 20
Askrigg	45	N 21
Aspatria	44	K 19
Aspley Guise	29	S 27
Assynt (Loch)	72	E 9
Aston Clinton	19	R 28
Aston Rowant	18	R 28
Aston Tirrold	18	Q 29
Astwood Bank	27	O 27
Atcham	26	L 25
Athelhampton Hall	8	N 31
Athelney	7	L 30
Atherington	6	H 31
Atherstone	27	P 26
Atherton	38	M 23
Atholl (Forest of)	61	H 13
Attleborough	30	X 26
Auchenblae	63	M 13
Auchencairn	43	I 19
Auchinleck	48	H 17
Auchleven	69	M 12
Auchnagatt	69	N 11
Auchterarder	55	I 15
Auchterderran	56	K 15
Auchtermuchty	56	K 15
Auchtertyre	66	D 12
Auckengill	74	K 8
Audenshaw	39	N 23
Audlem	34	M 25
Audley	34	N 24
Audley End	29	U 27
Aughton (Lancs.)	38	L 23
Aughton (South Yorks.)	40	Q 23
Auldearn	67	I 11
Auldhouse	55	H 16

Aultbea	66	D 10
Aust	16	M 29
Austwick	39	M 21
Avebury	17	O 29
Aveley	21	U 29
Avening	17	N 28
Aveton Gifford	4	I 33
Aviemore	67	I 12
Avoch	67	H 11
Avon (County)	16	M 29
Avon (Glen)	62	J 12
Avon (River)	9	O 31
Avon (River) (R. Severn)	27	N 27
Avonbridge	55	I 16
Avonmouth	16	L 29
Awe (Loch)	54	E 15
Awliscombe	7	K 31
Awre	17	M 28
Axbridge	16	L 30
Axminster	8	L 31
Axmouth	5	K 31
Aylesbury	18	R 28
Aylesford	12	V 30
Aylesham	13	X 30
Aylsham	31	X 25
Aymestrey	26	L 27
Aynho	28	Q 28
Ayr	48	G 17
Aysgarth	45	O 21
Ayton	47	S 21

B

Bà (Loch)	59	C 14
Babbacombe Bay	4	J 32
Backaland	75	L 6
Backwater Reservoir	62	K 13
Baconsthorpe	31	X 25
Bacton	31	Y 25
Bacup	39	N 22
Bad a' Ghaill (Loch)	72	E 9
Bad an Sgalaig (Loch)	66	D 10
Badachro	66	C 10
Badanloch (Loch)	73	H 9
Badcaul	66	D 10
Baddidarach	72	E 9
Badenoch	61	H 13
Badluarach	72	D 10
Badminton	17	N 29
Badrallach	66	E 10
Bae Colwyn/ Colwyn Bay	33	I 24
Bagh nam Faoileann	64	Y 11
Bagillt	33	K 24
Bagshot	19	R 29
Baile Mór	59	A 15
Bainbridge	45	N 21
Bainton	41	S 22
Bakewell	35	O 24
Bala	33	J 25
Balallan	70	A 9
Balbeggie	62	J 14
Balblair	67	H 10
Balcary Point	43	I 19
Balchrick	72	E 8
Balcombe	11	T 30
Balderton	36	R 24
Baldock	29	T 28
Balemartine	58	Z 14
Balephetrish Bay	58	Z 14
Balephuil Bay	58	Z 14
Baleshare	64	X 11
Balfour	74	L 6
Balfron	55	H 15
Balintore	67	I 10
Balivanich	64	X 11
Ballabeg	42	F 21
Ballachulish	60	E 13
Ballantrae	48	E 18
Ballasalla	42	G 21
Ballater	62	K 12
Ballaugh	42	G 21
Ballingry	56	K 15
Balmaha	55	G 15
Balmedie	69	N 12
Balmoral Castle	62	K 12
Balmullo	56	L 14

ABERDEEN

BATH

Gay Street ....**AV**
Green Street ....**BV** 21
Milsom Street ....**BV**
New Bond Street ....**BV** 31

Ambury ....**BX** 2
Argyle Street ....**BV** 3
Bennett Street ....**AV** 4
Bridge Street ....**BVX** 6
Broad Quay ....**BX** 7
Chapel Row ....**AVX** 9

Charles Street ....**AX** 10
Charlotte Street ....**AV** 12
Cheap Street ....**BX** 13
Churchill Bridge ....**BX** 14
Circus Place ....**AV** 16
Grand Parade ....**BX** 17
Great Stanhope Street ....**AV** 18
Guinea Lane ....**BV** 23
Henry Street ....**BX** 24
Lower Borough Walls ....**BX** 26
Monmouth Place ....**AVX** 28
Monmouth Street ....**AX** 30
New Orchard Street ....**BX** 32
Nile Street ....**AV** 34

Northgate Street ....**BVX** 35
Old Bond Street ....**BX** 36
Orange Grove ....**BX** 38
Pierrepont Street ....**BX** 39
Quiet Street ....**BV** 41
Russell Street ....**AV** 42
Southgate Street ....**BX** 43
Stanley Road ....**BX** 45
Terrace Walk ....**BX** 46
Upper Borough Walls ....**BX** 48
Westgate Buildings ....**AX** 49
Westgate Street ....**ABX** 50
Wood Street ....**AV** 52
York Street ....**BX** 53

BATH

BIRMINGHAM CENTRE

Bull Ring Centre ....**KZ**
Corporation Street ....**KYZ**
New Street ....**JKZ**

Albert Street ....**KZ** 2
Bull Street ....**KY** 13

Dale End ....**KZ** 21
Hall Street ....**JY** 29
Holloway Circus ....**JZ** 32
James Watt Queensway ......**KY** 35
Jennen's Road ....**KY** 36
Lancaster Circus ....**KY** 39
Lancaster Street ....**KY** 41
Masshouse Circus ....**KY** 43
Moor Street Queensway ......**KZ** 46
Navigation Street ....**JZ** 49
Newton Street ....**KY** 52

Paradise Circus ....**JZ** 56
Priory Queensway ....**KY** 57
St Chads Circus ....**JKZ** 62
St Chads Ringway ....**KY** 63
St Martin's Circus ....**KZ** 64
Shadwell Street ....**KY** 70
Smallbrook Queensway ......**KZ** 71
Snow Hill Queensway ....**KY** 73
Summer Row ....**JY** 77
Temple Row ....**KZ** 80
Waterloo Street ....**JZ** 84

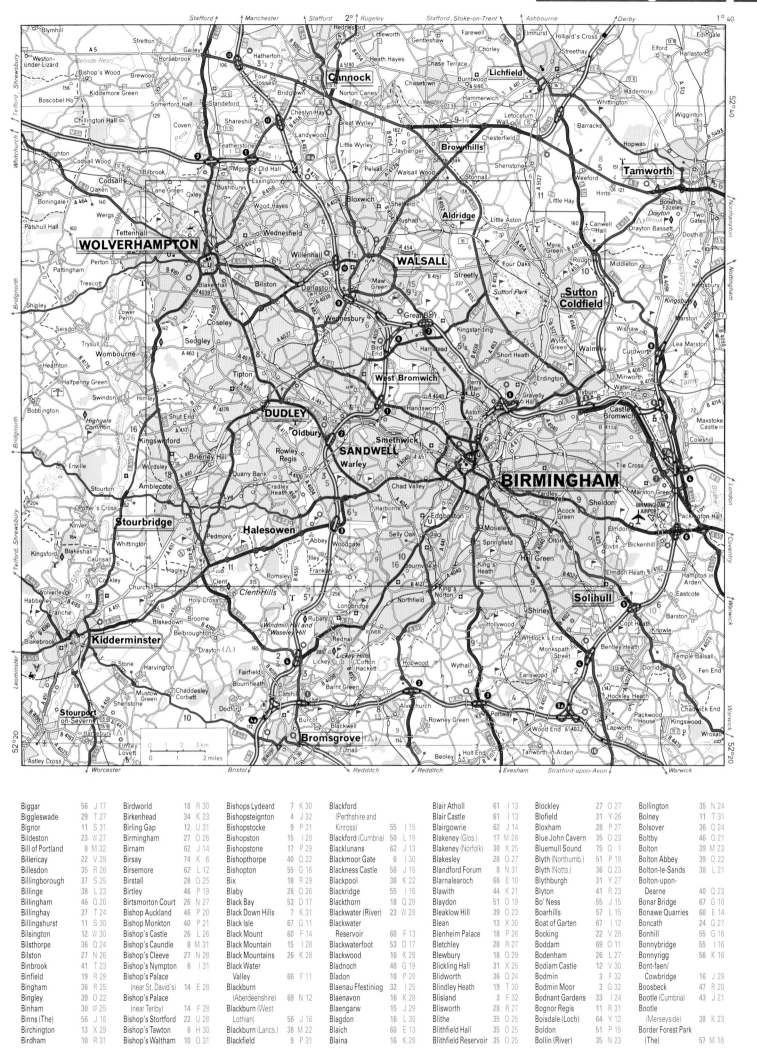

BLACKPOOL
CENTRE

Church Street

Abingdon Street	2
Adelaide Street	3
Caunce Street	7
Clifton Street	12
Cookson Street	14
Deansgate	15
George Street	17
Grosvenor Street	21
High Street	22
King Street	23
Lark Hill Street	24
New Bonny Street	25
Pleasant Street	27
South King St.	35
Talbot Square	39
Topping Street	40

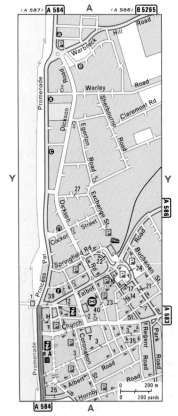

Bordon Camp	10	R 30
Boreham	22	V 28
Boreham Street	12	V 31
Borehamwood	20	T 29

Borgue	43	H 19
Borness	43	H 19
Borough Green	21	U 30

Boroughbridge	40	P 21
Borrobol Forest	73	H 9
Borrowash	35	P 25
Borth	24	H 26
Borve (Barra Isle)	64	X 13
Borve (Isle of Lewis)	70	A 8
Bosbury	26	M 27
Boscastle	3	F 31
Boscombe	9	O 31
Bosham	10	R 31
Bosherston	14	F 29
Boston	37	T 25
Boston Spa	40	P 22
Botesdale	30	W 26
Bothel	44	K 19
Bothwell	55	H 16
Botley	10	Q 31
Bottesford	36	R 25
Bottisham	29	U 27
Boughton	36	Q 24
Boughton House	28	R 26
Boughton Street	12	W 30
Boultham	36	S 24
Bourne	37	S 25
Bournemouth	9	O 31
Bourton	8	N 30
Bourton-on-the-Water	17	O 28
Bovey Tracey	4	I 32
Bovingdon	19	S 28
Bowerchalke	9	O 30
Bowes	45	N 20
Bowhill	50	L 17
Bowland (Forest of)	38	M 22
Bowmore	52	B 16
Bowness-on-Windermere	44	L 20
Bowness-on-Solway	44	K 19
Bowood House	17	N 29
Box	17	N 29
Box Hill	20	T 30
Boxford	23	W 27
Boxworth	29	T 27
Brabourne Lees	12	W 30
Bracadale (Loch)	65	A 12
Bracebridge Heath	36	S 24
Brackley	28	Q 27
Bracknell	19	R 29
Braco	55	I 15
Bradan Resr (Loch)	48	G 18
Bradfield	18	Q 29
Bradford	39	O 22
Bradford Abbas	8	M 31
Bradford-on-Avon	17	N 29
Brading	10	Q 31
Bradwell	35	O 24
Bradwell-on-Sea	23	W 28
Bradworthy	6	G 31

Brae	75	P 2
Brae Roy Lodge	60	F 13
Braemar	62	J 12
Braeriach	61	I 12
Braich y Pwll	32	F 25
Bràigh Mór	70	Y 9
Brailes	27	P 27
Brailsford	35	P 25
Braintree	22	V 28
Braishfield	9	P 30
Braithwell	40	Q 23
Bramcote	36	Q 25
Bramfield	31	Y 27
Bramford	23	X 27
Bramhall	35	N 23
Bramham	40	P 22
Bramhope	39	P 22
Bramley (South Yorks.)	36	Q 23
Bramley (Surrey)	19	S 30
Brampton (Cambs.)	29	T 27
Brampton (Cumbria)	50	L 19
Brampton (South Yorks.)	40	P 23
Brampton (Suffolk)	31	Y 26
Brancaster	30	V 25
Branderburgh	68	K 10
Brandesburton	41	T 22
Brandon (Durham)	46	P 19
Brandon (Suffolk)	30	V 26
Branscombe	5	K 31
Bransgore	9	O 31
Branston	37	S 24
Bratton Fleming	6	I 30
Braughing	22	U 28
Braunston	28	Q 26
Braunstone	28	Q 26
Braunton	6	H 30
Bray-on-Thames	18	R 29
Bray Shop	3	G 32
Brayton	40	Q 22
Breadalbane	61	G 14
Bream	17	M 28
Breamore House	9	O 31
Breasclete	70	Z 9
Breaston	36	Q 25
Brechin	63	M 13
Breckland	30	V 26
Brecon/Aberhonddu	25	J 28
Brecon Beacons National Park	15	J 28
Bredbury	39	N 23
Brede	12	V 31
Bredenbury	26	M 27
Bredon	27	N 27
Bredwardine	26	L 27
Brenchley	12	V 30
Brendon Hills	7	J 30
Brenig Reservoir	33	J 24

BOURNEMOUTH

Old Christchurch Road	DY
Square (The)	CY 63
Westover Road	DZ 75
Branksome Wood Road	CY 9
Commercial Road	CY 13
Durley Road	CZ 17
Exeter Road	CDZ 20
Fir Vale Road	DY 23
Gervis Place	DY 24
Hinton Road	DZ 27
Lansdowne (The)	DY 28
Lansdowne Road	DY 30
Madeira Road	DY 34
Manor Road	EY 35
Meyrick Road	EYZ 36
Post Office Road	CY 43
Priory Road	CZ 45
Richmond Hill	CY 47
Russell Cotes Road	DZ 49
St. Michael's Road	CZ 51
St. Paul's Road	EY 52
St. Peter's Road	DY 53
St. Stephen's Road	CY 55
St. Swithuns Road	EY 56
South Suffolk Road	EY 64
Triangle (The)	CY 67
Upper Hinton Road	DZ 68
West Cliff Promenade	CZ 71

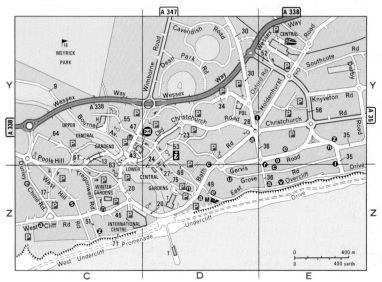

BRADFORD
CENTRE

Bank Street	AZ 4
Broadway	BZ 8
Charles Street	BZ 13
Kirkgate Centre	AZ 26
Market Street	AZ 28
Canal Road	BZ 10
Cheapside	BZ 14
Darley Street	AZ 18
Drewton Road	AZ 19
East Parade	BZ 22
Harris Street	BZ 23
Ivegate	AZ 25
Otley Road	BZ 31
Peckover Street	BZ 32
Prince's Way	BZ 33
School Street	BZ 35
Stott Hill	BZ 39

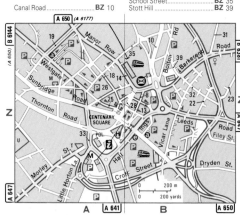

Brent (London Borough)	20	T 29
Brent Knoll	16	L 30
Brent Pelham	22	U 28
Brentwood	21	U 29
Brenzett	12	W 30
Bressay	75	Q 3
Bretherton	38	L 22
Brewlands Bridge	62	K 13
Brewood	27	N 25
Bride	42	G 20
Bridestowe	3	H 31
Bridge	13	X 30
Bridge of Allan	55	I 15
Bridge of Avon	68	J 11
Bridge of Craigisla	62	K 13
Bridge of Don	69	N 12
Bridge of Earn	56	J 14
Bridge of Forss	73	J 8
Bridge of Gairn	62	K 12
Bridge of Orchy	60	F 14
Bridgemary	10	Q 31
Bridgend/Pen-y-bont (Bridgend)	15	J 29
Bridgend (Perthshire and Kinross)	62	J 14
Bridgend (Islay)	52	B 16
Bridgend of Lintrathen	62	K 13
Bridgnorth	26	M 26
Bridgwater	7	L 30
Bridlington	41	T 21
Bridport	8	L 31
Brierfield	39	N 22
Brierley Hill	27	N 26
Brig	41	S 23
Brighouse	39	O 22
Brighstone	9	P 32
Brightlingsea	23	X 28
Brighton	11	T 31
Brightwell	18	Q 29
Brigstock	29	S 26
Brill	18	Q 28
Brimfield	26	L 27
Brimham Rocks	39	O 21
Brimington	35	P 24
Brinkburn Priory	51	O 18
Brinklow	28	P 26
Brinkworth	17	O 29
Brinyan	74	L 6
Brisley	30	W 25
Bristol	17	M 29
Briston	30	X 25
Briton Ferry	15	I 29
Brittle (Loch)	65	B 12
Brixham	4	J 32
Brixworth	28	R 27
Brize Norton	18	P 28
Broad Bay	71	B 9
Broad Blunsdon	17	O 29
Broad Chalke	9	O 30
Broad Law	49	J 17
Broadclyst	4	J 31
Broadford	65	C 12
Broadlands	9	P 31

Broadmayne	8	M 31
Broadstairs	13	Y 29
Broadstone	9	O 31
Broadwas	26	M 27
Broadway	27	O 27
Broadwey	8	M 32
Broadwindsor	8	L 31
Broch of Gurness	49	J 17
Brockenhurst	9	P 31
Brockley	16	L 29
Brockworth	17	N 28
Brodick	53	E 17
Brodick Castle	53	E 17
Brodick Bay	53	E 17
Brodie Castle	67	I 11
Brolass	59	B 14
Bromborough	34	L 24
Brome	31	X 26
Bromfield	26	L 26
Bromham	17	N 29
Bromley (London Borough)	21	U 29
Brompton (near Northallerton)	46	P 20
Brompton-by-Sawdon	47	S 21
Brompton (Kent)	12	V 29
Brompton on Swale	45	O 20
Brompton Regis	7	J 30
Bromsgrove	27	N 26
Bromyard	26	M 27
Bronllys	25	K 27
Brooke	31	Y 26
Brookland	12	W 30
Brookmans Park	19	T 28
Broom (Loch)	66	E 10
Broomfield	7	K 30
Broomhaugh	51	O 19
Brora	73	H 9
Brotherton	40	Q 22
Brotton	47	R 20
Brough	45	N 20
Brough Head	74	J 6
Brough Lodge	75	R 2
Brough of Birsay	74	J 6
Broughton (Cumbria)	43	J 19
Broughton (Hants.)	9	P 30
Broughton (Humberside)	40	S 23
Broughton (Lancs.)	38	L 22
Broughton (Northants.)	28	R 26
Broughton (Oxon.)	28	P 27
Broughton-in-Furness	38	K 21
Broughty Ferry	62	L 14
Brownhills	27	O 26
Brownsea Island	9	O 31
Broxbourne	19	T 28
Broxburn	56	J 16
Bruichladdich	52	A 16
Brundall	31	Y 26
Brushford	7	J 30
Bruton	8	M 30

Brymbo	33	K 24
Brympton d'Evercy	8	L 31
Brynamman	15	I 28
Brynbuga/Usk	16	L 28
Bryncethin	15	J 29
Bryn-Henllan	14	F 27
Brynmawr	16	K 28
Bubwith	41	R 22
Buchlyvie	55	H 15
Buckden (Cambs.)	29	T 27
Buckden (North Yorks.)	45	N 21
Buckfast Abbey	4	I 32
Buckfastleigh	4	I 32
Buckhaven	56	K 15
Buckie	68	L 10
Buckingham	28	Q 27
Buckinghamshire (County)	18	R 28
Buckland (Herts.)	29	T 28
Buckland (Oxon.)	18	P 28
Buckland Abbey	3	H 32
Buckland Newton	8	M 31
Buckland St. Mary	7	K 31
Bucklers Hard	9	P 31
Buckley/Bwcle	33	K 24
Buckminster	36	R 25
Bucknell	26	L 26
Bucksburn	69	N 12
Bude	6	G 31
Budleigh Salterton	4	K 32
Bugle	3	F 32
Bugthorpe	40	R 21
Buildwas Abbey	26	M 26
Builth Wells/Llanfair-ym-Muallt	25	J 27
Bulford	17	O 30
Bulkington	27	P 26
Bulwell	36	Q 24
Bunarkaig	60	F 13
Bunessan	59	B 15
Bungay	31	Y 26
Buntingford	29	T 28
Burbage (Leics.)	28	P 26
Burbage (Wilts.)	17	O 29
Bures	23	W 28
Burford	18	P 28
Burgess Hill	11	T 31
Burgh-by-Sands	44	K 19
Burgh-le-Marsh	37	U 24
Burghead	68	J 10
Burghley House	29	S 26
Burley	9	O 31
Burley-in-Wharfedale	39	O 22
Burneside	44	L 20
Burnham	20	S 29
Burnham Market	30	W 25
Burnham-on-Crouch	23	W 29
Burnham-on-Sea	7	L 30
Burnhaven	69	O 11
Burniston	47	S 21
Burnley	39	N 22
Burntisland	56	K 15
Burpham	20	S 31

BRIGHTON AND HOVE

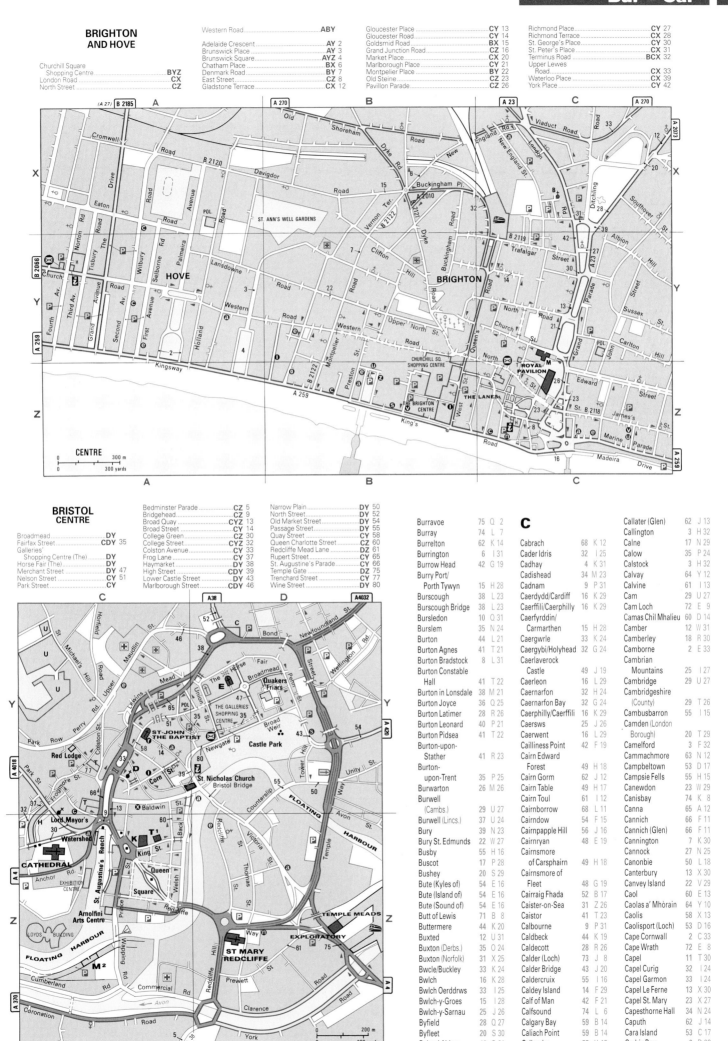

BRISTOL CENTRE

CAMBRIDGE

Grafton Centre .... Y
Lion Yard Centre .... Z
Market Hill .... Z 18
Market Street .... Z 19
Petty Cury .... Y 27
Rose Crescent .... Y 28
St. Andrew's St. .... Z 30
Sidney Street .... Y 34
Trinity Street .... Y 36

Bridge Street .... Y 2
Corn Exchange
    Street .... Z 6
Downing Street .... Z 7
Free School Lane .... Z 12

Hobson Street .... Y 14
King's Parade .... Z 15
Madingley Rd. .... Y 16
Magdalene St. .... Y 17
Milton Road .... Y 20
Newmarket Road .... Y 21
Northampton
    Street .... Y 22
Parker Street .... Z 23
Peas Hill .... Z 25
Pembroke Street .... Z 26
St John's Street .... Y 31
Short Street .... Z 32
Trumpington Road .... Z 37
Wheeler Street .... Z 39

COLLEGES

CHRIST'S .... Y A
CLARE .... Z B
CORPUS
    CHRISTI .... Z G
DARWIN .... Z D
DOWNING .... Z E
EMMANUEL .... Z F
GONVILLE
    AND CAIUS .... Y G
HARVEY COURT .... Z K
HUGHES HALL .... Y J
JESUS .... Y K
KING'S .... Y

LUCY
    CAVENDISH .... Y O
MAGDALENE .... Y N
PEMBROKE .... Z O
PETERHOUSE .... Z O
QUEENS' .... Y
RIDLEY HALL .... Z Q
ST CATHARINE'S .... Z R
ST EDMUNDS
    HOUSE .... Y U
ST JOHN'S .... Y
SIDNEY SUSSEX .... Y P
TRINITY V
TRINITY HALL .... V V
WESTMINSTER .... V W

CARDIFF / CAERDYDD

Duke Street .... BZ 26
High Street .... BZ
Queen Street .... BZ
Queens Arcade
    Shopping Centre .... BZ 54
St. David's Shopping Centre .. BZ
St. Mary Street .... BZ

Working Street .... BZ 67
Castle Street .... BZ 9
Cathays Terrace .... BY 10
Central Square .... BZ 12
Church Street .... BZ 14
City Hall Road .... BY 15
College Road .... BY 20
Corbett Road .... BY 21
Customhouse Street .... BZ 23
David Street .... BZ 25
Dumfries Place .... BY 28

Greyfriars Road .... BY 29
Guilford Street .... BZ 30
Hayes (The) .... BZ 32
King Edward VII Avenue ...... BY 36
Mary Ann Street .... BZ 39
Moira Terrace .... BY 42
Nantes (Boulevard de) .... BY 44
Penarth Road .... BZ 49
St. Andrews Place .... BY 56
St. John Street .... BZ 58
Station Terrace .... BZ 61
Stuttgart Street .... BY 62

CANTERBURY

Burgate .... Y
Butchery Lane .... Y 5
Guildhall Street .... Y 6
High Street .... Y 8
Mercery Lane .... Y 12

Palace Street .... Y
St. George's Street .... Z 17
St. Margaret's Street .... YZ 18
St. Peter's Street .... Y 20

Beercart Lane .... YZ 2
Borough (The) .... Y 4
Lower Bridge Street .... Z 9

Lower Chantry Lane .... Z 10
Rhodaus Town .... Z 13
Rosemary Lane .... Z 14
St. George's Place .... Z 16
St. Mary's Street .... Z 19
St. Radigund's Street .... Y 21
Upper Bridge Street .... Z 23
Watling Street .... Z 25

CARLISLE

Botchergate .... BZ
Castle Street .... BY 6
English Street .... BY 10
Scotch Street .... BY 19

Annetwell Street .... AY 2

Bridge Street .... AY 3
Brunswick Street .... BZ 4
Cecil Street .... BZ 5
Charlotte Street .... AZ 7
Chiswick Street .... BY 8
Church Street .... AY 10
Eden Bridge .... BY 11
Lonsdale Street .... BY 14
Lowther Street .... BY 15

Port Road .... AY 16
St. Marys Gate .... BY 17
St. Nicholas Street .... BZ 18
Spencer Street .... BY 20
Tait Street .... BZ 22
Victoria Viaduct .... ABZ 24
West Tower Street .... BY 26
West Walls .... ABY 27
Wigton Road .... AZ 29

CHESTER

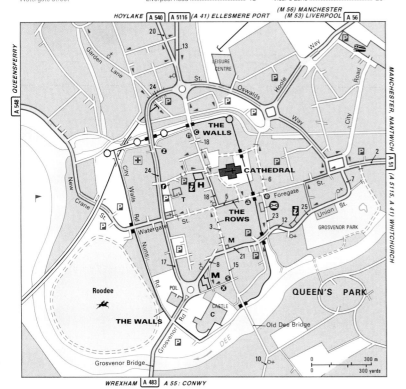

COVENTRY

DERBY

DOVER

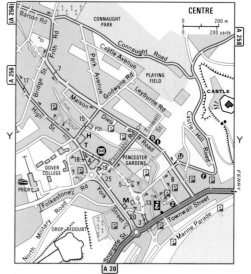

DUNDEE

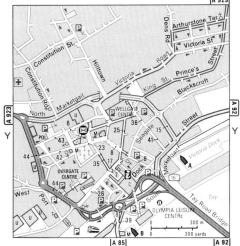

DURHAM

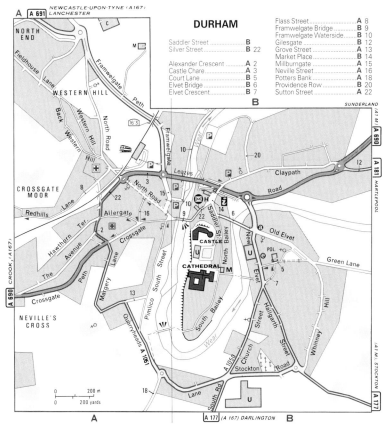

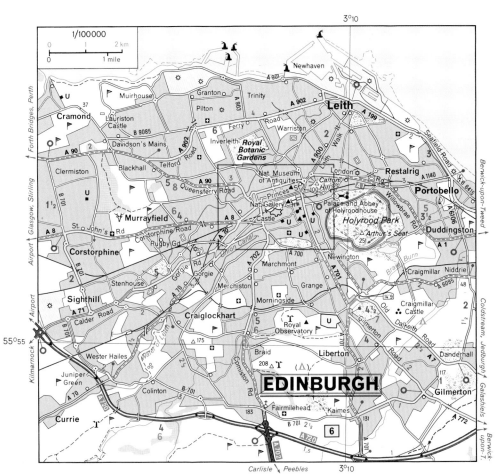

EDINBURGH
CENTRE

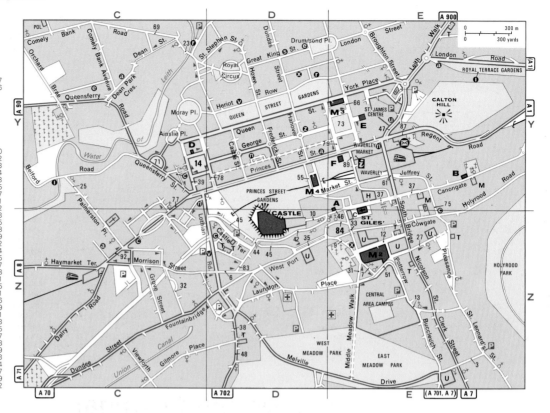

EXETER
CENTRE

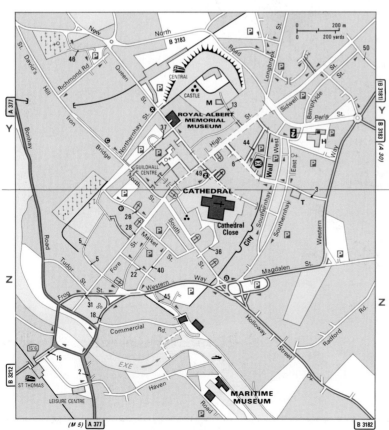

F

Folkestone Terminal

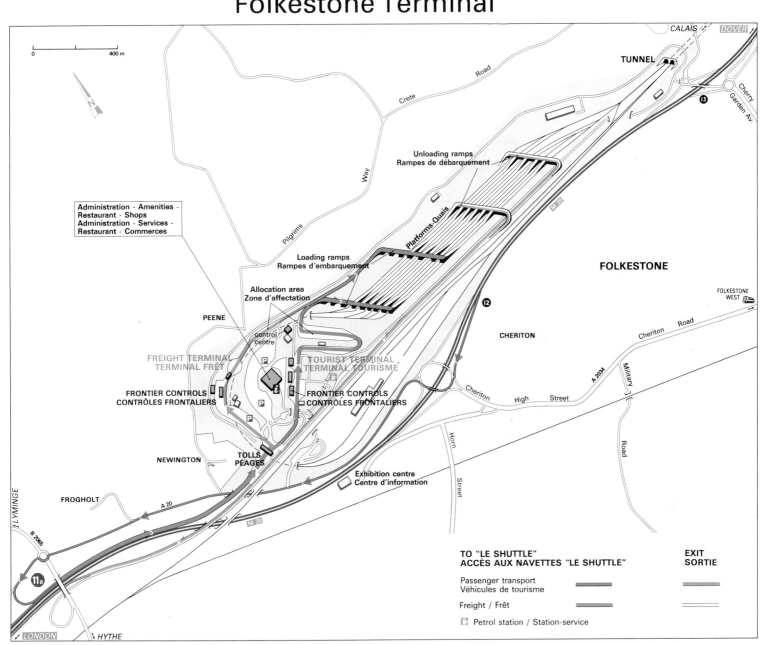

Calais Terminal

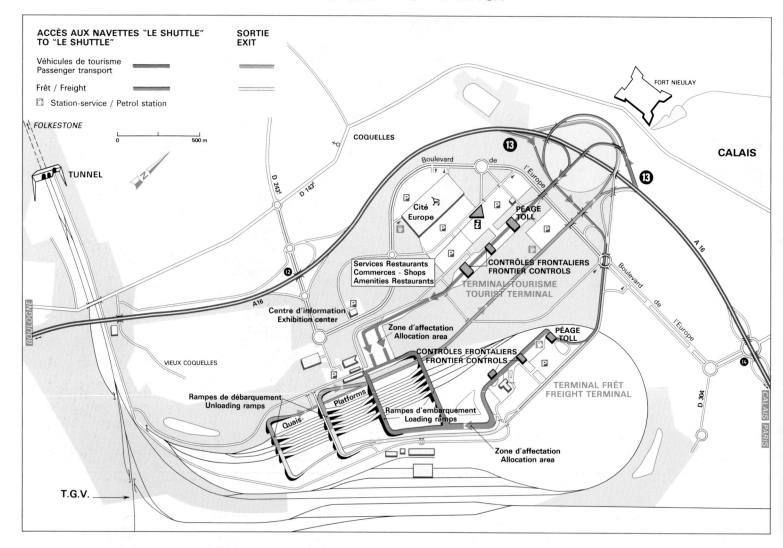

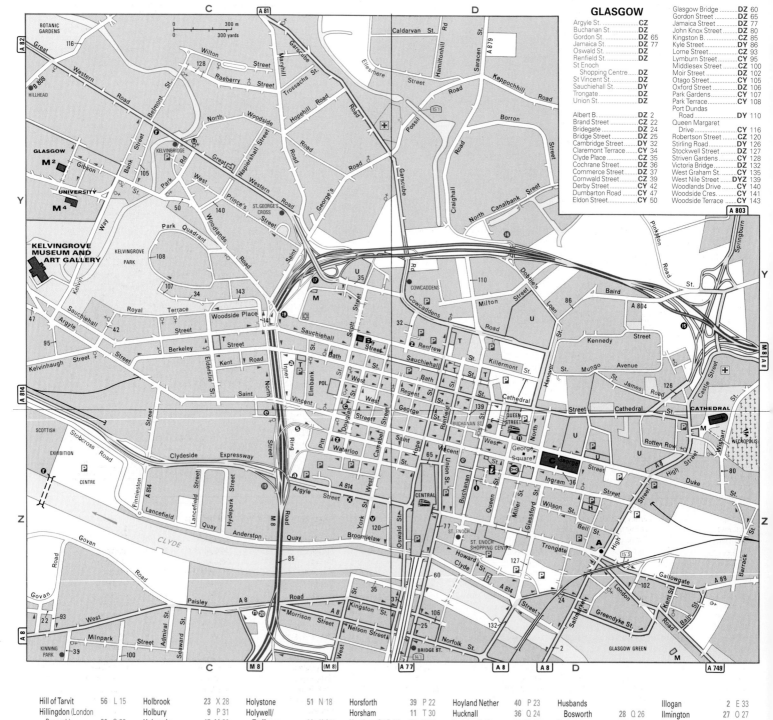

IPSWICH

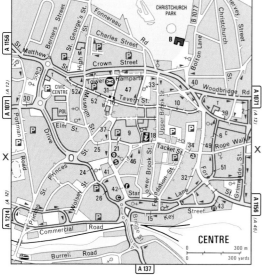

CENTRE

KINGSTON-UPON-HULL

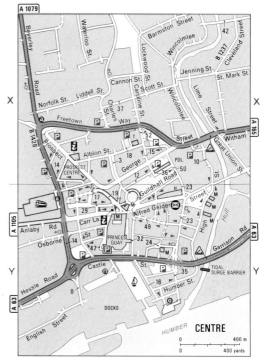

CENTRE

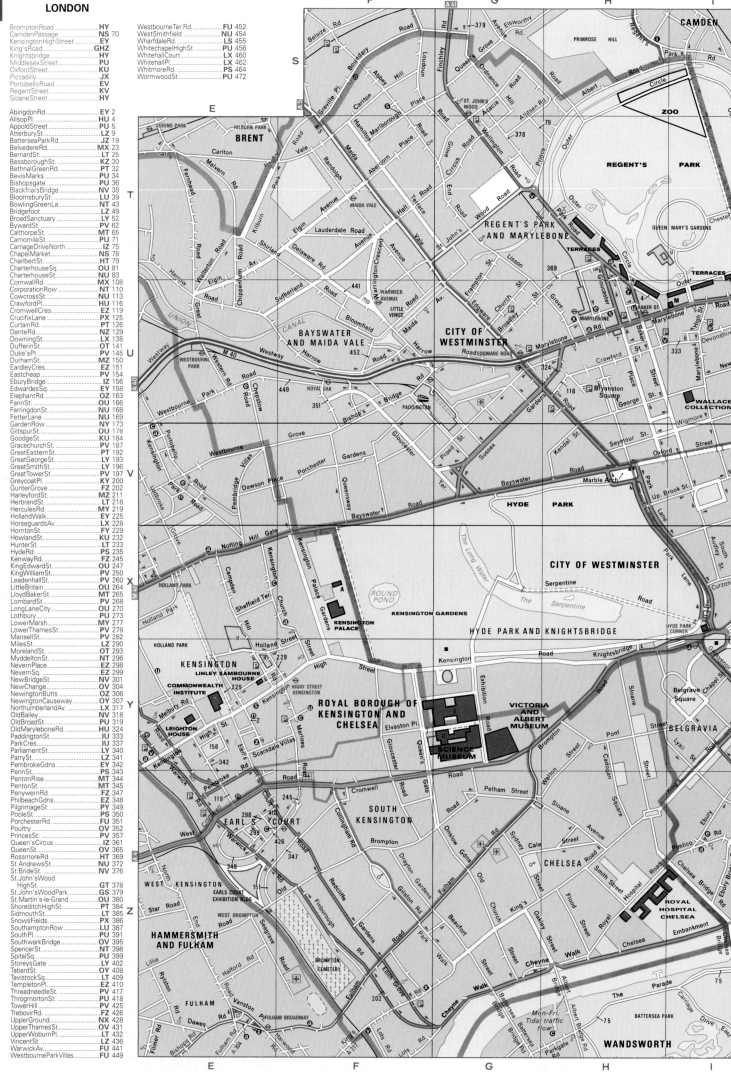

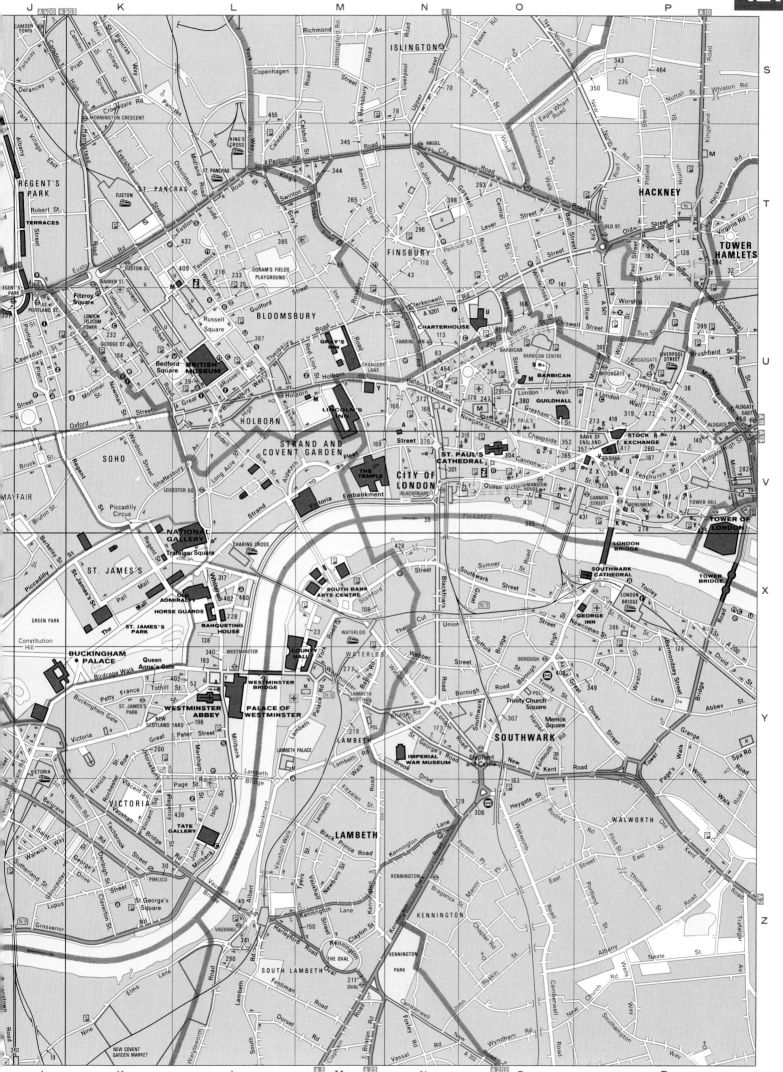

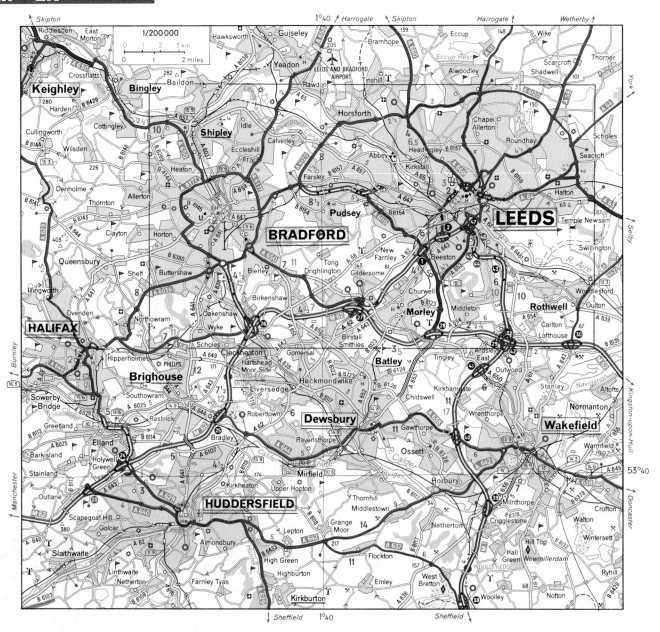

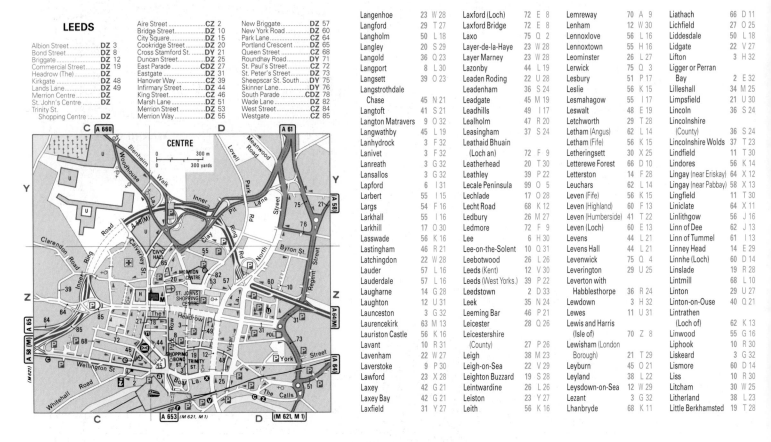

LEICESTER
CENTRE

Belgrave Gate CX
Church Gate .... BCX
Gallowtree Gate .... CY 24
High Street .... BXY
Market Street .... CY 42
Market (The) .... CY 43
St Martin's .... BY 55
Shires (The)
Shopping Centre .... BX

Belvoir Street .... CY 5
Bishop Street .... CY 7
Blackbird Road .... BX 8
Braunstone Gate .... BY 12
Cank Street .... BCY 15
Causeway Lane .... BX 16
Duns Lane .... BY 19
East Bond Street .... BCX 20

Fleet Street .... CX 21
Great Central Street .... BX 27
Hinckley Road .... BY 30
Horsefair Street .... CY 31
Humberstone Gate .... CX 33
Humberstone Road .... CX 34
Infirmary Road .... BCY 36
Lee Street .... CX 39
Millstone Lane .... BY 45
Narborough Road North .... BY 46

Newarke (The) .... BY 47
Peacock Lane .... BY 50
St. Augustine Road .... BY 51
St. Nicholas Circle .... BY 57
Southgate Street .... BY 63
Sparkenhoe Street .... CY 65
Swain Street .... CY 67
Welford Place .... CY 72
Western
Boulevard .... BY 74

LINCOLN

Guildhall Street .... Z 8
High Street .... Z
St. Swithin's Square .... Z 21
Saltergate .... Z 22
Waterside Centre .... Z 27

Avenue (The) .... Z 2
Carholme Road .... Z 3
Clasketgate .... Z 4
Corporation Street .... Z 5
Eastgate .... Y 6
High Bridge .... Z 9
Melville Street .... Z 10
Oxford Street .... Z 14
Pottergate .... Y 15
Steep Hill .... Y 17
Strait .... Z 19
St. Rumbolds's Street .... Z 20
South Park Avenue .... Z 23
Upper Avenue .... Y 25

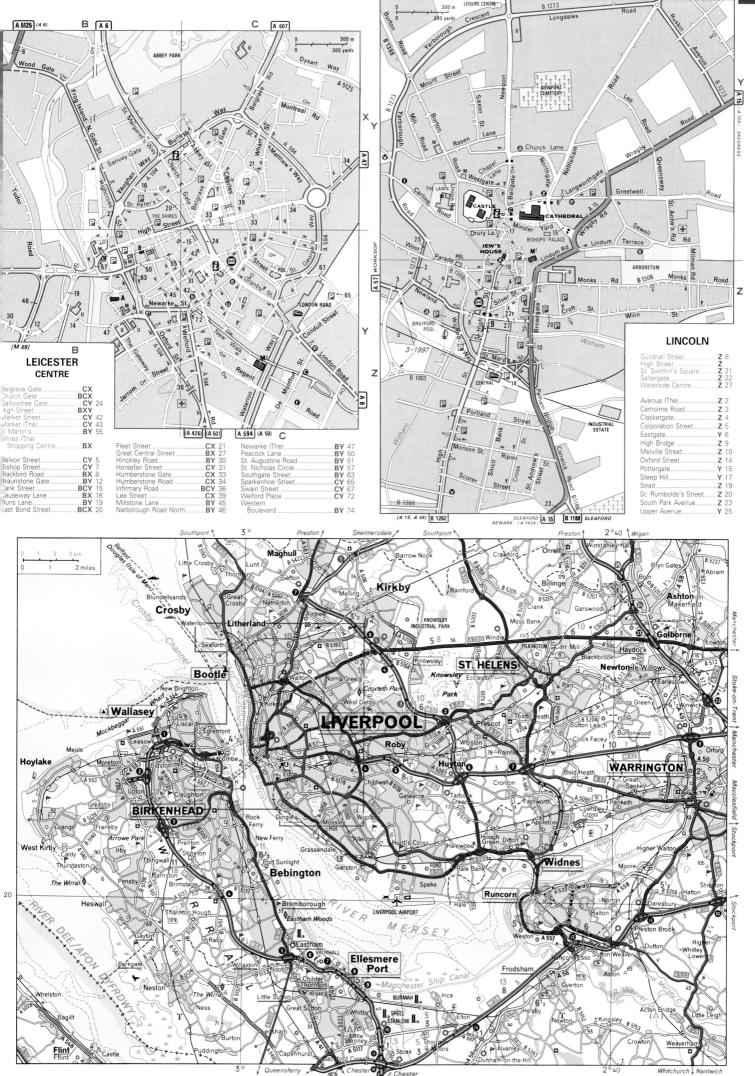

LIVERPOOL CENTRE

Place	Page	Grid	Place	Page	Grid
Lowick	57	Q 17	Luthrie	56	K 14
Lowick Bridge	44	K 21	Luton	19	S 28
Lowther	49	I 17	Luton Hoo	19	S 28
Lowther Hills	49	J 18	Lutterworth	28	Q 26
Loxwood	11	S 30	Luxborough	7	J 30
Loyal (Loch)	73	G 8	Lybster	74	K 9
Loyne (Loch)	60	E 12	Lydbury North	26	L 26
Lùb Score	65	A 10	Lydd	12	W 31
Lubenham	28	R 26	Lydd-on-Sea	12	W 31
Lubnaig (Loch)	55	H 15	Lydford	3	H 32
Luccombe	7	J 30	Lydham	26	L 26
Luce Bay	42	F 19	Lydiard Park	17	O 29
Ludgershall (Bucks.)	18	Q 28	Lydney	17	M 28
Ludgershall (Wilts.)	17	P 30	Lyme Bay	5	L 32
Ludgvan	2	D 33	Lyme Park	35	N 23
Ludham	31	Y 25	Lyme Regis	7	L 31
Ludlow	26	L 26	Lyminge	13	X 30
Lugton	55	G 16	Lymington	9	P 31
Luichart (Loch)	67	F 11	Lymm	34	M 23
Luing	54	D 15	Lympne	13	X 30
Lulworth Cove	8	N 32	Lympstone	4	J 32
Lumphanan	69	L 12	Lyndhurst	9	P 31
Lunanhead	62	L 14	Lyneham	17	O 29
Lundie (Loch)	66	C 11	Lyness	74	K 7
Lundin Links	56	L 15	Lynmouth	6	I 30
Lundy	6	G 30	Lynton	6	I 30
Lune (River)	44	L 20	Lyon (Glen)	61	H 14
Lurgainn (Loch)	72	E 9	Lyon (Loch)	61	G 14
Luss	55	G 15	Lyonshall	26	L 27
			Lytchett Minster	8	N 31
			Lytes Cary	8	L 30
			Lytham	38	L 22
			Lytham St. Anne's	38	K 22

M

Place	Page	Grid	Place	Page	Grid
Maaruig	70	Z 10	Mainland (Orkney Islands)	74	J 6
Mablethorpe	37	U 23	Mainland (Shetland Islands)	75	R 3
Mc Arthur's Head	52	B 16	Maisemore	17	N 28
Macaskin (Island)	54	D 15	Malborough	4	I 33
Macclesfield	35	N 24	Malden Bradley	8	N 30
Macduff	69	M 10	Maldon	22	W 28
Machars (The)	42	G 19	Malham	39	N 21
Machir Bay	52	A 16	Mallaig	65	C 12
Machrihanish	53	C 17	Mallory Park Circuit	28	P 26
Machrihanish Bay	53	C 17	Mallwyd	25	I 25
Machynlleth	25	I 26	Malmesbury	17	N 29
Madderty	61	I 14	Malpas	34	L 24
Maddy (Loch)	64	Y 11	Maltby	36	Q 23
Madeley (Salop)	26	M 26	Maltby-le-Marsh	37	U 24
Madeley (Staffs.)	26	M 25	Malton	40	R 21
Madingley	29	U 27	Malvern Wells	26	N 27
Madron	2	D 33	Mamble	26	M 26
Maenclochog	14	F 28	Mamore Forest	60	F 13
Maentwrog	25	I 25	Man (Isle of)	42	G 21
Maerdy	15	J 28	Manaton	4	I 32
Maes Howe	74	K 7	Manchester	39	N 23
Maesteg	15	J 29	Manderston	57	O 16
Maghull	38	L 23	Manea	29	U 26
Magor	16	L 29	Mangotsfield	17	M 29
Maiden Bradley	8	N 30	Manningtree	23	X 28
Maiden Castle	8	M 31	Manorbier	14	F 29
Maiden Newton	8	M 31	Mansfield	36	Q 24
Maidenhead	19	R 29	Mansfield Woodhouse	36	Q 24
Maidens	48	F 17	Manton	28	R 26
Maidford	28	Q 27	Manuden	22	U 28
Maidstone	12	V 30			

Place	Page	Grid	Place	Page	Grid
Mapledurham	18	Q 29	Marshchapel	41	U 23
Mar (Forest of)	62	J 12	Marshfield	17	N 29
Marazion	2	D 33	Marske-by-the-Sea	46	Q 20
March	29	U 26	Marston Magna	8	M 31
Marcham	18	P 29	Marston Moretaine	29	S 27
Marchwood	9	P 31	Martham	31	Y 25
Marden	12	V 30	Martin	9	O 31
Maree (Loch)	66	D 10	Martin (Isle)	66	E 10
Mareham-le-Fen	37	T 24	Martley	26	M 27
Maresfield	12	U 31	Martock	8	L 31
Margam	15	I 29	Marwell Zoological Park	10	Q 31
Margaretting	22	V 28	Mary Arden's House	27	O 27
Margate	13	Y 29	Mary Tavy	3	H 32
Margnaheglish	53	E 17	Maryburgh	67	G 11
Market Bosworth	27	P 26	Maryculter	69	N 12
Market Deeping	29	T 25	Marykirk	63	M 13
Market Drayton	34	M 25	Marypark	68	J 11
Market Harborough	28	R 26	Maryport	44	J 19
Market Lavington	17	O 30	Marywell	63	M 14
Market Rasen	37	T 23	Masham	46	P 21
Market Weighton	40	S 22	Matlock	35	P 24
Markfield	28	Q 25	Matlock Bath	35	P 24
Markinch	56	K 15	Mattishall	30	X 26
Marks Tey	23	W 28	Mauchline	48	G 17
Markyate	19	S 28	Maud	69	N 11
Marlborough	17	O 29	Maughold Head	42	H 21
Marldon	4	J 32	Mawbray	44	J 19
Marlow	19	R 29	Maybole	48	F 17
Marnhull	8	N 31	Mayfield (East Sussex)	12	U 30
Marple	35	N 23			
Marsden	39	O 23			
Marshall	8	N 31			
Marsham	31	X 25			

Place	Page	Grid
Mayfield (Staffs.)	35	O 24
Meadie (Loch)	72	G 8
Mealsgate	44	K 19
Meare	8	L 30
Measach (Falls of)	66	E 10
Measham	27	P 25
Medbourne	28	R 26
Medmenham	18	R 29
Medway (River)	12	W 29
Meidrim	14	G 28
Meigle	62	K 14
Melbost	71	B 9
Melbourn	29	U 27
Melbourne	35	P 25
Melfort	54	D 15
Melksham	17	N 29
Mellerstain	50	M 17
Melling	38	M 21
Mellon Udrigle	71	D 10
Melmerby	45	M 19
Melrose	50	L 17
Meltham	39	O 23
Melton Mowbray	36	R 25
Melvaig	66	C 10
Melvich	73	I 8
Menai Bridge/ Porthaethwy	32	H 24
Menai Strait	32	H 24
Mendip Hills	16	L 30
Menston	39	O 22
Menteith Hills	55	H 15
Mentmore	19	R 28
Meonstoke	10	Q 31

MANCHESTER
CENTRE

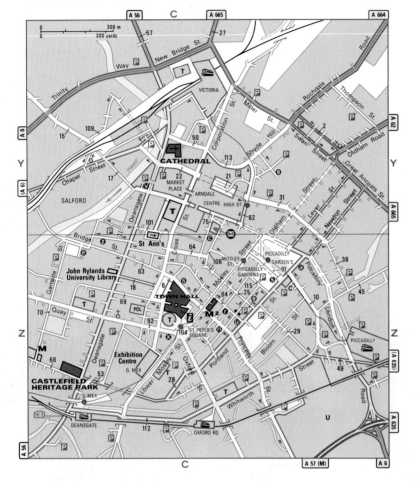

N

NEWCASTLE-UPON-TYNE

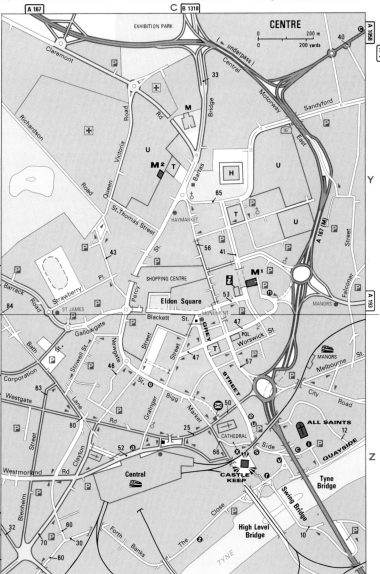

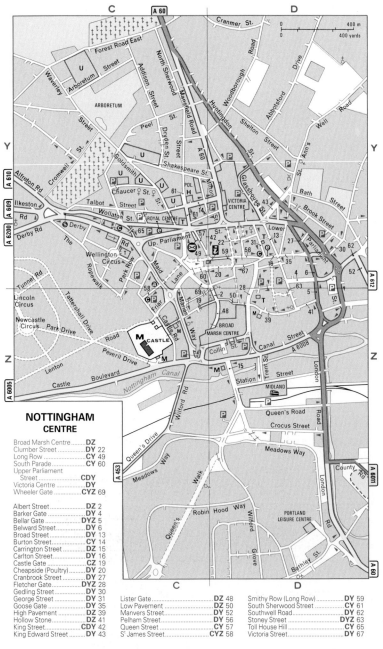

NOTTINGHAM CENTRE

Broad Marsh Centre	DZ
Clumber Street	DY 22
Long Row	CY 49
South Parade	CY 60
Upper Parliament Street	CDY
Victoria Centre	DY
Wheeler Gate	CYZ 69
Albert Street	DZ 2
Barker Gate	DY 4
Bellar Gate	DYZ 5
Belward Street	DY 6
Broad Street	DY 13
Burton Street	CY 14
Carrington Street	DZ 15
Carlton Street	DY 16
Castle Gate	CZ 19
Cheapside (Poultry)	DY 20
Cranbrook Street	DY 27
Fletcher Gate	DYZ 28
Gedling Street	DY 30
George Street	DY 31
Goose Gate	DY 35
High Pavement	DZ 39
Hollow Stone	DZ 41
King Street	CDY 42
King Edward Street	DY 43

Lister Gate	DZ 48
Low Pavement	DZ 50
Manvers Street	DY 52
Pelham Street	DY 56
Queen Street	CY 57
St James Street	CYZ 58

Smithy Row (Long Row)	DY 59
South Sherwood Street	CY 61
Southwell Road	DY 62
Stoney Street	DYZ 63
Toll House Hill	CY 65
Victoria Street	DY 67

Northiam	12 V 31	Oathlaw	62 L 13	Old Windsor	20 S 29
Northleach	17 O 28	Oban	60 D 14	Oldany Island	72 E 9
Northop	33 K 24	Ochil Hills	55 I 15	Oldbury	27 N 26
Northton	70 Y 10	Ochiltree	48 G 17	Oldcotes	36 Q 23
Northumberland (County)	50 M 18	Ockley	11 S 30	Oldham	39 N 23
		Odiham	18 R 30	Oldmeldrum	69 N 11
Northumberland National Park	51 N 18	Offa's Dyke Path	26 K 26	Ollaberry	75 P 2
		Ogbourne St. George	17 O 29	Ollay (Loch)	64 X 12
Northwich	34 M 24			Ollerton	36 Q 24
Northwold	30 V 26	Ogmore Vale	15 J 29	Olney	28 R 27
Norton	40 R 21	Ogmore-by-Sea	15 J 29	Olveston	17 M 29
Norton Fitzwarren	7 K 30	Oich (Loch)	60 F 12	Ombersley	27 N 27
Norton St. Philip	17 N 30	Oidhche (Loch na h-)	66 D 11	Onchan	42 G 21
Norwich	31 X 26	Oigh-Sgeir	58 Z 13	Onich	60 E 13
Noss Head	74 K 8	Oigh-Sgeir	58 Z 13	Orchy (Glen)	60 F 14
Noss (Isle of)	75 Q 3	Okeford Fitzpaine	8 N 31	Ord	65 C 12
Nottingham	36 Q 25	Okehampton	4 H 31	Orford	23 Y 27
Nottinghamshire (County)	36 Q 24	Old Alresford	10 Q 30	Orford Ness	23 Y 27
Nuneaton	27 P 26	Old Bolingbroke	37 U 24	Ormesby	46 Q 20
Nunney	17 M 30	Old Burghclere	18 Q 29	Ormesby St. Margaret	31 Z 25
Nunthorpe	46 Q 20	Old Deer	69 N 11	Ormskirk	38 L 23
Nunton	64 X 11	Old Fletton	29 T 26	Oronsay	52 B 15
Nutley	11 U 30	Old Harry Rocks	9 O 32	Orosay (near Fuday)	64 X 12
		Old Head	74 L 7	Orosay (near Lochboisdale)	64 X 12
		Old Kilpatrick	55 G 16		
O		Old Knebworth	19 T 28	Orphir	74 K 7
		Old Leake	37 U 24	Orrin (Glen)	66 F 11
Oa (The)	52 B 17	Old Man of Hoy	74 J 7	Orrin Reservoir	66 F 11
Oadby	28 Q 26	Old Man of Storr	65 B 11	Orsay	52 A 16
Oakengates	26 M 25	Old Radnor	25 K 27	Orsett	21 V 29
Oakham	28 R 25	Old Rayne	69 M 11	Orston	36 R 25
Oakhill	17 M 30	Old' Sarum	9 O 30	Orton	45 M 20
Oare	12 W 30	Old Sodbury	17 M 29	Orwell	29 T 27
		Old Warden	29 S 27	Orwell (River)	23 X 28

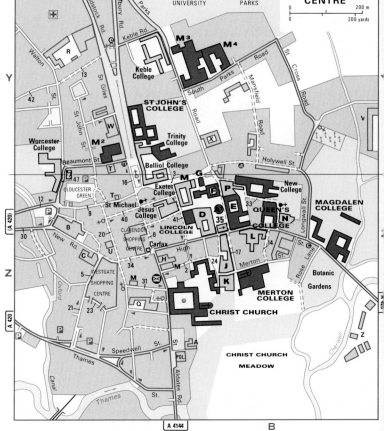

Osborne House	10 Q 31	Owslebury	10 Q 30	Parbold	38 L 23
Osdale	65 A 11	Oxburgh Hall	30 V 26	Parc Cefn Onn	16 K 29
Osgaig (Loch)	72 E 9	Oxford	18 Q 28	Parham House	11 S 31
Osmington	8 M 32	Oxfordshire		Park Gate	10 Q 31
Ossett	39 P 22	(County)	18 P 28	Park of Pairc	70 A 9
Oswaldtwistle	39 M 22	Oxted	21 T 30	Parkeston	23 X 28
Oswestry	33 K 25	Oxwich Bay	15 H 29	Parkhurst	10 Q 31
Otford	21 U 30	Oykel (Glen)	72 F 9	Parnham House	8 L 31
Othery	8 L 30	Oykel Bridge	72 F 10	Parrett (River)	7 K 30
Otley (Suffolk)	23 X 27	Oyne	69 M 12	Partney	37 U 24
Otley (West Yorks.)	39 O 22			Parton	43 J 20
Otterbourne	9 P 30			Partridge Green	11 T 31
Otterburn	51 N 18	**P**		Pass of LLanberis	32 H 24
Otterswick	75 Q 2			Patchway	17 M 29
Otterton	4 K 32	Pabay	65 C 12	Pateley Bridge	39 O 21
Ottery St. Mary	4 K 31	Pabbay (near Harris)	70 Y 10	Path of Condie	56 J 15
Oulton Park Circuit	34 M 24	Pabbay (near Mingulay)	58 X 13	Pathhead	56 L 16
Oulton Broad	31 Z 26	Pabbay (Sound of)	70 Y 10	Patna	48 G 17
Oundle	29 S 26	Padbury	28 R 28	Patrington	41 T 22
Ouse (River) (English Channel)	11 T 30	Paddock Wood	12 V 30	Patrixbourne	13 X 30
Ouse (River) (North Sea)	40 Q 21	Padiham	39 N 22	Patterdale	44 L 20
Out Skerries	75 R 2	Padstow	2 F 32	Pattingham	27 N 26
Outer Hebrides	70 W 10	Pagham	10 R 31	Paulerspury	28 R 27
Outwell	29 U 26	Paignton	4 J 32	Paull	41 T 22
Overseal	35 P 25	Painscastle	25 K 27	Paulton	17 M 30
Overstrand	31 Y 25	Painswick	17 N 28	Peacehaven	11 T 31
Overton (Wrexham)	34 L 25	Paisley	55 G 16	Peak District	
Overton (Hants.)	18 Q 30	Palnackie	43 I 19	National Park	35 O 23
Overton (Lancs.)	38 L 21	Pangbourne	18 Q 29	Peaseedown St.	
Overtown	55 I 16	Papa Stour	75 O 3	John	17 M 30
Ower	9 P 31	Papa Westray	74 L 5	Peasenhall	31 Y 27
Owermoigne	8 N 32	Paps of Jura	52 B 16	Peasmarsh	12 W 31
		Parbh (The)	72 F 8	Peat Inn	56 L 15
				Peatknowe	69 M 11

OXFORD

Broad Street	BZ 3
Clarendon Shopping Centre	BZ
Cornmarket Street	BZ 6
George Street	BZ 9
High Street	BZ
Queen Street	BZ 34
Westgate Shopping Centre	BZ

Blue Boar Street	BY 2
Castle Street	BZ 5
Hythe Bridge Street	BZ 12
Little Clarendon Street	BY 13
Logic Lane	BZ 14
Magdalen Street	BYZ 16
Magpie Lane	BZ 17
New Inn Hall Street	BZ 20
Norfolk Street	BZ 21
Old Greyfriars Street	BZ 23

Oriel Square	BZ 24
Park End Street	BZ 30
Pembroke Street	BZ 31
Queen's Lane	BZ 33
Radcliffe Square	BZ 35
St. Michael Street	BZ 40
Turl Street	BZ 41
Walton Crescent	BY 42
Worcester Street	BZ

COLLEGES

ALL SOULS	BZ E	LINCOLN	BZ	ST CROSS	BY W
BALLIOL	BY	MAGDALEN	BZ	ST EDMUND'S	BZ N
BRASENOSE	BZ D	MANSFIELD	BY E	ST HILDA'S	BZ Z
CHRIST CHURCH	BZ	MERTON	BZ	ST JOHN'S	BY
CORPUS CHRISTI	BZ K	NEW	BZ	ST PETER'S	BZ U
EXETER	BZ	NUFFIELD	BZ B	SOMERVILLE	BY R
HERTFORD	BZ P	ORIEL	BZ J	TRINITY	BY
JESUS	BZ	PEMBROKE	BZ Q	UNIVERSITY	BZ
KEBLE	BY	QUEEN'S	BZ	WADHAM	BY X
LINACRE	BZ A	ST CATHERINE'S	BY V	WORCESTER	BY

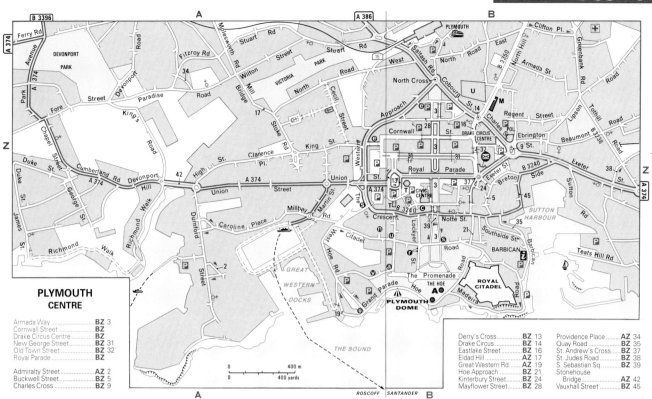

PLYMOUTH
CENTRE

Armada Way	BZ	3
Cornwall Street	BZ	
Drake Circus Centre	BZ	
New George Street	BZ	31
Old Town Street	BZ	32
Royal Parade	BZ	
Admiralty Street	AZ	2
Buckwell Street	BZ	5
Charles Cross	BZ	9

Derry's Cross	BZ	13
Drake Circus	BZ	14
Eastlake Street	BZ	16
Eldad Hill	AZ	17
Great Western Rd	AZ	19
Hoe Approach	BZ	21
Kinterbury Street	BZ	24
Mayflower Street	BZ	28

Providence Place	AZ	34
Quay Road	BZ	35
St. Andrew's Cross	BZ	37
St. Judes Road	BZ	38
S. Sebastian Sq.	BZ	39
Stonehouse Bridge	AZ	42
Vauxhall Street	BZ	45

ROSCOFF   SANTANDER
THE SOUND

PORTSMOUTH
AND SOUTHSEA

Arundel Street	CY 5
Cascade Centre	CY
Charlotte St.	CY 7
Commercial Rd.	CZ
Palmerston Rd	CZ
Tricorn Centre	CY
Alec Rose Lane	CY 2

Anglesea Rd	CY 3
Bellevue Terrace	CZ 6
Eldon St.	CY 10
Great Southsea St.	CZ 15
Guildhall Walk	CY 17
Hampshire Terrace	CY 18
Hard (The)	BY 20
High St.	BYZ 21
Isambard Brunel Rd.	CY 22
Landport Terrace	CY 25
Lombard St.	BYZ 29
Main Rd.	BY 31

Norfolk St.	CYZ 32
Ordnance Row	BY 34
Paradise St.	CY 35
Penny St.	BZ 36
St. Michael's Rd.	CY 41
Southsea Terrace	CZ 43
Spring St.	CY 45
Stanhope Rd.	CY 48
Unicorn Rd.	CY 49
Warblington St.	BY 53
White Hart Rd.	BYZ 57
Wiltshire St.	CY 59

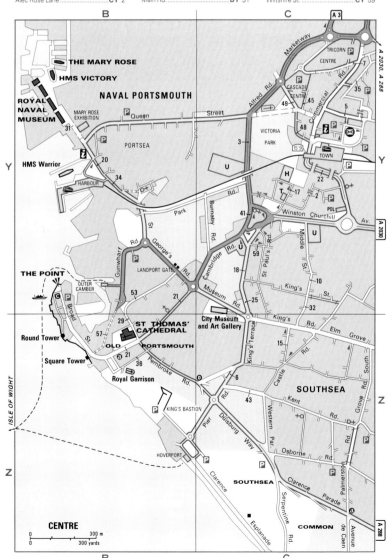

CENTRE

SHEFFIELD
CENTRE

Angel Street	DY 3
Commercial Street	DZ 16
Fargate	CZ
High Street	DZ
Leopold Street	CZ 31
West Street	CZ
Blonk Street	DY 6
Castle Gate	DY 13
Charter Row	CZ 14
Church Street	CZ 15
Cumberland Street	CZ 17
Fitzwilliam Gate	CZ 19
Flat Street	DZ 20
Furnival Gate	CZ 21
Furnival Street	CZ 22
Haymarket	DY 25
Moorfields	CY 35
Pinstone Street	CZ 37
Queen Street	CY 38
St. Mary's Gate	CZ 40
Shalesmoor	CY 41
Snig Hill	DY 42
Waingate	DY 44
West Bar Green	CY 45

SOUTHAMPTON
CENTRE

Above Bar Street
High Street

Avenue (The)	3
Bargate Street	4
Brunswick Place	6
Central Bridge	7
Central Station Bridge	8
Civic Centre Road	13
Cumberland Place	14
Hanover Buildings	17
Houndwell Place	20
Inner Avenue	22
Marsh Lane	26
Mountbatten Way	27
Orchard Place	32
Oxford Avenue	33
Portland Street	34
Pound Tree Road	35
Queen's Terrace	38
Queen's Way	39
Radcliffe Road	41
St. Andrew's Road	43
South Front	48
Terminus Terrace	52
Threefield Lane	56
Town Quay	57

Shepshed	36	Q 25
Shepton Mallet	8	M 30
Sherborne	8	M 31
Sherborne St. John	18	Q 30
Sherburn	47	S 21
Sherburn-in-Elmet	40	Q 22
Shere	20	S 30
Sheriff Hutton	40	Q 21
Sheriffhales	34	M 25
Sheringham	31	X 25
Sherston	17	N 29
Sherwood Forest	36	Q 24
Shiant (Sound of)	70	A 10
Shiel (Glen)	66	D 12
Shiel (Loch)	60	D 13
Shieldaig	66	D 11
Shieldaig (Loch)	66	C 11
Shifnal	26	M 25
Shilbottle	51	O 17
Shildon	46	P 20
Shillingford	7	J 30
Shillington	29	S 28
Shimpling	31	X 26
Shin (Loch)	72	G 9
Shinfield	18	R 29
Shipdham	30	W 26
Shipley (Salop)	27	N 26
Shipley (West Yorks.)	39	O 22
Shipston-on-Stour	27	P 27
Shipton	26	M 26
Shipton-under-Wychwood	18	P 28
Shira (Lochan)	60	F 14
Shirebrook	36	Q 24
Shirley	27	O 26
Shobdon	26	L 27
Shoeburyness	23	W 29
Shoreham	11	T 31
Shorne	12	V 29
Shorwell	9	P 32
Shotley Bridge	45	O 19
Shotley Gate	23	X 28
Shottermill	10	R 30
Shotton Colliery Thornley	46	P 19
Shotts	55	I 16
Shrewsbury	26	L 25
Shrewton	17	O 30
Shrivenham	17	P 29
Shropshire (County)	26	M 26
Shuna Sound	54	D 15
Shurdington	17	N 28
Sible Hedingham	22	V 28
Sibsey	37	U 24
Sidbury	5	K 31
Siddington	35	N 24
Sidford	5	K 31
Sidlaw Hills	62	K 14
Sidlesham	10	R 31
Sidmouth	5	K 31
Sighthill	56	K 16
Sileby	36	Q 25
Silecroft	44	K 21
Silkstone	35	P 23
Silloth	49	J 19
Silsden	39	O 22
Silver End	22	V 28
Silverdale	38	L 21
Silverstone Circuit	28	Q 27
Silverton	7	J 31
Simonsbath	7	I 30
Sinclair's Bay	74	K 8
Sionascaig (Loch)	72	E 9
Sissinghurst	12	V 30
Sittingbourne	12	W 29
Skara Brae	74	J 6
Skares	48	H 17
Skeabost	65	B 11
Skegness	37	V 24
Skellingthorpe	36	S 24
Skelmanthorpe	35	P 23
Skelmersdale	38	L 23
Skelmorlie	54	F 16
Skelton (Cleveland)	46	R 20
Skelton (Cumbria)	44	L 19
Skelwith Bridge	44	K 20
Skenfrith	16	L 28
Skerray	73	H 8
Skervuile Lighthouse	53	C 16
Skiddaw	44	K 20
Skilgate	7	J 30
Skipness	53	D 16
Skipport (Loch)	64	Y 12
Skipsea	41	T 22

Skipton	39	N 22
Skirza	74	K 8
Skokholm Island	14	E 28
Skomer Island	14	E 28
Skye (Isle of)	65	B 12
Slaidburn	39	M 22
Slaithwaite	39	O 23
Slamannan	55	I 16
Slapin (Loch)	65	B 12
Slapton	4	J 33
Sleaford	37	S 25
Sleat (Sound)	65	C 12
Sledmere	40	S 21
Sleekburn	51	P 18
Sleights	47	S 20
Sligachan	65	B 12
Sligachan (Loch)	65	B 12
Slimbridge	17	M 28
Slindon	11	S 31
Slockavullin	54	D 15
Slough	20	S 29
Sloy (Loch)	54	F 15
Small Hythe	12	W 30
Smallfield	11	T 30
Smarden	12	W 30
Smedmore	8	N 32
Snaefell	42	G 21
Snainton	47	S 21
Snaith	40	Q 22
Snape	23	Y 27
Snetterton Circuit	30	W 26
Snettisham	30	V 25
Snizort (Loch)	65	A 11
Snodland	12	V 30
Snowdon	32	H 24
Snowdonia Forest and National Park	32	I 24
Snowshill	27	O 27
Soa	58	Z 14
Soa Island	59	A 15
Soar (River)	36	Q 25
Soay	65	B 12
Soay Sound	65	B 12
Soham	30	V 26
Solent (The)	10	Q 31
Solihull	27	O 26
Sollas	64	X 11
Solva	14	E 28
Solway Firth	43	J 19
Somercotes	35	P 24
Somerset (County)	8	M 30
Somersham	29	U 26
Somerton (Norfolk)	31	Y 25
Somerton (Oxon.)	28	Q 28
Somerton (Somerset)	8	L 30
Sompting	11	S 31
Sonning	18	R 29
Sonning Caversham	18	R 29
Sonning Common	18	R 29
Sopley	9	O 31
Sorbie	42	G 19
Sorn	48	H 17
Sound (The)	3	H 32
South Brent	4	I 32
South Cave	40	S 22
South Cerney	17	O 28
South Downs	10	R 31
South Elmsall	40	Q 23
South Esk (River)	63	L 13
South Foreland	13	Y 30
South Hanningfield	22	V 29
South Harris	70	Z 10
South Harris Forest	70	Z 10
South Hayling	10	R 31
South Kelsey	41	S 23
South Kirkby	40	Q 23
South Lancing	11	T 31
South Leverton	36	R 24
South Lopham	30	X 26
South Mimms	20	T 28
South Molton	6	I 30
South Morar	59	C 13
South Normanton	35	P 24
South Ockendon	21	U 29
South Oxhey	20	S 29
South Petherton	8	L 31
South Petherwin	3	G 32
South Queensferry	56	J 16
South Ronaldsay	74	L 7
South Shields	51	P 19
South Stack	32	F 24
South Tawton	6	I 31
South Uist	64	X 12

South Walls	74	K 7
South Warnborough	18	R 30
South Woodham Ferrers	22	V 29
South Yorkshire (County)	39	O 23
South Zeal	6	I 31
Southam	28	P 27
Southampton	9	P 31
Southborough	12	U 30
Southbourne (Dorset)	9	O 31
Southbourne (West Sussex)	10	R 31
Southend	53	D 18
Southend-on-Sea	22	W 29
Southery	30	V 26
Southminster	23	W 29
Southport	38	K 23
Southsea	10	Q 31
Southwark (London Borough)	20	T 29
Southwater	11	S 30
Southwell	36	R 24
Southwick (West Sussex)	11	T 31
Southwick (Wilts.)	17	N 30
Southwick Widley	10	Q 31
Southwold	31	Z 27
Sowerby Bridge	39	O 22
Spalding	37	T 25
Spaldwick	29	S 26
Spanish Head	42	F 21
Sparkford	8	M 30
Spean (Glen)	60	F 13
Spean Bridge	60	F 13
Spelve (Loch)	59	C 14
Spennymoor	46	P 19
Spey (River)	61	G 12
Spey Bay	68	K 10
Speymouth Forest	68	K 11
Spilsby	37	U 24
Spinningdale	67	H 10
Spithead	10	Q 31
Spittal (Highland)	73	J 8
Spittal (Northumb.)	57	O 16
Spittal of Glenshee	62	J 13
Spofforth	40	P 22
Spondon	35	P 25
Spreyton	6	I 31
Springfield	56	K 15
Sprotbrough	40	Q 23
Spurn Head	41	U 23
St. Nicholas (Pembrokes)	14	E 28
St. Nicholas (Vale of Glamorgan)	16	K 29
Stack (Loch)	72	F 8
Stack Island	64	Y 12
Stacks Rocks	14	E 28
Staffa	59	A 14
Staffin Bay	65	B 11
Stafford	35	N 25
Staffordshire (County)	35	N 25
Staindrop	45	O 20
Staines	20	S 29
Stainforth (North Yorks.)	39	N 21
Stainforth (South Yorks.)	40	Q 23
Staithes	47	R 20
Stalbridge	8	M 31
Stalham	31	Y 25
Stalmine	38	L 22
Stalybridge	39	N 23
Stamford	29	S 26
Stanbridge	19	S 28
Standing Stones	70	Z 9
Standish	38	M 23
Standlake	18	P 28
Standon	22	U 28
Standford-in-the-Vale	18	P 29
Stanford-le-Hope	22	V 29
Stanford-on-Avon	28	Q 26
Stanhope	45	N 19
Stanley (Perthshire and Kinross)	62	J 14
Stanley (Durham)	46	O 19
Stanley (West Yorks.)	40	P 22
Stanmer Park	11	T 31
Stanstead Abbotts	22	U 28

STOKE-ON-TRENT
BUILT UP AREA

Alexandra Road	U 3	Elder Road	U 24
Bedford Road	U 4	Etruria Vale Road	U 27
Brownhills Road	U 12	Grove Road	V 30
Church Lane	U 19	Hanley Road	U 31
Cobridge Road	U 21	Heron Street	V 34
Davenport Street	U 23	High Street	U 35
		Higherland	V 37
		Manor Street	V 44
		Mayne Street	V 45

Moorland Road	U 48	Victoria Park Road	U 75
Park Hall Road	V 54	Watlands View	U 76
Porthill Road	U 59	Williamson Street	U 77
Snow Hill	U 63		
Stoke Road	U 68		
Strand (The)	V 69		

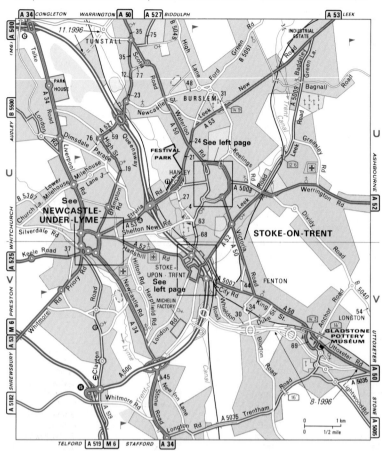

STOKE-ON-TRENT

Church Street	
Campbell Place	14
Elenora Street	26
Fleming Road	28
Hartshill Road	33
London Road	42
Shelton Old Road	62
Station Road	66
Vale Street	72

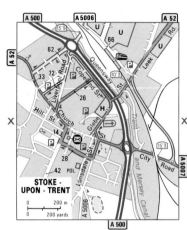

Stourbridge	27	N 26	
Stourhead House	8	N 30	
Stourport-on-Severn	27	N 26	
Stow	56	L 16	
Stow-on-the-Wold	17	O 28	
Stowe School	28	Q 27	
Stowmarket	23	W 27	
Strachan	63	M 12	
Strachur	54	E 15	
Stradbroke	31	X 28	
Stradishall	22	V 27	
Stradsett	30	V 26	
Straiton	48	G 18	
Straloch	62	J 13	
Stranraer	42	E 19	
Strata Florida	25	I 27	
Stratfield Saye	18	Q 29	
Stratford St. Mary	23	W 28	
Stratford-upon-Avon	27	O 27	
Strath Brora	73	H 9	
Strath Dearn	67	I 11	
Strath Halladale	73	I 8	
Strath Isla	68	K 11	
Strath More	66	E 10	
Strath Mulzie	72	F 10	
Strath of Kildonan	73	I 9	
Strath Oykel	72	F 10	
Strath Skinsdale	73	H 9	
Strath Tay	62	J 14	
Strathallan	55	I 15	
Strathardle	62	J 13	
Strathaven	55	H 16	
Strathbeg (Loch of)	69	O 11	
Strathblane	55	H 16	
Strathbogie	68	L 11	
Strathbraan	61	I 14	
Strathcarron	66	D 11	
Strathconon	66	F 11	
Strathconon Forest	66	F 11	
Strathdon	68	K 12	
Strathearn	55	I 14	
Stratherrick	67	G 12	
Strathkinness	56	L 14	
Strathmiglo	56	K 15	
Strathmore	62	K 14	
Strathnairn	67	H 11	
Strathnaver	73	H 8	

Stoke Gabriel	4	J 32	
Stoke Lacy	26	M 27	
Stoke Mandeville	18	R 28	
Stoke-on-Trent	35	N 24	
Stoke Poges	20	S 29	
Stoke sub Hamdon	8	L 31	
Stokenchurch	18	R 29	
Stokenham	4	I 33	
Stokesay	26	L 26	
Stokesley	46	Q 20	
Stone (Bucks.)	18	R 28	
Stone (Staffs.)	35	N 25	
Stonehaven	63	N 13	
Stonehenge	9	O 30	
Stonehouse (South Lanarkshire)	55	I 16	
Stonehouse (Devon)	3	H 32	
Stonehouse (Glos.)	17	N 28	
Stonesfield	18	P 28	
Stoneybridge	64	X 12	
Stoneykirk	42	E 19	
Stoneywood	69	N 12	
Stony Stratford	28	R 27	
Stornoway	70	A 9	
Storr (The)	65	B 11	
Storrington	11	S 31	
Stort (River)	22	U 28	
Stotfold	29	T 27	
Stottesdon	26	M 26	
Stour (River) (English Channel)	8	N 31	
Stour (River) (North Sea)	22	V 27	
Stour (River) (R. Severn)	27	N 26	

Stansted Mountfitched	22	U 28	
Stanton	30	W 27	
Stanton Harcourt	18	P 28	
Stanwell	20	S 29	
Stapleford (Notts.)	36	Q 25	
Stapleford (Wilts.)	9	O 30	
Staplehurst	12	V 30	
Start Point	4	J 33	
Startforth	45	O 20	
Stathern	36	R 25	
Staughton Highway	29	S 27	
Staunton	26	N 28	
Staveley (Cumbria)	44	L 20	
Staveley (Derbs.)	35	P 24	
Staxigoe	74	K 8	
Staxton	47	S 21	
Staylittle	25	J 26	
Stedham	10	R 31	
Steeple	22	W 28	
Steeple Ashton	17	N 30	
Steeple Aston	18	Q 28	
Steeple Bumpstead	22	V 27	
Steeple Claydon	18	R 28	
Steeple Morden	29	T 27	
Stenhousemuir	55	I 15	
Stenness (Orkney Islands)	74	K 7	
Stenness (Shetland Islands)	75	P 2	
Stevenage	19	T 28	
Stevenston	54	F 17	
Steventon	18	Q 29	
Stewartby	29	S 27	
Stewarton	55	G 16	
Stewkley	19	R 28	
Steyning	11	T 31	
Sticklepath	4	I 31	
Stilligarry	64	X 12	
Stillington	40	Q 21	
Stilton	29	T 26	
Stirling	55	I 15	
Stithians	2	E 33	
Stob Choire Clauigh	60	F 13	
Stock	22	V 29	
Stockbridge	9	P 30	
Stockland	7	K 31	
Stockport	35	N 23	
Stocksbridge	39	P 23	
Stockton Heath	34	M 23	
Stockton-on-Tees	46	P 20	
Stockton-on-Teme	26	M 27	
Stoer	72	D 9	
Stogumber	7	K 30	
Stogursey	7	K 30	
Stoke Albany	28	R 26	
Stoke-by-Nayland	23	W 28	
Stoke Climsland	3	H 32	
Stoke Fleming	4	J 33	

STRATFORD-UPON-AVON

Bridge Street	B	8
Henley Street	A	29
High Street	A	31
Sheep Street	AB	35
Wood Street	A	47
Banbury Road	B	2
Benson Road	B	3
Bridge Foot	B	6
Chapel Lane	A	13
Chapel Street	A	14

Church Street	A	16
Clopton Bridge	B	18
College Lane	A	19
Ely Street	A	22
Evesham Place	A	24
Great William Street	A	25
Greenhill Street	A	27
Guild Street	A	28
Rother Street	A	32
Scholars Lane	A	33
Tiddington Road	B	38
Trinity Street	A	40
Warwick Road	B	42
Waterside	B	43
Windsor Street	A	45

SUNDERLAND

Fawcett Street		15
High Street West		
Holmeside		16
John Street		
The Bridges		
Albion Place		2
Bedford Street		4

Borough Road	5
Bridge Street	6
Chester Road	10
Crowtree Road	11
Derwent Street	12
Livingstone Road	18
New Durham Road	19
Park Lane	23
St. Mary's Way	27
Southwick Road	30
Vine Place	36

SWANSEA/ ABERTAWE

College Street 13
Kingsway (The)
Oxford Street
Parc Tawe Shopping Centre
Princess Way
Quadrant Centre
St. David's Square

Alexandra Road 2
Belle Vue Way 4
Carmarthen Road 7
Christina Street 9
Clarence Terrace 10
De La Beche Street 14
Dillwyn Street 15
East Bank Way 16
Fabian Way 17
Grove Place 18
Nelson Street 20
New Cut Bridge 21
St. Mary's Square 28
Tawe Bridge 29
Union Street 32
Wellington Street 37
West Way 38
William Street 39

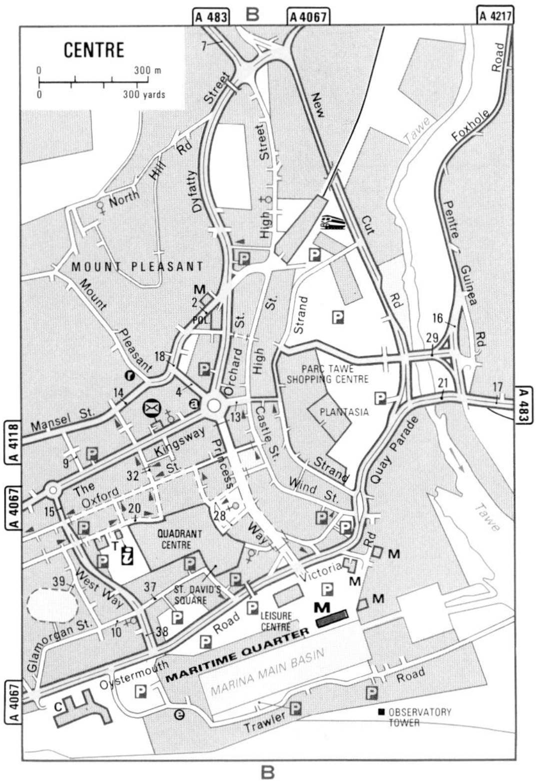
CENTRE
300 m
300 yards
A 483
B
A 4067
A 4217
A 4118
MOUNT PLEASANT
PARC TAWE SHOPPING CENTRE
PLANTASIA
QUADRANT CENTRE
ST. DAVID'S SQUARE
LEISURE CENTRE
MARITIME QUARTER
MARINA MAIN BASIN
OBSERVATORY TOWER

Strathpeffer 67 G 11
Strathspey 68 J 11
Strathvaich Lodge 66 F 10
Strathy 73 I 8
Strathy Point 73 H 8
Strathyre 55 H 15
Stratton (Cornwall) 6 G 31
Stratton (Glos.) 17 O 28
Stratton-on-the-Fosse 17 M 30
Stratton-St. Margaret 17 O 29
Streatley 18 Q 29
Street 8 L 30
Strensall 40 Q 21
Stretford 39 N 23
Stretham 29 U 26
Stretton (Cheshire) 34 M 23
Stretton (Staffs.) 27 N 25
Strichen 69 N 11
Striven (Loch) 54 E 16
Stroma (Island of) 74 K 7
Stromeferry 66 D 11
Stromemore 66 D 11
Stromness 74 K 7
Stronachlachar 55 G 15
Stronchreggan 60 E 13
Stronsay 75 M 6
Stronsay Firth 74 L 6
Strontian 59 D 13
Stroud 17 N 28
Strumble Head 14 E 27
Stuart Castel 67 H 11
Stuartfield 69 N 11
Stubbington 10 Q 31
Studland 9 O 32
Studley (Warw.) 27 O 27
Studley (Wilts.) 17 N 29
Studley Royal Gardens 39 P 21
Stuley 64 Y 12
Sturminster Marshall 8 N 31
Sturminster Newton 8 N 31
Sturry 13 X 30
Sturton-le-Steeple 36 R 23
Suainaval (Loch) 70 Z 9
Sudbury (Derbs.) 35 O 25
Sudbury (Suffolk) 22 W 27
Sudbury Hall 35 O 25
Sudeley Castle 17 O 28
Suffolk (County) 30 X 27
Sùil Ghorm 59 A 13
Sulby 42 G 21
Sulgrave 28 Q 27
Sullom Voe 75 P 2
Sumburgh 75 Q 4
Sumburgh Roost 75 P 4
Summer Bridge 39 O 21
Summer Island 72 D 9
Summercourt 2 F 32
Sunart 59 D 13
Sunart (Loch) 59 C 13
Sunbury 20 S 29
Sunderland 46 P 19
Sunningdale 20 S 29
Sunninghill 20 S 29
Surfleet 37 T 25
Surrey (County) 11 S 30
Sutterton 37 T 25
Sutton (Cambs.) 29 U 26
Sutton (London Borough) 20 T 29
Sutton (Salop) 34 M 25
Sutton Bank 46 Q 21
Sutton Benger 17 N 29
Sutton Bridge 37 U 25
Sutton Coldfield 27 O 26
Sutton Courtenay 18 Q 29
Sutton-in-Ashfield 36 Q 24
Sutton-on-Forest 40 Q 21
Sutton-on-Hull 41 T 22
Sutton-on-Sea 37 U 24
Sutton-on-Trent 36 R 24
Sutton Scotney 9 P 30
Sutton Valence 12 V 30
Swadlincote 35 P 25
Swaffham 30 W 26
Swaffham Bulbeck 29 U 27
Swale (River) 40 P 21
Swale (The) 12 W 29
Swale Dale 45 O 20
Swallow 41 T 23
Swallow Falls 33 I 24
Swanage 9 O 32
Swanland 41 S 22
Swanley 21 U 29
Swanscombe 21 U 29
Swansea/Abertawe 15 I 29
Swarbacks Minn 75 P 2
Sway 9 P 31
Swaythling 9 P 31
Swimbridge 6 I 30
Swinbrook 18 P 28
Swindon 17 O 29
Swineshead 37 T 25
Swinton (Scottish Borders) 57 N 16
Swinton (South Yorks.) 40 Q 23
Swynnerton 35 N 25
Symbister 75 Q 2
Symonds Yat 16 M 28
Symonds Yat Rock 16 M 28
Symondsbury 8 L 31
Syresham 28 Q 27
Syston 28 Q 25

T

Tadcaster 40 Q 22
Tadley 18 Q 29
Tadmarton 27 P 27
Tadworth 20 T 30
Taff (River) 16 K 29
Taibach 15 I 29
Tain 67 H 10
Takeley 22 U 28
Tal-y-bont (Dyfed) 24 I 26
Tal-y-Llyn Lake 33 I 25
Talgarth 25 K 28
Talke 34 N 24
Talladale 66 D 10
Talley 15 I 28
Talsarnau 32 H 25
Talybont-on-Usk (Powys) 16 K 28
Tamanavay (Loch) 70 Y 9
Tamar (River) 6 G 31
Tamworth 27 O 26
Tan Hill 45 N 20
Tanera Beg 72 D 9
Tanera Mór 72 D 9
Tannadice 62 L 13
Tantallon Castle 57 M 15
Taransay 70 Y 10
Taransay (Sound of) 70 Z 10
Tarbat Ness 67 I 10
Tarbert (Argyll and Bute) 53 D 16
Tarbert (Western Isles) 70 Z 10
Tarbert (Loch) 53 C 16
Tarbet 54 F 15
Tarbolton 48 G 17
Tardy Gate 38 L 22
Tarland 68 L 12
Tarleton 38 L 22
Tarn (The) 44 L 20
Tarporley 34 M 24
Tarrant Hinton 8 N 31
Tarrant Keyneston 8 N 31
Tarrington 26 M 27
Tarskavaig Point 65 B 12
Tarves 69 N 11
Tarvin 34 L 24
Tattershall 37 T 24
Tatton Hall 34 M 24
Taunton 7 K 30
Taunton Deane 7 K 30
Taverham 31 X 25
Tavistock 3 H 32
Taw (River) 6 I 31
Tay (Firth of) 62 K 14
Tay (Loch) 61 H 14
Tay (River) 61 H 14
Tay Road Bridge 62 L 14
Taynuilt 60 E 14
Tayport 62 L 14
Tayvallich 54 D 15
Teacuis (Loch) 59 C 14
Tebay 45 M 20
Tedburn St. Mary 7 I 31
Tees (River) 46 P 20
Teesdale 45 N 20
Teifi (River) 24 G 27
Teignmouth 4 J 32
Telford 26 M 25
Teme (River) 26 M 27
Temple Ewell 13 X 30
Temple Sowerby 45 M 20
Templeton 14 F 28
Tempsford 29 T 27
Tenbury Wells 26 M 27
Tenby/Dinbych-y-pysgod 14 F 28
Tendring 23 X 28
Tenterden 12 W 30
Terling 22 V 28
Tern Hill 34 M 25
Terrington St. Clement 37 U 25
Test (River) 18 P 30
Tetbury 17 N 29
Tetford 37 T 24
Tetney 41 T 23
Tettenhall 27 N 26
Teviotdale 50 L 17
Tewin 19 T 28
Tewkesbury 27 N 28
Texa 52 B 17
Teynham 12 W 30
Thakeham 11 S 31
Thame 18 R 28
Thame (River) 18 R 28
Thames (River) 18 Q 29
Thanet (Isle of) 13 Y 29
Thatcham 18 Q 29
Thaxted 22 V 28
Theale (Berks.) 18 Q 29
Theale (Somerset) 16 L 30
Theddlethorpe St. Helen 37 U 23
Thetford 30 W 26
Theydon Bois 21 U 28
Thirsk 46 P 21
Thoralby 45 N 21
Thornaby-on-Tees 46 Q 20
Thornaganby 41 R 22
Thornbury (Avon) 17 M 29
Thornbury (Heref. and Worc.) 26 M 27
Thornby 28 Q 26
Thorne 41 R 23
Thorner 40 P 22
Thorney 29 T 26
Thornham 30 V 25
Thornhill (Stirling) 55 H 15
Thornhill (Dumfries and Galloway) 49 I 18
Thornley 46 P 19
Thornton (Fife) 56 K 15
Thornton (Lancs.) 38 K 22
Thornton Curtis 41 S 23
Thornton Dale 47 R 21
Thornton-in-Craven 39 N 22
Thornyhive Bay 63 N 13
Thorpe (Derbs.) 35 O 24
Thorpe (Essex) 23 W 29
Thorpe-le-Soken 23 X 28
Thorpe-on-the-Hill 36 S 24
Thorpeness 23 Y 27
Thorrington 23 X 28
Thorverton 7 J 31
Thrapston 29 S 26
Three Cocks 25 K 27
Threlkeld 44 K 20
Throckley 51 O 19
Throwleigh 4 I 31
Thruxton Circuit 18 P 30
Thundersley 22 V 29
Thurcroft 36 Q 23
Thurlby 37 S 25
Thurlestone 4 I 33
Thurlow 22 V 27
Thurmaston 28 Q 25
Thursby 44 K 19
Thurso 73 J 8
Thwaite 45 N 20
Tibberton (Glos.) 17 M 28
Tibberton (Salop) 34 M 25
Tibshelf 35 P 24
Ticehurst 12 V 30
Tickhill 36 Q 23
Ticknall 35 P 25
Tideswell 35 O 24
Tigerton 63 L 13
Tigharry 64 X 11
Tighnabruaich 54 E 16
Tilbury 21 V 29
Tillicoultry 55 I 15
Tillington 11 S 31
Tilshead 17 O 30
Tilt (Glen) 61 I 13
Tilton-on-the-Hill 28 R 26
Timberscombe 7 J 30
Timsbury 17 M 30
Tingwall (Loch) 75 P 3
Tintagel 3 F 32
Tintern Abbey 16 L 28
Tintinhull 8 L 31
Tipton 27 N 26
Tiptree 22 W 28
Tiree 58 Z 14
Tirga Mór 70 Z 10
Tiroran 59 B 14
Tisbury 8 N 30
Titchfield 10 Q 31
Tiumpan Head 71 B 9
Tiverton 7 J 31
Tobermory 59 B 14
Toberonochy 54 D 15
Tobson 70 Z 9
Toddington 19 S 28
Todmorden 39 N 22
Toe Head 70 Y 10
Toll of Birness 69 O 11
Tollerton 40 Q 21
Tollesbury 23 W 28
Tolleshunt d'Arcy 23 W 28
Tolpuddle 8 N 31
Tolsta 71 B 8
Tolsta Chaolais 70 Z 9
Tolsta Head 71 B 8
Tomatin 67 I 11
Tombreck 67 H 11
Tomintoul 68 J 12
Tonbridge 12 U 30
Tongland 43 H 19
Tongue 73 G 8
Tonna 15 I 28
Tonypandy 16 J 29
Tonyrefail 16 J 29
Topcliffe 46 P 21
Topsham 4 J 31
Tor Ness 74 K 7
Torbay 4 J 32
Torcross 4 J 33
Torksey 36 R 24
Torlundy 60 E 13
Torphichen 55 J 16
Torphins 69 M 12
Torpoint 3 H 32
Torquay 4 J 32
Torridon (Loch) 66 C 11
Torrisdale Bay 73 H 8
Torthorwald 49 J 18
Torver 44 K 20
Totland 9 P 31
Totnes 4 I 32
Totton 9 P 31
Tow Law 45 O 19
Towcester 28 R 27
Tower Hamlets (London Borough) 21 T 29
Town Yetholm 50 N 17
Towneley Hall 39 N 22
Traborton 48 G 17
Trallwng/Welshpool 25 K 26
Tranent 56 L 16
Traquair House 50 K 17
Trawden 39 N 22
Trawsfynydd 25 I 25
Trealaval (Loch) 70 A 9
Trearddur Bay 32 G 24
Trecastle 15 J 28
Trefaldwyn/Montgomery 25 K 26
Treffynnon/Holywell 33 K 24
Trefnant 33 J 24
Trefyclawdd/Knighton 25 K 26
Trefynwy/Monmouth 16 L 28
Tregaron 24 I 27
Tregony 3 F 33
Treharris 16 K 29
Treherbert 15 J 28
Treig (Loch) 60 F 13
Trelech 14 G 28
Trelissick Gardens 2 E 33
Trelleck 16 L 28
Tremadog 32 H 25
Tremadog Bay 32 H 25
Trengwainton Garden 2 D 33
Trent (River) 36 N 25
Trentham 35 N 25
Treorchy 15 J 29
Trerice 2 E 32
Treshnish Isles 59 A 14
Treshnish Point 59 A 14
Tretower 16 K 28
Trevone 2 F 32
Trevor 32 G 25
Trevose Head 2 E 32
Trewithen 3 F 33
Trimdon 46 P 19
Trimley Heath 23 X 28
Trimsaran 15 H 28
Tring 19 R 28
Trispen 2 E 33
Trochry 62 J 14
Troedyrhiw 16 J 28
Trollamarig (Loch) 70 Z 10
Tromie (Glen) 61 H 12
Troon 48 G 17
Trossachs (The) 55 G 15
Trotternish 65 B 11
Troutbeck 44 L 20
Trowbridge 17 N 30
Truim (Glen) 61 H 13
Trull 7 K 31
Trumpington 29 U 27
Truro 2 E 33
Trwyn Cilan 32 G 25
Tuath (Loch) 59 B 14
Tuddenham 30 V 27
Tudweiliog 32 G 25
Tugford 26 M 26
Tulla (Loch) 60 F 14
Tullibody 55 I 15
Tumble 15 H 28
Tummel (Loch) 61 I 13
Tunstall (Staffs.) 35 N 24
Tunstall (Suffolk) 31 Y 25
Turnberry 48 F 18
Turnditch 35 P 24
Turret (Loch and Reservoir) 61 I 14
Turriff 69 M 11
Turvey 29 S 27
Tusker Rock 15 I 29
Tutbury 35 O 25
Tuxford 36 R 24
Twatt 74 K 6
Tweed (River) 49 J 17
Tweeddale 49 J 17
Tweedmouth 57 N 16
Tweedsmuir Hills 49 J 17
Twickenham 20 S 29
Twyford (Berks.) 18 R 29
Twyford (Hants.) 10 Q 30
Twyford (Leics.) 28 R 25
Twynholm 43 H 19
Tyddewi/St. David's 14 E 28
Tyldesley 34 M 23
Tyne (River) 51 P 19
Tyne and Wear (Metropolitan County Newcastle) 51 P 19
Tynemouth 51 P 18
Tynewydd 15 J 28
Tytherington 17 M 29
Tywardreath 3 F 32
Tywi (River) 25 I 27
Tywyn 24 H 26

U

Uckfield 12 U 31
Uddingston 55 H 16
Uffculme 7 K 31
Ufford 23 Y 27
Ugadale Bay 53 D 17
Ugborough 4 I 32
Uig (Highland) 65 A 11
Uig (Western Isles) 70 Y 9
Uisg (Loch) 59 C 14
Uiskevagh (Loch) 64 Y 11
Uley 17 N 28
Ullapool 72 E 10
Ulleskelf 40 Q 22
Ullesthorpe 28 Q 26
Ullswater 44 L 20
Ulpha 44 K 21
Ulsta 75 Q 2
Ulva 59 B 14
Ulverston 44 K 21
Unapool 72 E 9
Unst 75 R 1
Upavon 17 O 30
Uphall 56 J 16
Uphill 16 L 30
Uplyme 7 L 31
Upottery 7 K 31
Upper Badcall 72 E 9
Upper Beeding 11 T 31
Upper Chapel 25 J 27
Upper Dicker 12 U 31
Upper Knockando 68 J 11
Upper Loch Torridon 66 D 11
Upper Poppleton 40 Q 22
Upper Tean 35 O 25
Uppertown 74 K 7
Uppingham 28 R 26
Upton (Dorset) 8 N 31
Upton (Notts.) 36 R 24
Upton Grey 18 Q 30
Upton House 27 P 27
Upton Magna 26 M 25
Upton-upon-Severn 27 N 27
Upwell 29 U 26
Urchfont 17 O 30
Ure (River) 40 Q 21
Urigill (Loch) 72 F 9
Urmston 39 M 23
Urquhart Castle 67 G 12
Urquhart (Glen) 67 G 11
Urrahag (Loch) 70 A 8
Urswick 38 K 21
Usk (River) 15 J 28
Usk/Brynbuga 16 L 28
Uttoxeter 35 O 25
Uyea 75 R 2
Uyeasound 75 R 1

WINCHESTER

WOLVERHAMPTON

YORK CENTRE

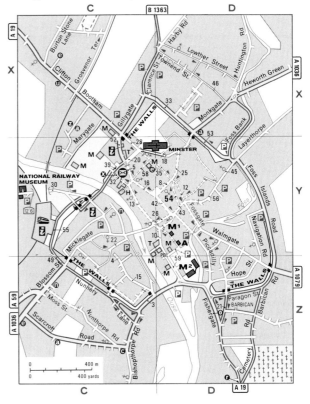

Ireland

A

Abbeydorney 82 C 10
Abbeyfeale 83 E 10
Abbeylara 91 J 6
Abbeyleix /
  Mainistir Laoise 86 J 9
Achill Head 94 B 6
Achill Island 94 B 6
Achill Sound /
  Gob an Choire 94 C 6
Achillbeg Island 94 B 6
Aclare 95 F 5
Acoose (Lough) 76 C 11
Adamstown 81 L 10
Adare 84 F 10
Adrigole 76 C 12
Aghaboe 86 J 9
Aghabullogue 78 F 12
Aghada 79 H 12
Aghalee 98 N 4
Aghavannagh 87 M 9
Aghaville 77 D 13
Aghla Mountain 100 H 3
Aglish 79 I 11
Ahakista 77 D 13
Ahascragh 89 G 7
Ahenny 80 J 10
Aherlow (Glen of) 85 H 10
Ahoghill 102 M 3
Aillwee Cave 89 E 8
Ailt an Chorráin /
  Burtonport 100 G 3
Aird Mhór /
  Ardmore 79 I 12
Allen (Bog of) 86 K 8
Allen (Lough) 96 H 5
Allenwood 86 L 8
Allihies 76 B 13
Allua (Lough) 77 E 12
Altan Lough 100 H 2
An Blascaod Mór /
  Blasket Islands 82 A 11
An Bun Beag /
  Bunbeg 100 H 2
An Cabhán / Cavan 97 J 6
An Caiseal / Cashel 88 C 7
An Caisleán Nua /
  Newcastle West 83 E 10
An Caisleán
  Riabhach /
  Castlerea 96 G 6
An Charraig /
  Carrick 100 G 4
An Chathair / Caher 85 I 10
An Cheathrú Rua /
  Carraroe 88 D 8
An Chloich
  Mhóir /
  Cloghmore 94 C 6
An Clochán /
  Clifden 88 B 7
An Clochán /
  Cloghan
  (Donegal) 100 I 3
An Clochán Liath /
  Dunglow 100 G 3
An Cloigeann /
  Cleegan 88 B 7
An Cóbh / Cobh 78 H 12
An Coimín /
  Commeen 100 I 3
An Coireán /
  Waterville 76 B 12
An Corrán / Currane 94 C 6
An Creagán /
  Mount Bellew 89 G 7
An Daingean /
  Dingle 82 B 11
An Droichead Nua /
  Newbridge 86 L 8
An Dúchoraidh /
  Doocharry 100 H 3
An Fál Carrach /
  Falcarragh 100 H 2
An Fhairche /
  Clonbur 88 D 7
An Geata Mór 94 B 5
An Gleann Garbh /
  Glengarriff 77 D 12
An Gort / Gort 89 F 8

An Gort Mór /
  Gortmore 88 D 7
An Leacht / Lahinch 88 D 9
An Longfort /
  Longford 91 I 6
An Mám /
  Maam Cross 88 D 7
An Mhala
  Raithní/Mulrany 94 C 6
An Móta / Moate 91 I 7
An Muileann
  gCearr/Mullingar 91 J 7
An Nás /
  Naas 87 M 8
An Ráth / Rath Luirc
  (Charleville) 84 F 10
An Ráth /
  Charleville 84 F 10
An Ros / Rush 93 N 7
An Scairbh /
  Scarriff 84 G 9
An Sciobairín /
  Skibbereen 77 E 13
An Seanchaisleán/
  Oldcastle 91 K 6
An Spidéal /
  Spiddal 88 E 8
An tAonach /
  Nenagh 84 H 9
An Teampall Mór/
  Templemore 85 I 9
An Tearmann /
  Termon 101 I 2

An tInbhear Mór/
  Arklow 87 N 9
An tSraith / Srah 95 E 6
An Tulach / Tullow 86 L 9
An Uaimh / Navan 92 L 7
Anascaul 82 B 11
Annacarriga 84 G 9
Annacotty 84 G 9
Annagary 100 H 2
Annagassan 93 M 6
Annageeragh 83 D 9
Annagh Head 94 B 5
Annaghdown 89 E 7
Annaghmore
  Lough 90 H 6
Annalee 97 J 5
Annalong 99 O 5
Annamoe 87 N 8
Annestown 80 K 11
Antrim 103 N 3
Antrim (County) 102 M 3
Antrim Coast 103 O 2
Antrim (Glens of) 103 N 2
Antrim Mountains 103 N 2
Anure (Lough) 100 H 3
Araglin 79 H 11
Árainn Mhór / Aran
  or Aranmore
  Island 100 G 2
Árainn (Oileáin) /
  Aran Islands 88 C 8
Aran Islands /
  Oileáin Árainn 88 C 8

Aran or Aranmore
  Island / Árainn
  Mhór 100 G 2
Archdale (Castle) 97 I 4
Ardagh 83 E 10
Ardara 100 G 3
Ardboe 98 M 4
Ardcath 93 M 7
Ardcrony 85 H 9
Ardea 76 C 12
Ardee / Baile
  Átha Fhirdhia 93 M 6
Ardfert 82 C 11
Ardfinnan 85 I 11
Ardglass 99 P 5
Ardgroom 76 C 12
Ardkeen 99 P 4
Ardmore / Aird
  Mhór 79 I 12
Ardrahan 89 F 8
Ardress House 98 M 4
Ards Forest Park 101 I 2
Ards Peninsula 99 P 4
Argideen 78 F 13
Argory (The) 98 M 4
Arigna 96 H 5
Arklow /
  An tInbhear Mór 87 N 9
Armagh 98 M 4
Armagh (County) 98 L 5
Armoy 103 N 2
Arney 97 I 5
Arrow (Lough) 96 H 5

Arthurstown 80 L 11
Arvagh 97 J 6
Ashbourne 93 M 7
Ashford 87 N 8
Ashford Castle 89 E 7
Askeaton 84 F 10
Astee 83 D 10
Áth Cinn / Headford 89 E 7
Athassel Abbey 85 I 10
Athboy 92 L 7
Athea 83 E 10
Athenry /
  Baile Átha an Rí 89 F 8
Athleague 90 H 7
Athlone /
  Baile Átha Luain 90 I 7
Athy / Baile Átha Í 86 L 9
Attymon 89 G 8
Audley's Castle 99 P 4
Augher 97 K 4
Aughils 82 C 11
Aughnacloy 97 L 4
Aughnanure Castle 89 E 7
Aughrim (Galway) 90 H 8
Aughrim
  (Wicklow) 87 N 9
Aughris Head 95 F 5
Avoca 87 N 9
Avoca (River) 87 N 9
Avoca (Valle of) 87 N 9
Avonbeg 87 M 9
Avondale Forest
  Park 87 N 9

B

Bagenalstown 86 L 9
Baile an
  Fheirtéaraigh /
  Ballyferriter 82 A 11
Baile an Mhóta /
  Ballymote 96 G 5
Baile an Róba /
  Ballinrobe 89 E 7
Baile an Sceilg /
  Ballinskelligs 76 B 12
Baile Átha an Rí /
  Athenry 89 F 8
Baile Átha Cliath /
  Dublin 87 N 8
Baile Átha Fhirdhia /
  Ardee 93 M 6
Baile Átha Í / Athy 86 L 9
Baile Átha Luain /
  Athlone 90 I 7
Baile Átha Troim /
  Trim 92 L 7
Baile Bhuirne /
  Ballyvourney 77 E 12
Baile Brigín /
  Balbriggan 93 N 7
Baile Chláir /
  Claregalway 89 F 7
Baile Locha Riach /
  Loughrea 89 G 8
Baile Mhic Andáin /
  Thomastown 80 K 10

Baile Mhic Íre /
  Ballymakeery 77 E 12
Baile Mhistéala /
  Mitchelstown 79 H 11
Baile na Finne /
  Fintown 100 H 3
Baile na Lorgan /
  Castleblayney 98 L 5
Baile Uí Bhuaigh /
  Ballyvoge 77 E 12
Baile Uí Fhiacháin /
  Newport 94 D 6
Baile Uí Mhatháin /
  Ballymahon 91 I 7
Bailieborough /
  Coill an Chollaigh 97 L 6
Balbriggan /
  Baile Brigín 92 N 7
Baldoyle 93 N 7
Balla 95 E 6
Ballagan Point 99 N 5
Ballaghaderreen 96 G 6
Ballaghbeama
  Gap 76 C 12
Ballaghisheen Pass 76 C 12
Ballina / Béal an
  Átha 95 E 5
Ballina
  (Tipperary) 84 G 9
Ballinaboy 88 B 7
Ballinadee 78 G 12
Ballinafad 96 G 5

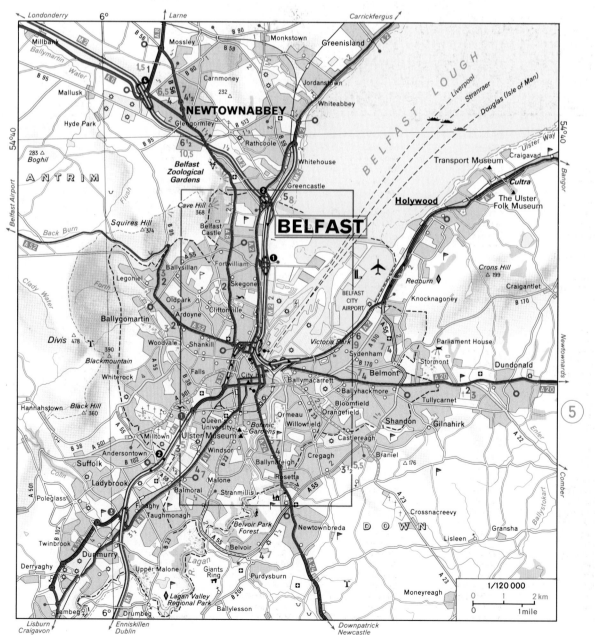

BELFAST

Castlecourt Shopping Centre ..... BYZ
Castle Place ..... BZ
Donegal Place ..... BZ
Royal Avenue ..... BYZ

Albert Square ..... BY 3
Ann Street ..... BZ 5
Bridge Street ..... BZ 12
Clifton Street ..... BY 15
Corporation Square ..... BY 16
Donegall Quay ..... BYZ 19
Donegall Square ..... BZ 20
Great Victoria Street ..... BZ 26
High Street ..... BYZ 28
Howard Street ..... BZ 29
Lagan Bridge ..... BY 32
Queen Elizabeth Bridge ..... BZ 40
Queen's Bridge ..... BZ 41
Queen's Square ..... BY 42
Rosemary Street ..... BZ 44
Waring Street ..... BY 54
Wellington Place ..... BZ 55

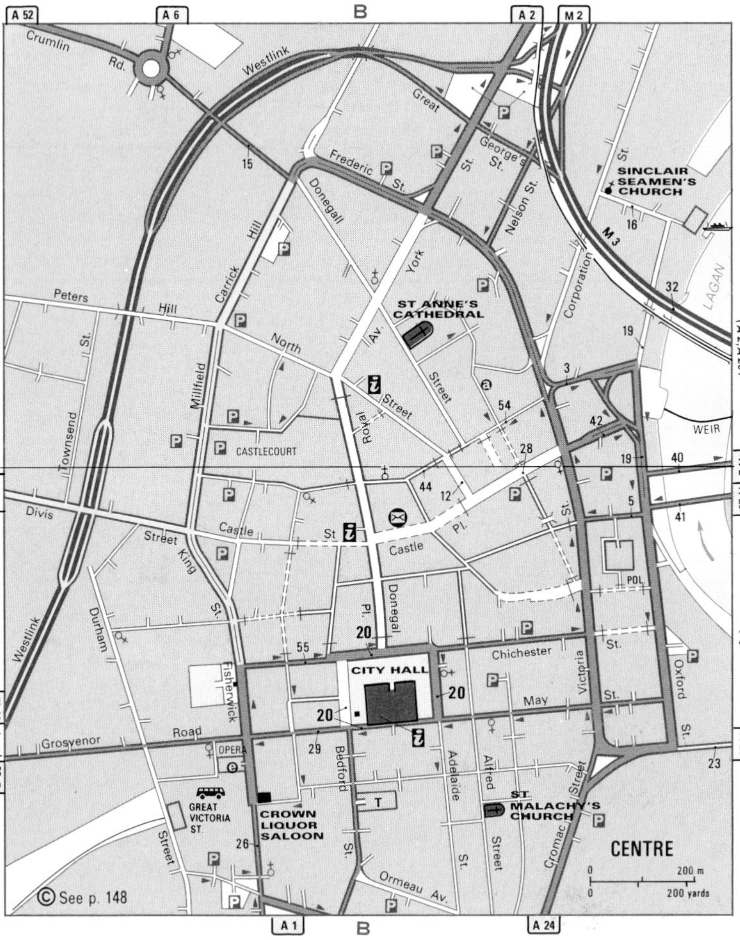

A 52
A 6
B
A 2
M 2
Crumlin Rd.
Westlink
Great
George's St.
Frederic St.
Donegall
Nelson St.
SINCLAIR SEAMEN'S CHURCH
M 3
Y
Hill
Carrick
York
Corporation
LAGAN
Peters Hill
ST ANNE'S CATHEDRAL
(A 2, A 20)
North
Millfield
Street
Townsend St.
Royal Av.
CASTLECOURT
WEIR
A 2
A 20
A 501
Divis Street
Castle St
Castle Pl.
King St.
POL.
Durham St.
Z
Westlink
Chichester
Donegall Pl.
CITY HALL
May St.
Victoria
Oxford
Fisherwick
A 12
(M1) B 38
Grosvenor Road
OPERA
Bedford
Adelaide
Alfred Street
Cromac St.
A 23
GREAT VICTORIA ST.
CROWN LIQUOR SALOON
ST. MALACHY'S CHURCH
CENTRE
Street
Ormeau Av.
200 m
200 yards
© See p. 148
A 1
A 24

Ballinagar 86 J 8
Ballinakill 86 K 9
Ballinalack 91 J 7
Ballinalea 87 N 8
Ballinalee 91 J 6
Ballinamallard 97 J 4
Ballinamore / Béal an Átha Mhóir 96 I 5
Ballinamore Bridge 89 G 7
Ballinascarty 78 F 12
Ballinasloe / Béal Átha na Sluaighe 90 H 8
Ballincollig 78 G 12
Ballincrea 80 K 11
Ballincurrig 79 H 12
Ballindarragh 97 J 5
Ballinderry 85 H 8
Ballindine 95 F 6
Ballineen 78 F 12
Ballingarry (Galway) 85 H 8
Ballingarry (Limerick) 84 F 10
Ballingarry (Tipperary) 80 J 10
Ballingeary / Béal Átha an Ghaorthaidh 77 E 12
Ballinhassig 78 G 12
Ballinlough 96 G 6
Ballinrobe / Baile an Róba 89 E 7
Ballinskelligs / Baile an Sceilg 76 B 12
Ballinskelligs Bay 76 B 12
Ballinspittle 78 G 12
Ballintober (Roscommon) 96 G 6
Ballintogher 96 G 5
Ballintoy 103 M 2
Ballintra 96 H 4
Ballinure 85 I 10
Ballitore 86 L 8
Ballivor 92 L 7
Ballon 86 L 9
Ballyagran 84 F 10
Ballybay 97 L 5
Ballybofey / Bealach Féich 101 I 3
Ballyboghil 93 N 7
Ballyboy 91 I 8
Ballybrittas 86 K 8
Ballybrophy 86 J 9
Ballybunnion 83 D 10
Ballycanew 81 N 10
Ballycarney 81 M 10
Ballycastle (Antrim) 103 N 2
Ballycastle (Mayo) 95 D 5
Ballycastle Bay 103 N 2
Ballyclare (Antrim) 103 N 3
Ballyclare (Roscommon) 90 I 6
Ballyclogh 78 F 11
Ballycolla 86 J 9
Ballyconneely 88 B 7
Ballyconneely Bay 88 B 7
Ballyconnell 97 J 5
Ballycotton 79 H 12
Ballycotton Bay 79 H 12
Ballycroy 94 C 5
Ballydavid 82 A 11
Ballydavid Head 82 A 11
Ballydavis 86 K 8
Ballydehob 77 D 13
Ballydesmond 83 E 11
Ballydonegan 76 B 13
Ballyduff (Dingle) 82 B 11
Ballyduff (Kerry) 83 D 10
Ballyduff (Waterford) 79 H 11
Ballyeighter Loughs 84 F 9
Ballyfarnan 96 H 5
Ballyferriter/Baile an Fheirtéaraigh 82 A 11
Ballyforan 90 H 7
Ballygalley 103 O 3
Ballygalley Head 103 O 3
Ballygar 90 H 7
Ballygawley (Sligo) 96 G 5
Ballygawley (Tyrone) 97 K 4
Ballygorman 101 K 1
Ballygowan 99 O 4
Ballyhack 80 L 11
Ballyhahill 83 E 10
Ballyhaise 97 K 5
Ballyhalbert 99 P 4
Ballyhale 80 K 10
Ballyhaunis / Béal Átha hAmhnais 95 F 6
Ballyhean 95 E 6
Ballyheige 82 C 10
Ballyheige Bay 82 C 10
Ballyhoe Lough 92 L 6
Ballyhooly 78 G 11
Ballyhoura Mountains 84 G 11
Ballyjamesduff 91 K 6
Ballykeeran 90 I 7
Ballykelly 102 K 2
Ballylanders 84 G 10
Ballylickey 77 D 12
Ballyliffin 101 J 2
Ballylongford 83 D 10
Ballylongford Bay 83 D 10
Ballylynan 86 K 9
Ballymacarbry 79 I 11
Ballymacoda 79 I 12
Ballymagorry 101 J 3
Ballymahon / Baile Uí Mhatháin 91 I 7
Ballymakeery / Baile Mhic Íre 77 E 12
Ballymartin 99 O 5
Ballymena 103 N 3
Ballymoe 96 G 6
Ballymoney 102 M 2
Ballymore 91 I 7
Ballymore Eustace 87 M 8
Ballymote / Baile an Mhóta 96 G 5
Ballymurphy 81 L 10
Ballynabola 81 L 10
Ballynacarrigy 91 J 7
Ballynacorra 79 H 12
Ballynagore 91 J 7
Ballynagree 78 F 12
Ballynahinch 99 O 4
Ballynahinch Lake 88 C 7
Ballynahown 88 D 8
Ballynakill Harbour 88 B 7
Ballyneety 84 G 10
Ballynoe 79 H 11
Ballynure 103 O 3
Ballyorgan 84 G 11
Ballypatrick 80 J 10
Ballyporeen 79 H 11
Ballyquintin Point 99 P 5
Ballyragget 86 J 9
Ballyroan 86 K 9
Ballyronan 102 M 3
Ballyroney 99 N 5
Ballysadare 96 G 5
Ballyshannon / Béal Átha Seanaidh 96 H 4
Ballysteen 84 F 10
Ballyteige Bay 81 L 11
Ballyvaughan 89 E 8
Ballyvaughan Bay 89 E 8
Ballyvourney / Baile Bhuirne 77 E 12
Ballywalter 99 P 4
Ballywilliam 81 L 10
Balrath 93 M 7
Baltimore 77 D 13
Baltinglass / Bealach Conglais 87 L 9
Baltray 93 N 6
Banagher 90 I 8
Banbridge 98 N 4
Bandon / Droichead na Bandan 78 F 12
Bandon River 77 F 12
Bangor (Down) 103 O 4
Bangor (Mayo) 94 C 5
Bann (River) (Lough Neagh) 99 N 5
Bann (River) (R. Slaney) 81 M 10
Banna Strand 82 C 11
Bannow 81 L 11
Bansha 85 H 10
Banteer 78 F 11
Bantry / Beanntrai 77 D 12
Bantry Bay 76 C 13
Barefield 84 F 9
Barley Cove 76 C 13
Barna / Bearna 89 E 8
Barnaderg 89 F 7
Barnatra / Barr na Trá 94 C 5
Barnesmore Gap 100 I 3
Baronscourt Forest 101 J 3
Barra (Lough) 100 H 3
Barraduff 77 D 11
Barr na Trá / Barnatra 94 C 5
Barrow 86 J 8
Barrow Harbour 82 C 11
Barrow (River) 86 K 8
Beagh (Lough) 101 I 2
Béal an Átha / Ballina 95 E 5
Béal an Átha Mhóir / Ballinamore 96 I 5
Béal an Mhuirthead / Belmullet 94 C 5
Béal Átha an Ghaorthaidh / Ballingeary 77 E 12
Béal Átha hAmhnais / Ballyhaunis 95 F 6
Béal Átha na Muice / Swinford 95 F 6
Béal Átha na Sluaighe / Ballinasloe 90 H 8
Béal Átha Seanaidh / Ballyshannon 96 H 4
Béal Deirg / Belderrig 94 D 5
Béal Tairbirt / Belturbet 97 J 5
Bealach an Doirín / Ballaghaderreen 96 G 6
Bealach Conglais / Baltinglass 87 L 9
Bealach Féich / Ballybofey 101 I 3
Bealaclugga 89 E 8
Bealadangan 88 D 8
Bealaha 83 D 9
Beanntraí / Brantry 77 D 12
Beara 76 C 12
Bearna / Barna 89 E 8
Beaufort 77 D 11
Beehive Huts 82 A 11
Beenoskee 82 B 11
Beg (Lough) 102 M 3
Behy 76 C 11
Belcarra 95 E 6
Belclare 89 F 7
Belcoo 96 I 5
Belderrig / Béal Deirg 94 D 5
Belfast 103 O 4
Belfast Lough 103 O 3
Belgooly 78 G 12
Belhavel Lough 96 H 5
Bellacorick 94 D 5
Bellaghy 102 M 3
Bellanagare 96 G 6
Bellanaleck 97 J 5
Bellananagh 97 J 6
Bellavary 95 E 6
Belleek (Armagh) 98 M 5
Belleek (Fermanagh) 96 H 4
Belmullet / Béal an Mhuirthead 94 C 5
Beltra 95 D 6
Beltra Lough 94 D 6
Belturbet / Béal Tairbirt 97 J 5
Benbane Head 102 M 2
Benbrack 96 I 5
Benbulben 96 G 4
Benburb 98 L 4
Bencroy or Gubnaveagh 96 I 5
Benmore or Fair Head 103 N 2
Benettsbridge 80 K 10
Benwee Head 94 C 4
Beragh 97 K 4
Bere Island 76 C 13
Bernish Rock 98 M 5
Bertraghboy Bay 88 C 7
Bessbrook 98 M 5
Bettystown 93 N 6
Binevenagh 102 L 2
Binn Éadair / Howth 93 N 7
Biorra / Birr 90 I 8
Birdhill 84 G 9
Birr / Biorra 90 I 8
Black Head (Antrim) 103 O 3
Black Head (Clare) 89 E 8
Black Ball Head 76 B 13
Black Bull 93 M 7
Black Gap (The) 96 I 4
Blacklion 96 I 5
Blackrock 87 N 8
Blackrock (Louth) 98 M 6
Blacksod Bay 94 B 5
Blacksod Point 94 B 5
Blackstairs Mountains 81 L 10
Blackwater 81 M 10
Blackwater Bridge 76 C 12
Blackwater (River) (Cork) 78 F 11
Blackwater (River) (Lough Neagh) 98 L 4
Blackwater (River) (R. Boyne) 92 L 6
Blarney 78 G 12
Blasket Islands / An Blascaod Mór 82 A 11
Blennerville 83 C 11
Blessington 87 M 8
Bloody Foreland 100 H 2
Blue Ball 86 J 8
Blue Stack Mountains 100 H 3
Boderg (Lough) 96 I 6
Bodyke 84 G 9
Bofin (Lough) (Galway) 88 D 7
Bofin (Lough) (Roscommon) 96 I 6
Boggeragh Mountains 77 E 12
Boheraphuca 85 I 8
Boherboy 77 E 11
Bohermeen 92 L 7
Bola (Lough) 88 C 7
Boley 86 L 8
Boliska Lough 88 E 8
Bolus Head 76 A 12
Bonet 96 H 5
Boobyglass 80 K 10
Borris 80 L 10
Borris in Ossory 86 J 9
Borrisokane / Buiríos Uí Chéin 85 H 9
Borrisoleigh 85 I 9
Bouladuff 85 I 9
Boyle / Mainistir na Búille 96 H 6
Boyle (River) 96 H 6
Boyne (River) 91 K 7
Bracklin 91 K 7
Brandon / Cé Bhréanainn 82 B 11
Brandon Bay 82 B 11
Brandon Head 82 B 11
Brandon Hill 81 L 10
Bray / Bré 87 N 8
Bray Head (Kerry) 76 A 12
Bray Head (Wicklow) 87 N 8
Bré / Bray 87 N 8
Breenagh 100 I 3
Bride (River) 79 I 11
Bridebridge 79 H 11
Bridge End 101 J 2
Bridgeland 87 M 9
Bridget Lough 84 G 9
Bridgetown 81 M 11
Briensbridge 84 G 9
Brinlack / Bun na Leaca 100 H 2
Brittas 87 M 8
Brittas Bay 87 N 9
Broad Haven 94 C 5
Broad Meadow 93 N 7
Broadford (Clare) 84 G 9
Broadford (Limerick) 84 F 10
Broadway 81 M 11
Brookeborough 97 J 5
Brosna (River) 90 I 8
Brosna 83 E 11
Broughshane 103 N 3
Brow Head 76 C 13
Brown Flesk 83 D 11
Brownstown Head 80 K 11
Bruff 84 G 10
Bruree 84 G 10
Buckode 96 H 4
Buiriós Uí Chéin / Borrisokane 85 H 9
Bull Point 103 N 2
Bull's Head 82 B 11
Bullaun 89 G 8
Bun an Phobail / Moville 101 K 2
Bun Cranncha / Buncrana 101 J 2
Bun Dobhráin / Bundoran 96 H 4
Bun na hAbhna / Bunnahowen 94 C 5
Bun na Leaca / Brinlack 100 H 2
Bunacurry 94 C 6
Bunbeg / An Bun Beag 100 H 2
Bunclody 81 M 10
Buncrana / Bun Cranncha 101 J 2
Bundoran / Bun Dobhráin 96 H 4
Bunmahon 80 J 11
Bunnahowen / Bun na hAbhna 94 C 5
Bunnanaddan 96 G 5
Bunny (Lough) 89 F 8
Bunnyconnellan 95 E 5
Bunowen 94 C 6
Bunratty 84 F 9
Burncourt 85 H 11
Burnfort 78 G 11
Burren (The) 89 E 8
Burrishoole Abbey 94 D 6
Burtonport / Ailt an Chorráin 100 G 3
Bush 102 M 2
Bushfield 84 G 9
Bushmills 102 M 2
Butler's Bridge 97 J 5
Butlerstown 78 F 13
Buttevant 84 F 11
Bweeng 78 F 11

C

Caha Mountains 76 C 12
Caher / An Chathair 85 I 10
Caher Island 94 B 6
Caherbarnagh 77 E 11
Caherconlish 84 G 10
Caherdaniel 76 B 12
Cahersiveen / Cathair Saidhbhín 76 B 12
Cahore Point 81 N 10
Caiseal / Cashel 85 I 10
Caisleán an Bharraigh / Castlebar 95 E 6
Caisleán an Chomair / Castlecomer 86 K 9
Calafort Ros Láir / Rosslare Harbour 81 M 11
Caledon 98 L 4
Callainn / Callan 80 J 10
Callan / Callainn 80 J 10
Caltra 89 G 7
Camlough 98 M 5
Camolin 81 M 10
Camp 82 C 11
Campile 80 L 11
Canglass Point 76 B 12

CORK / CORGAICH

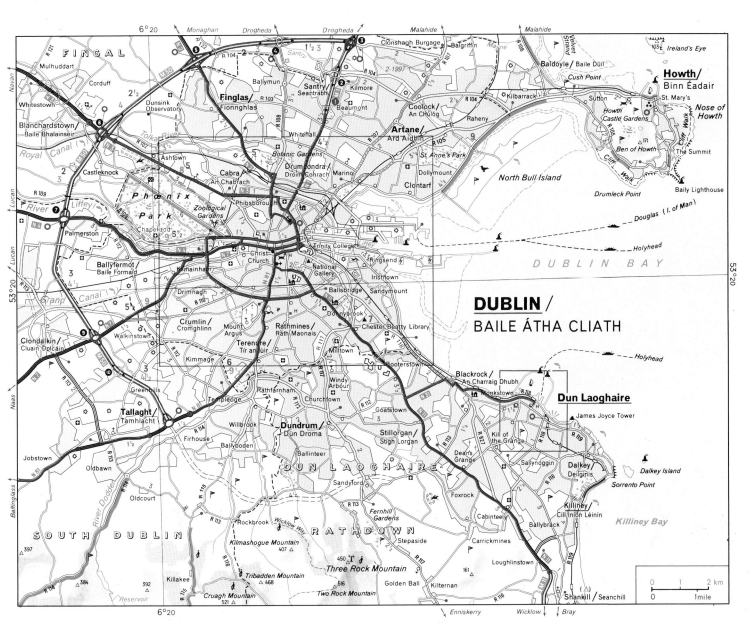

DUBLIN / BAILE ÁTHA CLIATH

DUBLIN/ BAILE ÁTHA CLIATH CENTRE

Town plans : the names of main shopping streets are indicated in red at the beginning of the list of streets.

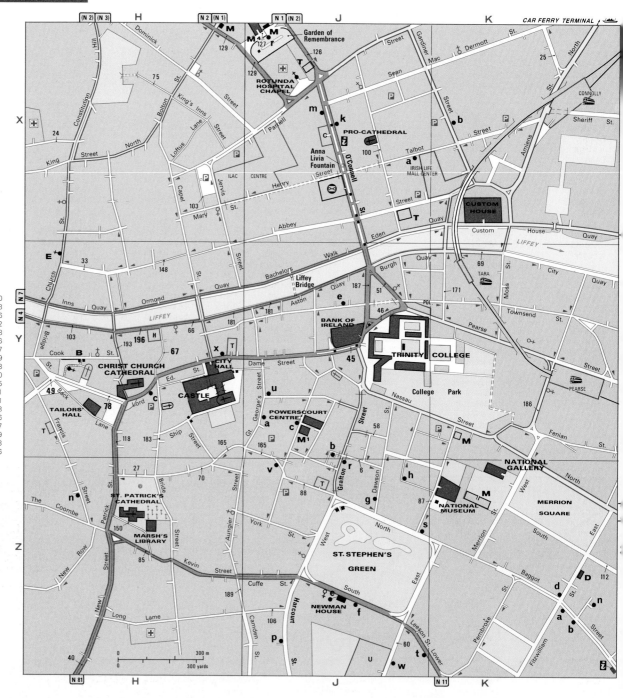

Grange (Kilkenny) 80 K 10
Grange (Louth) 98 N 5
Grange (Sligo) 96 G 4
Gransha 103 O 3
Great Island 78 H 12
Great Blasket Island 82 A 11
Great Newtown Head 80 K 11
Great Skellig 76 A 12
Greenan 87 N 9
Greencastle (Donegal) 101 L 2
Greencastle (Down) 99 N 5
Greencastle (Tyrone) 102 K 3
Greenfield 89 E 7
Greenisland 103 O 3
Greenore 99 N 5
Greenore Point 81 N 11
Grey Point 103 O 3
Greyabbey 99 P 4
Greystones / Na Clocha Liatha 87 N 8
Grianan of Aileach 101 J 2
Groomsport 99 P 3
Guaire / Gorey 87 N 9
Gulladoo Lough 97 J 6
Gullion (Slieve) 98 M 5
Gur (Lough) 84 G 10
Gurteen 89 G 7
Gwebarra Bridge 100 H 3
Gweebarra Bay 100 G 3
Gweedore / Gaoth Dobhair 100 H 2
Gweestin 77 D 11
Gyleen 79 H 12

H

Hacketstown 87 M 9
Hags Head 88 D 9
Headford / Áth Cinn 89 E 7
Healy Pass 76 C 12
Helvick Head 80 J 11
Herbertstown 84 G 10
Hillsborough 99 N 4
Hilltown 99 N 5
Hog's Head 76 B 12
Hollyford 85 H 10
Hollyfort 87 M 9
Hollymount 89 E 7
Hollywood 87 M 8
Holy Cross 85 I 10
Holy Island 84 G 9
Holycross 84 G 10
Holywood 103 O 4
Hook Head 80 L 11
Hore Abbey 85 I 10
Horn Head 100 I 2
Horseleap 91 J 7
Hospital 84 G 10
Howth / Binn Éadair 93 N 7
Hugginstown 80 K 10
Hungry Hill 76 C 12
Hurlers Cross 84 F 9
Hyne (Lough) 77 E 13

I

Ilen 77 E 13
Inagh 83 E 9
Inagh (Lough) 88 C 7
Inch 76 C 11
Inch Abbey 99 O 4
Inch Island 101 J 2
Inchigeelagh 77 E 12
Inchiquin Lough (Kerry) 77 D 12
Inchydoney Island 78 F 13
Indreabhán / Inverin 88 D 8
Inis / Ennis 84 F 9
Inis Bó Finne / Inishbofin 100 H 2
Inis Córthaidh / Enniscorthy 81 M 10
Inis Díomáin / Ennistimon 88 E 9
Inis Meáin / Inishmaan 88 D 8
Inis Mór / Inishmore 88 C 8
Inis Oírr / Inisheer 88 D 8
Inishannon 78 G 12
Inishbofin / Inis Bó Finne (Donegal) 100 H 2
Inishbofin (Galway) 88 B 7
Inishcarra Reservoir 78 F 12
Inishcrone 95 E 5
Inisheer / Inis Oírr 88 D 8
Inishfree Bay 100 G 2
Inishglora 94 B 5
Inishkea North 94 B 5
Inishkea South 94 B 5
Inishmaan / Inis Meáin 88 D 8
Inishmore / Inis Mór 88 C 8
Inishmurray 96 G 4
Inishnabro 82 A 11
Inishowen 101 J 2
Inishowen Head 102 L 2
Inishshark 88 B 7
Inishtrahull 101 K 1
Inishtrahull Sound 101 K 1
Inishturk 94 B 6
Inistioge 80 K 10
Innfield 92 L 7
Inniskeen 98 M 5
Inny (River) 91 J 6
Inver 100 H 4
Inver (Mayo) 94 C 5
Inverin / Indreabhán 88 D 8
Ireland's Eye 93 N 7
Irishtown 89 F 7
Iron (Lough) 91 J 7
Iron Mountains 96 I 5
Irvinestown 97 J 4
Iveragh 76 B 12

J

Jamestown 96 H 6
Japanese Gardens 86 L 8
Jerpoint Abbey 80 K 10
Johnstown 86 J 9
Johnstown Castle 81 M 11
Jonesborough 98 M 5
Joyce 88 D 7
Joyce Country 88 C 7
Julianstown 93 N 6

K

Kanturk / Ceann Toirc 78 F 11
Katesbridge 98 N 5
Keadew 96 H 5
Keady 98 L 5
Kealduff 76 C 12
Kealkill 77 D 12
Kearney 99 P 4
Keel 94 B 6
Keel Lough 94 B 6
Keem Strand 94 B 6
Keimaneigh (The pass of) 77 E 12
Kells (Antrim) 103 N 3
Kells (Kerry) 76 B 12
Kells (Ceanannus Mor) / Ceanannas (Meath) 92 L 6
Kells Bay 76 B 11
Kenmare / Neidín 77 D 12
Kenmare River 76 B 12
J. F. Kennedy Park 80 L 11
Kerry (County) 77 D 11
Kerry Head 82 C 10
Kerry (Ring of) 76 B 12
Kesh 97 I 4
Key (Lough) 96 H 5
Key (Lough) Forest Park 96 H 6
Kilbaha 82 C 10
Kilbeggan 91 J 7
Kilbeheny 84 H 11
Kilberry 92 L 6
Kilbricken 86 J 9
Kilbride (near Blessington) 87 M 8
Kilbrittain 78 F 12
Kilcar 100 G 4
Kilchreest 89 G 8
Kilclief 99 P 5
Kilcock 92 L 7
Kilcolgan 89 F 8
Kilconly (Galway) 89 F 7
Kilcoo 99 N 5
Kilcormac 90 I 8
Kilcrohane 76 C 13
Kilcullen 86 L 8
Kilcummin (Kerry) 82 B 11
Kildare / Cill Dara 86 L 8
Kildare (County) 86 L 8
Kildorrery 78 G 11
Kilfenora 89 E 9
Kilfinnane 84 G 10
Kilgarvan 77 D 12
Kilglass 95 E 5
Kilglass Lough 90 H 6
Kilgobnet 76 C 11
Kilgory Lough 84 F 9
Kilkee / Cill Chaoi 83 D 9
Kilkeel 98 N 5
Kilkeeran High Crosses 80 J 10
Kilkenny / Cill Chainnigh 80 K 10
Kilkenny (County) 80 J 10
Kilkieran / Cill Chiaráin 88 C 8
Kilkishen 84 F 9
Kill 80 J 11
Killadoon 94 C 6
Killadysert 83 E 9
Killala 95 E 5
Killala Bay 95 E 5
Killaloe / Cill Dalua 84 G 9
Killamery 80 J 10
Killann 81 L 10
Killard Point 99 P 5
Killarga 96 H 5
Killarney / Cill Airne 77 D 11
Killarney National Park 83 D 11
Killary Harbour 88 C 7
Killashandra 97 J 5
Killavally 95 D 6
Killavullen 78 G 11
Killeagh 79 H 12
Killeigh 86 J 8
Killenagh 81 N 10
Killenaule 85 I 10
Killerrig 86 L 9
Killeshin 86 K 9
Killeter 101 I 3
Killeter Forest 101 I 3
Killevy Churches 98 M 5
Killimer 83 D 10
Killimor 90 H 8
Killinaboy 89 E 9
Killiney Bay 87 N 8
Killiney (Dublin) 87 N 8
Killinick 81 M 11
Killinure Lough 90 I 7
Killkelly 95 F 6
Killmuckbridge 81 N 10
Killorglin / Cill Orglan 76 C 11
Killough 99 P 5
Killucan 91 K 7
Killurin 81 M 10
Killybegs / Na Cealla Beaga 100 G 4
Killygordon 101 I 3
Killykeen Forest Park 97 J 5
Killylea 98 L 4
Killyleagh 99 P 4
Kilmacduagh Monastery 89 F 8
Kilmacow 80 K 11
Kilmacrenan 101 I 2
Kilmacthomas 80 J 11
Kilmaganny 80 K 10
Kilmaine 89 E 7
Kilmalkedar 82 B 11
Kilmallock / Cill Mocheallóg 84 G 10
Kilmanagh 80 J 10
Kilmeage 86 L 8
Kilmeedy 84 F 10
Kilmessan 93 M 7
Kilmichael 77 E 12
Kilmichael Point 87 N 9
Kilmihil 83 E 9
Kilmore 81 M 11
Kilmore Quay 81 M 11
Kilmurry (near Kilkishen) 84 F 9
Kilmurvy 88 C 8
Kilnaleck 91 K 6
Kilrane 81 M 11
Kilrea 102 M 3
Kilreekill 89 G 8
Kilronan / Cill Rónáin 88 C 8
Kilrush / Cill Rois 83 D 10
Kilshanny 88 E 9
Kilsheelan 80 J 10
Kiltamagh 95 E 6
Kiltealy 81 L 10
Kiltegan 87 M 9
Kilternan 87 N 8
Kiltoom 90 H 7
Kiltormer 90 H 8
Kiltyclogher 96 H 4
Kilworth 79 H 11
Kilworth Mountains 79 H 11
Kinale (Lough) 91 J 6
Kincasslagh 100 G 2
Kings River 80 J 10
Kingscourt 97 L 6
Kinlough 96 H 4
Kinnegad 91 K 7
Kinnitty 90 I 8
Kinsale / Cionn tSáile 78 G 12
Kinsale (Old Head of) 78 G 13
Kinvarra 89 F 8
Kinvarra Bay 89 F 8
Kinvarra (near Screeb) 88 D 7
Kippure 87 N 8
Kircubbin 99 P 4
Kitconnell 89 G 8
Knappagh 94 D 6
Knappogue Castle 84 F 9
Knight's Town 76 B 12
Knock (Clare) 83 E 10
Knock (Mayo) 95 F 6
Knockadoon Head 79 I 12
Knockainy 84 G 10
Knockalongy 95 F 5
Knockcroghery 90 H 7
Knockferry 89 E 7
Knocklayd 103 N 2
Knocklong 84 G 10
Knockmealdown 79 I 11
Knockmealdown Mountains 79 H 11
Knockmoy Abbey 89 F 7
Knocknadobar 76 B 12
Knocknagree 77 E 11
Knockraha 78 G 12
Knocktopher 80 K 10
Knowth 93 M 6
Kylemore Abbey 88 C 7
Kylemore Lough 88 C 7

L

Labasheeda 83 E 10
Lack 97 J 4
Ladies View 77 D 12
Lady's Island Lake 81 M 11
Ladysbridge 79 H 12
Lagan (River) 99 N 4
Lagan Valley 99 O 4
Laghy 100 H 4
Lahinch / An Leacht 88 D 9
Lamb's Head 76 B 12
Lambay Island 93 N 7
Lanesborough 90 I 6
Laois (County) 86 J 9
Laragh 87 N 8
Larne 103 O 3
Larne Lough 103 O 3
Laune (River) 76 C 11
Lauragh 76 C 12
Laurencetown 90 H 8
Lavagh More 100 H 3
Lawrencetown 98 N 4
Laytown 99 N 6
League (Slieve) 100 F 4
Leamaneh Castle 89 F 9
Leane (Lough) 77 D 11
Leannan 101 I 2
Leap 77 E 13
Leap (The) 81 M 10
Lecarrow (Leitrim) 96 H 5
Lecarrow (Roscommon) 90 H 7
Leckanvy 94 C 6
Leckavrea Mountain 88 D 7
Lee 82 C 11
Lee (River) 78 G 12
Leenane 88 C 7
Legananny Dolmen 99 N 5
Leighlinbridge 86 L 9
Leinster (Mount) 81 L 10
Leitir Ceanainn / Letterkenny 101 I 3
Leitir Mealláin / Lettermullan 88 C 8
Leitir Mhic an Bhaird / Lettermacaward 100 H 3
Leitrim 96 H 6
Leitrim (County) 96 I 6
Leixlip 93 M 7
Lemybrien 80 J 11
Lene (Lough) 91 K 7
Letterfrack 88 C 7
Letterkenny / Leitir Ceanainn 101 I 3
Lettermacaward / Leitir Mhic an Bhaird 100 H 3
Lettermore 88 D 8
Lettermore Island 88 C 8
Lettermullan / Leitir Mealláin 88 C 8
Licky 79 I 11
Liffey (River) 87 M 8
Lifford 101 J 3
Limavady 102 L 2
Limerick / Luimneach 84 G 9
Limerick (County) 84 F 10
Limerick Junction 84 H 10
Lios Dúin Bhearna / Lisdoonvarna 88 E 8
Lios Mór / Lismore 79 I 11
Lios Póil / Lispole 82 B 11
Lios Tuathail / Listowel 83 D 10
Lisbellaw 97 J 5
Lisburn 99 N 4
Liscannor 88 D 9
Liscannor Bay 83 D 9
Liscarroll 84 F 11
Lisdoonvarna / Lios Dúin Bhearna 88 E 8

LIMERICK/ LUIMNEACH

Arthur Quay Shopping Centre Y
O'Connell Street Z
Patrick Street YZ 32
Roches Street Z
Sarfield Street Y 39
William Street Z
Arthur Quay Y 2
Baal's Bridge Y 4
Bank Place Y 5
Barrington Street Z 6
Bridge Street Y 7
Broad Street Y 8
Castle Street Y 10
Cathedral Place Z 12
Charlotte's Quay Y 13
The Crescent Z 14
Cruises Street Z 15
Gerald Griffen St. Z 16
Grattan Street Y 17
High Street Z 18
Honan's Quay Y 19
John Square Z 20
Lock Quay Y 21
Lower Cecil Street Z 22
Lower Mallow Street Z 23
Mathew Bridge Y 24
Mount Kenneth Z 26
Newtown Mahon Z 28
North Circular Rd Z 29
O'Dwyer Bridge Y 30
Penniwell Road Z 33
Rutland Street Y 34
St Alphonsus St. Z 35
St Gerard St. Z 36
St Lelia Street YZ 37
Sexton Street North Y 40
Shannon Street Z 42
South Circular Rd Z 43
Thomond Bridge Y 45
Wickham Street Z 47

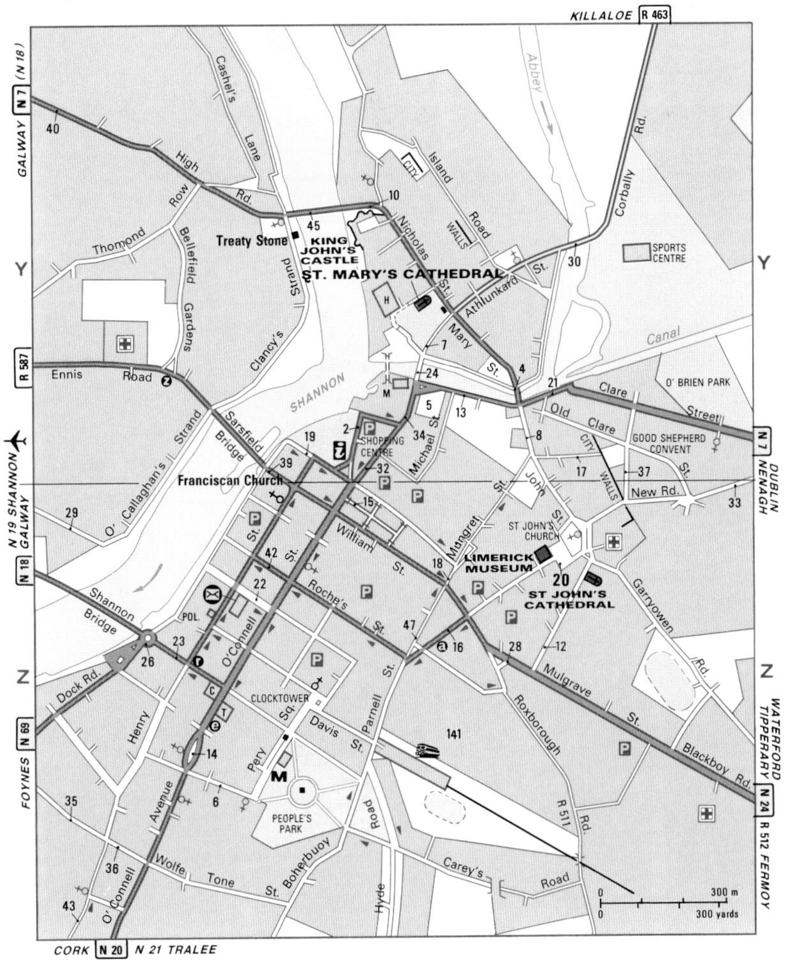

KILLALOE R 463
GALWAY N 7 (N 18)
N 19 SHANNON GALWAY N 18
R 587
FOYNES N 69
DUBLIN NENAGH N 7
WATERFORD TIPPERARY N 24
R 512 FERMOY
CORK N 20 N 21 TRALEE
High Rd.
Thomond
Treaty Stone
KING JOHN'S CASTLE
ST. MARY'S CATHEDRAL
Bellefield Gardens
Ennis Road
SHANNON
Franciscan Church
Shannon Bridge
O' Callaghan's Strand
Sarsfield Bridge
Clancy's Strand
Island Road
Nicholas St.
Athlunkard St.
Mary St.
Abbey
Corbally Rd.
SPORTS CENTRE
Canal
O' BRIEN PARK
Clare Street
Old Clare
GOOD SHEPHERD CONVENT
City Walls
New Rd.
SHOPPING CENTRE
William St.
Mungret St.
John St.
ST JOHN'S CHURCH
LIMERICK MUSEUM
ST JOHN'S CATHEDRAL
Garryowen Rd.
Mulgrave St.
Roxborough Rd.
Blackboy Rd.
Rochs St.
O'Connell St.
CLOCKTOWER Sq.
Davis St.
Parnell St.
Dock Rd.
Henry St.
Perry St.
Avenue
PEOPLE'S PARK
Boherbuoy
Hyde Road
Wolfe Tone St.
Carey's Road
R 511
POL
0 300 m
0 300 yards

LONDONDERRY

Orchard Lane ....X 25

Barrack Street ....X 2	Francis Street..............................X 13
Clooney Terrace ....X 5	Glendermott Road.......................X 14
Creggan Street ....X 6	Harbour Square...........................X 15
Custom House Street ....X 7	Infirmary Road.............................X 17
Dungiven Road ....X 8	John Street..................................X 18
Duke Street ....X 9	Lecky Road...................................X 19
Foyle Road ....X 10	Limavady Road.............................X 20
Foyle Street ....X 12	Long Tower Street.......................X 22
	Lower James Street....................X 23
	Sackville Street............................X 26
	Simpsons Brae.............................X 29
	Water Street..................................X 32
	William Street...............................X 34

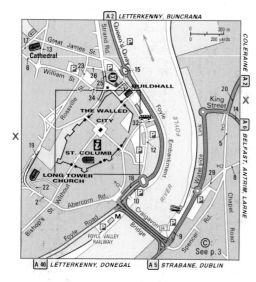

Lismacaffry	91 J 6			
Lismore / Lios Mór	79 I 11			
Lisnacree	99 N 5			
Lisnarrick	97 J 4			
Lisnaskea	97 J 5			
Lispole / Lios Póil	82 B 11			
Lissadell House	96 G 4			
Lissatinnig Bridge	76 C 12			
Lisselton	83 D 10			
Lissycasey	83 E 9			
Listowel / Lios Tuathail	83 D 10			
Little Island	78 G 12			
Little Skellig	76 A 12			
Littleton	85 I 10			
Lixnaw	83 D 10			
Loch Garman / Wexford	81 M 10			
Loghill	83 E 10			
Londonderry	102 K 3			
Londonderry (County)	102 K 3			
Long Island	77 D 13			
Longford (County)	90 I 6			
Longford / An Longfort (Longford)	91 I 6			
Longford (Offaly)	85 I 8			
Loo Bridge	77 D 12			
Loop Head	82 C 10			
Lorrha	90 H 8			
Lough Gowna	97 J 6			
Loughgall	98 M 4			
Loughbrickland	98 N 5			
Loughglinn	96 G 6			
Loughinisland	99 O 4			
Loughrea / Baile Locha Riach	89 G 8			
Loughros More Bay	100 G 3			
Loughshinny	93 N 7			
Louisburgh	94 C 6			
Loup (The)	102 M 3			
Louth	98 M 6			
Louth (County)	98 M 6			
Lower Lake	81 N 8			
Lower Ballinderry	98 N 4			
Lucan	93 M 7			
Lugnaquillia Mountain	87 M 9			
Luimneach / Limerick	84 G 10			
Lullymore	86 L 8			
Lung	96 G 6			
Lurgan	98 N 4			
Lusk	93 N 7			
Lyracrumpane	83 D 10			

M

Maam Cross / An Teach Dóite	88 D 7
Maas	100 G 3
Macgillycuddy's Reeks	76 C 12
Macnean Upper (Lough)	96 I 5
Macroom / Maigh Chromtha	78 F 12
Maganey	86 L 9
Magee (Island)	103 O 3
Maghera (Donegal)	100 G 3
Maghera (Down)	99 O 5
Maghera (Londonderry)	102 L 3
Magherafelt	102 M 3
Magheralin	98 N 4
Maghery	98 M 4
Magilligan	102 L 2
Magilligan Strand	102 L 2
Maguiresbridge	97 J 5
Mahee Island	99 P 4
Mahon	80 J 11
Mahoonagh	83 E 10
Maigh Chromtha / Macroom	78 F 12
Maigh Cuilinn / Moycullen	89 E 7
Maigh Nuad / Maynooth	93 M 7
Maigue (River)	84 F 10
Main	103 N 3
Maine (River)	82 C 11
Mainistir Fhear Maí / Fermoy	78 H 11
Mainistir Laoise / Abbey Leix	86 J 9
Mainistir na Búille / Boyle	96 H 6
Mainistir na Corann / Midleton	79 H 12
Máistir Gaoithe / Mastergeehy	76 B 12
Mal Bay	83 D 9
Mala / Mallow	78 G 11
Malahide	93 N 7
Mullach Íde	93 N 7
Málainn Bhig / Malin Beg	100 F 3
Malin	101 K 2
Malin Bay	100 F 3
Malin Beg / Málainn Bhig	100 F 3
Malin Head	101 J 1

Malin More	100 F 3
Mallow / Mala	78 G 11
Mamore (Gap of)	101 J 2
Mangerton Mountain	77 D 12
Mannin Bay	88 B 7
Mannin Lake	95 F 6
Manorcunningham	101 J 3
Manorhamilton / Cluainín	96 H 5
Mansfieldstown	92 M 6
Manulla	95 E 6
Maothail / Mohill	96 I 6
Marble Arch Caves	96 I 5
Marble Hill	101 I 2
Markethill	98 M 5
Mask (Lough)	88 D 7
Mastergeehy / Máistir Gaoithe	76 B 12
Matrix (Castle)	84 F 10
Mattock	93 M 6
Maum	88 D 7
Maumeen Lough	88 D 7
Maumtrasna	88 D 7
Maumturk Mountains	88 C 7
Maynooth / Maigh Nuad	93 M 7
Mayo	95 E 6
Mayo (County)	95 E 6
Mayo (Plains of)	95 E 6
Mealagh	77 D 12
Meath (County)	92 L 7
Meela (Lough)	100 G 3
Meenaneary / Min na Aoire	100 G 3
Meenavean	100 F 3
Meeting of the Waters	87 N 9
Mellifont Abbey	93 M 6
Melmore Head	101 I 2
Melvin (Lough)	96 H 4
Menlough	89 G 7
Mew Island	99 P 3
Middletown (Armagh)	98 L 5
Middletown (Donegal)	100 H 2
Midleton / Mainistir na Corann	79 H 12
Milestone	85 H 9
Milford	84 F 10
Millford	101 I 2
Millisle	99 P 4
Millstreet	77 E 11
Milltown (Cavan)	97 J 5
Milltown (Galway)	89 F 7
Milltown (Kerry)	77 C 11

Milltown Malbay / Sráid na Cathrach	83 D 9
Mín na Aoire / Meenaneary	100 G 3
Minane Bridge	78 G 12
Minard Head	82 B 11
Mine Head	80 J 12
Mitchelstown / Baile Mhistéala	79 H 11
Mizen Head	76 C 13
Moate / An Móta	91 I 7
Moher (Cliffs of)	88 D 9
Moher Lough	94 D 6
Mohill / Maothail	96 I 6
Móinteach Mílic / Mountmellick	86 K 8
Moll's Gap	77 D 12
Monaghan / Muineachán	97 L 5
Monaghan (County)	97 K 5
Monasteraden	96 G 6
Monasteranenagh Abbey	84 G 10
Monasterboice	93 M 6
Monasterevin	86 K 8
Monavullagh Mountains	80 J 11
Mondello Park	86 L 8
Monea	97 I 4
Moneygall	85 I 9
Moneymore	102 L 3
Monivea	89 F 7
Monkstown (Antrim)	103 O 3
Monkstown (Cork)	78 G 12
Mooncoin	80 K 11
Moone	86 L 9
Moore Bay	83 C 9
Moorfields	103 N 3
Morley's Bridge	77 D 12
Mosney	93 N 7
Moss-Side	102 M 2
Mossley	103 O 3
Mostrim	91 J 6
Mount Bellew / An Creagán	89 G 7
Mount Melleray Monastery	79 I 11
Mount Norris	98 M 5
Mount Nuggent	91 K 6
Mount Stewart Gardens	99 P 4
Mount Usher Gardens	87 N 8
Mountcharles	100 H 4
Mountfield	97 K 4
Mountmellick / Móinteach Mílic	86 K 8
Mountrath	86 J 8
Mountshannon	84 G 9
Mourne (Lough)	103 O 3
Mourne Mountains	99 N 5
Mourne River	101 J 3
Moville / Bun an Phobail	101 K 2
Moy	98 L 4
Moy (River)	95 E 5
Moyard	88 B 7
Moyasta	83 D 9
Moycullen / Maigh Cuilinn	89 E 7
Moylough	89 G 7
Moynalty	92 L 6
Moyne Abbey	95 E 5
Moyvally	92 L 7
Moyvore	91 J 7
Muck (Isle of)	103 O 3
Muckamore	103 N 3
Muckanagh Lough	83 E 10
Muckish Mountain	100 H 2
Muckno Lake	98 L 5
Muckros Head	100 G 4
Muckross	77 D 11
Muff	101 K 2
Muggort's Bay	80 J 11
Muinchille / Cootehill	97 K 5
Muineachán / Monaghan	97 L 5
Muine Bheag	86 L 9
Muing	94 D 5
Muingnabo	94 C 5
Mulkear	84 G 10
Mullach Íde / Malahide	93 N 7

Mullagh (Cavan)	92 L 6
Mullagh (Meath)	93 M 7
Mullaghareirk Mountains	83 E 10
Mullaghcleevaun	87 M 8
Mullaghmore	96 G 4
Mullet Peninsula	94 B 5
Mullinahone	80 J 10
Mullinavat	80 K 10
Mullingar / An Muileann gCearr	91 J 7
Mulrany / An Mhala Raithní	94 C 6
Mulroy Bay	101 I 2
Multyfarnham	91 J 7
Mungret	84 F 10
Muntervary or Sheep's Head	76 C 13
Murlough Bay	103 N 2
Murntown	81 M 11
Murrisk	94 D 6
Murroe	84 G 10
Mussenden Temple	102 L 2
Mutton Island	83 D 9
Mweelrea Mountains	88 C 7
Myshall	86 L 9

N

Na Cealla Beaga / Killybegs	100 G 4
Na Clocha Liatha / Greystones	87 N 8
Na Dúnaibh / Downings	101 I 2
Na Sceirí / Skerries	93 N 7
Naas / An Nás	87 L 8
Nacung (Lough)	100 H 2
Nad	78 F 11
Nafooey (Lough)	88 D 7
Nagles Mountains	78 G 11
Naminn (Lough)	101 J 2
Namona (Lough)	76 B 12
Nanny	93 M 7
Naran	100 G 3
Narrow Water Castle	98 N 5
Naul	93 N 7
Navan / An Uaimh	92 L 7
Neagh (Lough)	98 M 4
Neale	89 E 7
Neidín / Kenmare	77 D 12
Nenagh / An tAonach	84 H 9
Nephin	95 D 5
Nephin (Glen)	95 D 6
Nephin Beg	94 D 5
Nephin Beg Range	94 C 5
New Inn (Cavan)	97 K 6
New Inn (Galway)	89 G 8
New Kildimo	84 F 10
New Ross / Ros Mhic Thriúin	80 L 10
Newbawn	81 L 10
New Birmingham	80 J 10
Newbliss	97 K 5
Newbridge	93 N 7
Newbridge / An Droichead Nua	86 L 8
Newcastle (Down)	99 O 5
Newcastle (Dublin)	87 M 8
Newcastle (Tipperary)	79 I 11
Newcastle (Wicklow)	87 N 8
Newcastle West / An Caisleán Nua	83 E 10
Newgrange	93 M 6
Newinn	85 I 10
Newmarket	84 F 11
Newmarket on Fergus	84 F 9
Newport / Baile Uí Fhiacháin (Mayo)	94 D 6
Newport (Tipperary)	84 G 9
Newport Bay	94 C 6
Newry	98 M 5
Newtown Cashel	90 I 7
Newtown-Crommelin	103 N 3
Newtown (Laois)	86 K 9
Newtown (Offaly)	90 H 8

Newtownabbey	103 O 4
Newtown Forbes	90 I 6
Newtown Gore	96 I 5
Newtown Mount Kennedy	87 N 8
Newtownards	99 O 4
Newtownbutler	97 J 5
Newtownhamilton	98 M 5
Newtownshandrum	84 F 10
Newtownstewart	101 J 3
Nier	80 J 11
Ninemilehouse	80 J 10
Nobber	92 L 6
Nohaval	78 G 12
Nore	86 J 9
Nore (River)	80 K 10
North Sound	88 C 8
North Ring	78 F 13
Nurney	86 L 8
Nurney (Carlow)	86 L 9

O

O'Brien's Tower	88 D 9
Offaly (County)	90 I 8
O'Grady (Lough)	84 G 9
Oileán Ciarraí / Castleisland	83 D 11
Oilgate	81 M 10
Oily	100 G 4
Old Head	94 C 6
Old Kildimo	84 F 10
Oldcastle / An Seanchaisleán	91 K 6
Oldleighlin	86 K 9
Old Ross	81 L 10
Omagh	97 K 4
Omeath	98 N 5
Omey Island	88 B 7
Oola	84 H 10
Oorid Lough	88 D 7
Oranmore	89 F 8
Ossian's Grave	103 N 2
Oughterard / Uachtar Ard	89 E 7
Ougther (Lough)	97 J 6
Ovens	78 G 12
Owel (Lough)	91 J 7
Owenascaul	82 B 11
Owenator	100 H 3
Owenavorragh	81 M 10
Owenbeg (River)	96 G 5
Owenboliska	88 E 8
Owencarrow	101 I 2
Owenea	100 G 3
Owengarve	94 D 6
Owenglin	88 C 7
Oweniny	94 D 5
Owenkillew	101 J 2
Owenkillew	102 K 3
Owenriff	88 D 7
Owentocker	100 H 3
Owey Island / Uaigh	100 G 2
Owvane	77 D 12
Oysterhaven	78 G 12

P

Pallasgreen	84 G 10
Pallaskenry	84 F 10
Paps (The)	77 E 11
Parke's Castle	96 H 5
Parkmore Point	82 A 11
Parknasilla	76 C 12
Partry	95 E 6
Partry Mountains	88 D 7
Passage East	80 L 11
Passage West	78 G 12
Patrickswell	84 F 10
Peake	78 F 12
Peatlands	98 M 4
Pettigoe	97 I 4
Phoenix Park	93 M 7
Piltown	80 K 10
Pluck	101 J 3
Plumbridge	102 K 3
Pomeroy	97 L 4
Pontoon	95 E 6
Port Durlainne / Porturlin	94 C 5
Port Láirge / Waterford	80 K 11

Port Laoise / Portlaoise	86 K 8
Port Omna / Portumna	90 H 8
Portacloy	94 C 5
Portadown	98 M 4
Portaferry	99 P 4
Portarlington / Cúil an tSúdaire	86 K 8
Portavogie	99 P 4
Port Ballintrae	102 M 2
Portglenone	102 M 3
Portlaoise / Port Laoise	86 K 8
Portlaw	80 K 11
Portmagee	76 A 12
Portmagee Channel	76 A 12
Portmarnock	93 N 7
Portmuck	103 O 3
Portnablagh	101 I 2
Portnoo	100 G 3
Portrane	93 N 7
Portroe	84 G 9
Portrush	102 M 2
Portsalon	101 J 2
Portstewart	102 L 2
Portumna / Port Omna	90 H 8
Porturlin / Port Durlainne	94 C 5
Poulaphouca Reservoir	87 M 8
Poulnasherry Bay	83 D 10
Powerscourt Demesne	87 N 8
Poyntz Pass	98 M 5
Prosperous	87 L 8
Puckaun	84 H 9
Puffin Island	76 A 12

Q

Quigley's Point	101 K 2
Quilty	83 D 9
Quin	84 F 9

R

Rae na nDoirí / Reananeree	77 E 12
Raghly	96 G 5
Raharney	91 K 7
Ram Head	79 I 12
Ramor (Lough)	91 K 6
Randalstown	103 N 3
Raphoe	101 J 3
Rasharkin	102 M 3
Rath	90 I 8
Ráth Caola / Rathkeale	84 F 10
Ráth Droma / Rathdrum	87 N 9
Rath Luirc (Charleville) / An Ráth	84 F 10
Rathangan	86 L 8
Rathcool	78 F 11
Rathcoole	87 M 8
Rathcormack	78 H 11
Rathcroghan	90 H 6
Rathdangan	87 M 9
Rathdowney	86 J 9
Rathdrum / Ráth Droma	87 N 9
Rathfriland	99 N 5
Rathgormuck	80 J 11
Rathkeale / Ráth Caola	84 F 10
Rathlackan	95 E 5
Rathlin Island	103 N 2
Rathlin Sound	103 N 2
Rathmelton	101 J 2
Rathmolyon	92 L 7
Rathmore	83 E 11
Rathmullan	101 J 2
Rathnew	87 N 9
Rathowen	91 J 7
Rathvilla	86 K 8
Rathvilly	87 L 9
Ratoath	93 M 7
Raven Point (The)	81 M 10
Ray	100 H 2
Rea (Lough)	89 G 8

Notes

THE WORLD
IN YOUR POCKET

These colourful, easy-to-use travel books provide an instant sight-seers guide to each destination in a handy pocket-sized format. They offer a wealth of information with detailed maps and city plans and stunning colour photographs. You'll also find ideas for enjoying your stay including food and entertainment, walks and excursions and a superb A-Z Factfinder so you know exactly where you are.

AMSTERDAM - BRITTANY - FLORIDA - GREEK ISLANDS
NEW YORK - PARIS - PRAGUE - ROME - SOUTH OF FRANCE
SOUTHERN SPAIN - TUSCANY - VENICE

RED HOTEL & RESTAURANT GUIDES

Red Hotel and Restaurant Guides
Before you book a restaurant or check into a hotel, check out Michelin Red Guides. World famous for their star food-ratings, they list thousands of hotels and restaurants across Europe, covering a wide range of prices and facilities. A system of symbols shows the service available, so you can instantly find the establishment to suit your needs. They include detailed town plans to help you on your way.

FRANCE-BENELUX-DEUTSCHLAND-ESPAÑA PORTUGAL
GREAT BRITAIN AND IRELAND-ITALIA-EUROPE
SUISSE SCHWEIZ SVIZZERA

GREEN TOURIST GUIDES
ENGLISH EDITIONS

Green Tourist Guides
Ideal travel companions for independent
sightseeing, Green Guides include time-
saving driving schedules, walking tours
and maps. Tourist attractions are described
and illustrated, in many cases with opening
times, so you can fully plan each day's
viewing. You will also find historical
and cultural outlines, with photographs
and drawings, giving you the full picture
of your destination.

ENGLAND : THE WEST COUNTRY - GREAT BRITAIN
IRELAND - LONDON - SCOTLAND - WALES

AUSTRIA - BELGIUM - BRUSSELS - FRANCE - GERMANY - GREECE
ITALY - NETHERLANDS - PORTUGAL - ROME - SCANDINAVIA FINLAND
SPAIN - SWITZERLAND - TUSCANY - VENICE

ATLANTIC COAST - AUVERGNE RHONE VALLEY - BRITTANY
BURGUNDY JURA - CHATEAUX OF THE LOIRE - DISNEYLAND PARIS - DORDOGNE
FLANDERS PICARDY AND THE PARIS REGION - FRENCH RIVIERA -
NORMANDY - PARIS - PROVENCE - PYRENEES LANGUEDOC TARN GORGES

CALIFORNIA - CANADA - CHICAGO - FLORIDA - MEXICO - NEW ENGLAND
NEW YORK CITY - QUEBEC - SAN FRANCISCO - WASHINGTON DC

First published 1990 by Manufacture Française des Pneumatiques Michelin
Société en commandite par actions au capital de 2 000 000 000 de Francs
Place des Carmes-Déchaux – 63 Clermont-Ferrand (France) – RCS Clermont-Fd B855200507
© Michelin et Cie, propriétaires-éditeurs 1997
Eighth edition 1997

Great Britain: the maps and town plans in the Great Britain section of this Atlas are based upon
the Ordnance Survey of Great Britain with the permission of the Controller of Her Majesty's
Stationery Office. Permit number 39923 X.

Northern Ireland: the maps and town plans in the Northern Ireland section of this Atlas are
based upon the Ordnance Survey of Northern Ireland with the permission of the Controller of
Her Majesty's Stationery Office. Permit number 949.

Republic of Ireland: the maps and town plans in the Republic of Ireland section of this Atlas are
based upon the Ordnance Survey of Ireland by permission of the Government of the Republic.
Permit number 6280.

In spite of the care taken in the production of this book, it is possible that a defective copy may
have escaped our attention. If this is so, please return it to your bookseller, who will exchange it
for you, or contact:

Michelin Tyre Public Limited Company
The Edward Hyde Building
38 Clarendon Road
WATFORD Herts WD1 1SX
Tel (01923) 415000

The representation of a road in this atlas is no evidence of a right of way.

ISBN Hardback 2-06-112008-3 – ISBN Softback 2-06-112108-X – ISBN Spiral 2-06-112208-6

Dépôt légal octobre 1996 – Printed in E.U. 09-96

Printed by Casterman